PENGUIN BOOKS

THE PENGUIN DICTIONARY OF JOKES

Fred Metcalf was born in Yorkshire and educated in Devon. He has worked as a freelance writer in London, Sydney and Los Angeles. He is also the editor of *The Penguin Dictionary of Modern Humorous Quotations*, which was first published in 1986.

THE PENGUIN DICTIONARY OF JOKES, WISECRACKS, QUIPS AND QUOTES

COMPILED BY FRED METCALF

PENGUIN BOOKS

PENGUIN BOOKS

Published by the Penguin Group
Penguin Books Ltd, 27 Wrights Lane, London W8 5TZ, England
Penguin Books USA Inc., 375 Hudson Street, New York, New York 10014, USA
Penguin Books Australia Ltd, Ringwood, Victoria, Australia
Penguin Books Canada Ltd, 10 Alcorn Avenue, Toronto, Ontario, Canada M4V 3B2
Penguin Books (NZ) Ltd, 182–190 Wairau Road, Auckland 10, New Zealand

Penguin Books Ltd, Registered Offices: Harmondsworth, Middlesex, England

First published by Viking 1993
Published by Penguin Books 1994
7 9 10 8 6

Printed in England by Clays Ltd, St Ives plc

FOREWORD

Experts agree that there are certain times in history when circumstances combine to produce the conditions in which a book is published at the precise moment when the world has expressed an unspoken need for it.

This is such a time. And this is such a book for such a time. A time when all of us need to come together and share the healing power of laughter.

Cometh the hour, a wise man once said, cometh the jokes.

This is a book which poses profound questions about the way we live – and laugh – in the final decade of the twentieth century.

Why do we laugh? What is funny and what is not? When does a witticism become a wisecrack? And why did the chicken cross the road?

This is a book for today. And tomorrow. A book to be laughed at. And with. A book to be read. And re-read. A book to be read out loud. And re-read out loud. Today. And tomorrow.

In compiling this collection, the enthusiastic interest of my friends has been a vital source of encouragement. While I toiled at the coalface of comedy, they were there, laughing in all the right places – London, Los Angeles, Bath, Bruges, Hong Kong, Exeter . . .

I am forever grateful to all of them, especially, Kate, Laura and Alice Patten and Kitty Dimbleby, Louise Bagshawe, Laurence Allen, John and Jane Birt, Carolyn Brakefield, Ben Butters, Guy and Lindsay Butters, Roger, Doris and John Cock, Emma and Craig Chapman, Judi and Xenia Brill, Ray and Richie Bradford, Bob Dean, Dudley Doolittle and Elaine, Jonathan Dimbleby and Bel Mooney, Danny Dimbleby, Martin Cunning, Andy, Peter and Lucy Dean, Nick and Gilly Elliott, John and Gina Florescu, Gillian and Nicholas Evans, Bruce Gowers, Carol Rosenstein, Sean and Katie, Beccy Goodhart, Laurence and Jessica Gorley, Ian Gordon, Yvonne Hawker, Ellie, Daisy and Poppy Hughes, Helen James, Marie and Daniel Jessel, Billie and Jessie Lever Taylor, Vijay Lakhani, Sue, Karla and Kathryn at Together Again Productions, Ket Lamb, Eugenia McGrath, Stefanie Metcalf, Bob, Rae and Jacqueline Metcalf, Andrew Mortimer,

Horatio, Matthew, Frances and Phoebe Mortimer, Gwen Metcalf, Sonia McDonald, Natalie and Kelly Metcalf, Andy and Tess Mayer, Chris and Missy Miller, Trevor and Fiona Poots, Mike and Pat Prout, Emily Rush, Chantal Rutherford Browne, Ivan Schutts, Neil Shand, Jules Slaughter, David and Lesley Taylor and Jane Thomas.

Finally, I would particularly like to thank Kathryn McMurray and Vivien Green at my agents Sheil Land, and Ravi Mirchandani, Judith Flanders and Lesley Levene at Penguin Books for, among other things, waiting, with varying degrees of patience, for this book.

I hope they feel it's worth its wait in gold.

Absence

1 I'm going now, but should I return during my absence, please wait for me till I come back.

2 I'm so miserable without her, it's almost like having her here.

See also Farewells, Retirement, Separation

Absent-minded

1 He's so absent-minded that he left home without his watch, then looked at it to see if he had time to go back and get it.

2 It worries me, I'm getting so absent-minded. I mean, sometimes in the middle of a sentence I . . .

3 One night I was so confused that I got into the bath without taking off my clothes. But it didn't matter, because I'd also forgotten to turn on the tap.

See also Amnesia, Memory

Accidents

1 First impressions are often lasting – especially if they're made by a car bumper.

2 If you fall out of that tree and break both your legs, don't come running to me!

3 My uncle was knocked 30 feet in the air by a speeding car – and the police charged him with leaving the scene of an accident.

4 The accident wasn't my fault. I had the right of way. Unfortunately, the other guy had the truck.

5 The cyclist injured in an accident with a bus is said from hospital this evening to be critical – especially of the bus driver.

6 CHILD: Mum, come quickly! I've knocked the ladder down outside!
MOTHER: Well, don't tell me. Tell your father.
CHILD: But he already knows – he's hanging from the roof!

7 Did your watch stop when it hit the floor?
Of course! Did you expect it to go straight through?

8 Have an accident?
No thanks, I've just had one.

9 How did you break your arm?
Well, do you see that broken step?
Yes.
Well, I didn't.

10 I broke my leg in three places.
I always told you not to go to those places.

11 I was walking past this building site when this brick came hurtling down, missing my shoulder by this much!
Thank goodness!
And landing smack on the top of my head!

12 I've just fallen in the water.
How did you come to fall in?
I didn't come to fall in. I came to fish!

13 MECHANIC: How did you smash up the wing like that?

DRIVER: I hit a pedestrian.

MECHANIC: You did all that damage just hitting a pedestrian?

DRIVER: Well, he was on a bus at the time.

14 SON: Remember that vase you were always worried I might break?

MOTHER: What about it?

SON: Well, your worries are over.

15 This morning I fell out of a tenth-storey window.

Well, it doesn't seem to have hurt you.

No. Fortunately the ground broke my fall!

16 What happened when you dropped the lighted candle in his lap?

He waxed eloquent!

17 What's the matter with your finger?

I hit the wrong nail!

18 A man falls headlong down a flight of stairs and as he's picking himself up and dusting himself down, a woman rushes over and says, 'Did you miss a step?'

'No,' the man replies, 'I hit every one of them!'

19 A nurse in hospital was chatting to one of her patients who was wrapped from head to toe in bandages. She said, 'So what do you do for a living?'

'I used to wash windows.'

'And when did you stop?'

'About half-way down!'

See Circus 2, Cosmetics 3, Drink 40, Fame 5, Farming 9, Flying 17, Golf 1, Husbands and Wives 44, Insurance 1, New York 2, Pessimism 7, Stupidity 15; see also Cars, Driving, Insurance, Mistakes, Motorcycling, Sympathy

Accountants

1 An accountant is someone who tells you exactly how much money you have and how much of it you owe to him.

2 An accountant is someone who tells you what to do with your money after you've done something else with it.

3 An accountant is someone who solves a problem you didn't know you had in a way you don't understand.

4 I've got an absolutely brilliant accountant. They've just named a loophole after him.

5 My accountant called me. He said, 'I've got some terrible news for you. Last year was the best you've ever had.'

6 My accountant told me my business is looking up. But only because it's flat on its back.

7 Our chief accountant is shy and retiring. He's half a million dollars shy, and that's why he's retiring!

8 This year's balance sheet is being brought to you in colour – red.

9 My company is looking for a new accountant.

Didn't you hire one just last week?

We did – and that's the one we're looking for.

10 What is an actuary?

Someone who is too boring to be an accountant.

11 A company was looking to employ a new accountant and had called in the last three candidates for their final interviews. The first candidate was invited into the chairman's office and asked, 'What's two plus two?'

'Four,' he replied.

The second candidate was invited in and she was asked, 'What's two plus two?'

She replied, 'Four.'

Finally, the third candidate was

invited in and he was asked, 'What's two plus two?'

He said, 'What do you want it to be?'

They said, 'You've got the job.'

12 A private detective was hired to find a missing accountant. He asked the boss, 'Was he tall or was he short?'

And the boss said, 'Both.'

13 A businessman attending a conference got talking to another delegate, who happened to be an accountant. The businessman said, 'Why don't we pop down to the bar? I'll buy you a drink.'

And the accountant replied, 'No, thanks. I tried alcohol once but I just didn't like it.'

So the businessman said, 'Fine, let's just sit here and talk. Would you like a cigarette?'

And the accountant replied, 'Sorry, I don't smoke. I tried it once and I hated it.'

So the businessman said, 'OK, but later tonight a gang of us are going to play a little poker. Would you care to join us?'

And the accountant replied, 'I'm afraid I don't gamble. I tried it once and it just didn't appeal. But my son is coming over tonight. Maybe he'd like to join in.'

And the businessman said, 'He's your *only* son, I assume!'

14 An accountant was going on a family holiday by train. As they were passing through the countryside, one of his children yelled, 'Look, Dad, a flock of sheep in that field – and they've just been shorn!'

And the accountant replied, 'Well, on this side anyway.'

15 A good accountant is someone who told you yesterday what the economists forecast for tomorrow.
Sir Miles Thomas

See Gold-diggers 5, Hard Times 11; *see also* Banks and Banking, Business, Consultants, Money, Professions, Taxes

Actors and acting

1 An actor is the only ham that can't be cured.

2 An agent is someone who believes that an actor takes 90 per cent of his money.

3 Did you see my 'Bottom' at Stratford-upon-Avon? Many people consider it my best part.

4 For him, the advent of television opened up a whole new area of unemployment.

5 He was born in the theatre. It went down so well, his mother kept it in the act.

6 I had a bit part in the last *Lassie* picture. I got bit.

7 I never turn down an acting job. My motto is, 'Better a small role than a long loaf.'

8 I used to suffer from terrible stage fright but I found a cure for it. I take a twenty-minute walk three minutes before I go on!

9 I've got a very ambitious agent – he's always opening up offices overseas. At the moment I'm out of work in seventeen countries.

10 The critics said that last night I did the most wonderful Hamlet they'd ever seen. The trouble was, I was playing Richard the Third!

11 You can always tell an actor, but you can't tell him much.

12 AGENT: Leave your number and I'll call you when I'm looking for someone to play an old man.
ACTOR: But I'm a young man!
AGENT: You won't be when I call you!

13 DIRECTOR: Well, I've been looking at your screen test and, quite frankly, it would take an act of Congress to get you into the movies.
YOUNG ACTRESS: Before I came to Hollywood, I was warned about men like you!

14 How did the audience like your act?
Difficult to say. I didn't mind them looking at their watches, but when they started shaking them, that was hard to take.

15 I hear you've got a leading part at the National Theatre.
That's right. I'm working as an usherette.

16 I heard you're in a new play. How's business?
Well, on the first night there was nobody there at all but on the second, attendance fell off completely. Last night we had our best night so far – we sent the audience home in a taxi.

17 I left the theatre to become an architect.
Are you drawing better houses?

18 I'll never forget my first words in the theatre.
What were they?
This way, please! Programmes!

19 I've been in films. Did you see *Dead Poets' Society*?
Yes?
So did I. Terrific, wasn't it?

20 Q: When is an actor not an actor?
A: Most of the time.

21 We're casting the drama school end-of-term production of *Romeo and Juliet*.
So what would you like me to play?
Truant.

22 DIRECTOR: Right, you've been stranded alone on a desert island for ten years. One day you're strolling along the beach and, to your surprise and delight, you meet a young blonde woman emerging from the sea. You take her in your arms and begin to kiss her passionately . . .
ACTOR: OK, OK, but what's my motivation?

23 If you want to be a good actor, you have to be able to laugh or cry on cue. I have a couple of techniques that work for me. If I want to laugh, I just think of my sex life.
And if you want to cry?
I just think of my sex life.

24 A famous actor bumped into a friend at a Hollywood party and started to tell him about the success of his latest film.
'They love it,' he said, 'and they love me in it! The audience reaction has been fantastic and you should read the reviews – they're calling me the new Laurence Olivier! We are talking Oscar nominations here! *And* they've got me on the front cover of *Time* next week!
'Anyway, Gerry, here I am going on about myself all the time and I haven't even asked about you. Tell me, what did *you* think of me in the film?'

25 An actor walked into a seedy café for a quick cup of coffee and was amazed to see another actor washing the dishes behind the counter.
'Good grief!' he cried, 'an actor of your talent and experience, working in a place like this!'
And the other actor replied, 'Well, at least I don't *eat* here!'

26 The waitress stared hard at the handsome young actor she was serving and finally said, 'Where have I seen you before?'
The actor replied, 'You may have seen me in the movies.'
'That's possible,' said the waitress. 'Where do you normally sit?'

27 The young actor really believed in immersing himself in the part. He'd spend days reading, researching and thinking himself into it. Then, one day, he got his big break: he was invited to audition for the starring role of Abraham Lincoln in a play about the president's life. The actor went to the library and read everything he could on the subject and then, on the day of the audition, rented a Lincoln outfit – right down to the black top hat and the beard. Looking in the mirror he could convince himself he *was* Abraham Lincoln.

But despite everything, he didn't get the job. On the way to the audition he was assassinated!

28 Acting is merely the art of keeping a large group of people from coughing.
Sir Ralph Richardson

29 An actor's success has the life expectancy of a small boy about to look into a gas tank with a lighted match.
Fred Allen

30 If you really want to help the American theater, don't be an actress, darling. Be an audience.
Tallulah Bankhead

31 One of my chief regrets during my years in the theatre is that I couldn't sit in the audience and watch me.
John Barrymore

32 You can pick out actors by the glazed look that comes into their eyes when the conversation wanders away from themselves.
Michael Wilding

See Landlords 3; *see also* Egotists, Films, Professions, Television, Theatre, Vanity

Addiction

1 I only play golf on days that have a 'd' in them.

2 I take these tablets. They're not habit-forming as long as you take one every day.

3 You should stop taking those pills. They might be habit-forming.
Nonsense. I've been taking them regularly for ten years!

See Water 1; *see also* Alcoholism, Drink, Drugs, Smoking

Adolescence

1 Adolescence is the age when a child feels that its parents should be taught the facts of life.

2 Adolescence is the time when you're always starting things you can't finish – like phone calls.

3 I really wish I was young enough to know everything.

See also Teenagers

Advertising

1 Advertising is what makes you think you've longed all your life for something you've never heard of before.

2 FOR SALE Television set. Hardly used. Owned by old lady with weak eyesight.

3 He had some brilliant ideas as an advertising man. Once he got a boxer to accept an ad for aspirins on the soles of his shoes.

4 I found something fascinating in the small ads today – FOR SALE Two single beds and a worn carpet.

5 I saw an ad on TV last night for a mouthwash that guarantees to kill all known germs. But who wants a mouthful of dead germs?

6 I saw an ad in my local paper. It read: 'Used gravestone for sale. Ideal gift for family called Ellsworth.'

7 There's no doubt advertising brings

quick results. Yesterday we advertised for a security guard and last night we were burgled.

8 WANTED Man to work forty hours a week to replace man who didn't.

9 Woman with mallet would like to meet man with bow legs. Object: croquet.

10 A company selling tins of red salmon was in trouble. People were buying twice as many tins of *pink* salmon. So the company called in an advertising agency, explained the problem and waited for them to come up with a solution – which they did.

The label, they suggested, should be changed to read: 'Authentic Red Salmon – Guaranteed Not to Turn Pink!'

11 The chewing-gum magnate R. J. Wrigley was on a flight to Chicago when the friend sitting next to him asked why, with Wrigley's chewing gum far outselling all other brands, he still needed to advertise.

The great man replied, 'For the same reason that the pilot keeps this plane's engines running even though we're already in the air.'

12 Bonzo Snax – the dog food so good, it doesn't need a slogan!
Bumper sticker

See Banks and Banking 6, Business 3, Dogs 1, Games 6, Hair 16, Smoking 11, Television 24; *see also* Newspapers, Public Relations, Radio, Sales and Selling, Television

Advice

1 A word of advice: don't give it.

2 Don't take any advice – including this.

3 The best way to save face is to keep the lower half shut.

4 LETTER TO PROBLEM PAGE: I am in love with a beautiful girl but she doesn't even know I'm alive.
REPLY: Show her your birth certificate.

5 LETTER TO PROBLEM PAGE: My husband and I have just qualified for our old age pensions and it's made him very passionate. He wants to make love to me every moment of the day. What am I to do? PS Please excuse the wobbly handwriting.

6 Advice is seldom welcome; and those who want it the most always like it the least.
Earl of Chesterfield

7 Always do right. This will surprise some people and astonish the rest.
Mark Twain

8 Don't give a woman advice: one should never give a woman anything she can't wear in the evening.
Oscar Wilde

9 Start every day with a smile – and get it over with.
W. C. Fields

10 When a man comes to me for advice, I find out the kind of advice he wants, and give it to him.
Josh Billings

See Banks and Banking 15, Wealth 24

Age

1 He says he's looking forward to his twenty-ninth birthday. But I'm afraid he's looking in the wrong direction.

2 Her age is a millinery secret: she keeps it under her hat.

3 I don't know how old you are but you certainly don't look it.

4 I'm as young as I've ever been – allowing for age.

5 I've known her for many years – in fact, since we were the same age.

6 My uncle lived to be 100 and he owed it all to mushrooms. He never ate them!

7 She says she's approaching thirty, but she won't say from which direction!

8 Some of the happiest years of a woman's life are when she's twenty-nine.

9 You're twelve years old? Heavens – when I was your age I was sixteen!

10 The best way to tell a woman's age is not to.

11 Twenty-five is always a nice age for a woman – especially if she happens to be forty.

12 Twenty-nine is a wonderful age for a man to be and a woman to stay.

13 Women who don't marry by the time they're twenty-eight usually stay that age until they do.

14 You know you're getting on when people call you young-looking instead of young.

15 You know you're an adult when you've ceased to grow vertically but not horizontally.

16 Some people think she's a bit hoity-toity.
Well, she may be hoity but, believe me, she'll never see toity again!

17 Did my wife tell you how old she was?
Partly.

18 FIRST WOMAN: How do you keep your youth?
SECOND WOMAN: I lock him in the wardrobe!

19 I don't look twenty-five, do I?
No, but you did when you were.

20 I used to be young once.
What a memory!

21 PERSONNEL MANAGER: I see that your birthday is on 30 September. May I ask what year?
WOMAN: Every year.

22 A woman is as old as she looks before breakfast.
Edgar Watson Howe

23 My mother is going to have to stop lying about her age because pretty soon I'm going to be older than she is.
Tripp Evans

24 There was no respect for youth when I was young, and now that I am old there is no respect for age. I missed it coming and going.
J. B. Priestley

See Children 31, Diplomacy 9; *see also* Birthday Parties, Birthdays, Experience, Middle Age, Old Age

Alcoholism

1 Alcoholics have one thing in common with arthritics – they're always stiff in one joint or another.

2 His problem is he doesn't just drink to excess, he drinks to anything.

3 If you're rich you're an alcoholic, if you're poor you're just a drunk.

4 What's the difference between a drunk and an alcoholic?
The drunk doesn't have to go to meetings.

5 An alcoholic is someone you don't like who drinks as much as you do.
Dylan Thomas

See also Addiction, Drink

Alimony

1 Alimony is the arrangement whereby two people make a mistake but only one pays for it.

2 Alimony is like having to pay instalments on a car after you've written it off.

3 First she gets your wages – that's your take-home pay. Then she gets your alimony – that's your leave-home pay.

4 How times change. Today, a faithful husband is one whose alimony cheques arrive on time.

5 I'm two months late with my alimony – one more month and my wife can repossess me!

6 My wife was delighted with the divorce settlement. She got custody of the money.

7 Paying alimony is like having the TV on after you've fallen asleep.

8 There's only one thing more expensive than a wife and that's an ex-wife.

9 What do you mean I'm not a good housekeeper? Every time I get divorced I keep the house, don't I?

10 JUDGE: I'm awarding your wife 200 pounds a month.
HUSBAND: Very generous. I might even chip in a few pounds myself!

See also Debt, Divorce, Money, Separation

Ambition

1 There's definitely a connection between getting up in the morning and getting up in the world.

2 I want to be what I was when I wanted to be what I am now.

See Bosses 6, Cannibals 1, Cars 2, Catholics 2, Gold-diggers 6; *see also* Incentives, Success

America and the Americans

1 America, where everyone would love to be able to run a big Cadillac convertible – especially the people who *own* a big Cadillac convertible!

2 America is proof that immigration is the sincerest form of flattery.

3 America is the only country in the world where the poor have a parking problem.

4 I'd much rather work in New York than Los Angeles. For a start, you get paid three hours earlier.

5 They say America was discovered before Christopher Columbus but they'd just kept quiet about it.

6 So how difficult could it be to discover America? Surely, it's too big to miss!

7 Christopher Columbus travelled 2,000 miles on a galleon, and we think it's great if our cars do fifty!

8 The Europeans were delighted when Christopher Columbus discovered America. At last they had somewhere to borrow money from.

9 America was founded in 1776. When was it losted?

10 We came across a Cherokee tribe. The chief greeted me. He said, 'How!'
    And I said, 'How!'
    Then he said, 'How!'
    And I said, 'How.'
I didn't know you could speak Cherokee.
It's easy when you know how.

11 All America has to do to get in bad all over the world is just to start out on what we think is a Good Samaritan mission.
Will Rogers

12 All the problems we face in the United States today can be traced to an unenlightened immigration policy on the part of the American Indian.
Pat Paulsen

13 An asylum for the sane would be empty in America.
George Bernard Shaw

14 I have just returned from Boston. It is the only thing to do if you find yourself up there.
Fred Allen

15 That's America for you. They won't let kids pray in school, but they put Bibles in motels.
Bob Hope

See Debt 2, Lawyers 14, Newspapers 9; *see also* California, Hollywood, Los Angeles, New York, Texas and the Texans

American football

1 At my institution we're determined to develop a school of which the football team can be proud.

2 Pro football is like nuclear warfare. There are no winners, only survivors.
Frank Gifford

See Failure 8, Politics and Politicians 48; *see also* Defeat, Losers, Sport, Victory

Amnesia

1 Amnesia is nature's way of saying 'Forget it!'

2 I found a cure for my amnesia but then I forgot what it was.

3 I'm losing my memory. It's got me terribly worried.
Never mind. Try and forget about it.

4 PATIENT: I'm suffering from amnesia.
DOCTOR: Have you ever had it before?

See Proposals 17, Stupidity 21; *see also* Absent-minded, Doctors, Memory, Psychiatry

Ancestors

1 The cheapest way of tracing your family tree is to run for public office.

2 The thing is, heredity runs in our family.

3 She says her family came over on the *Mayflower*.
Let's hope the immigration laws are stricter now.

4 I've traced my ancestors right back to royalty?
You mean King Kong?

5 My family's records go back at least eight centuries. How about yours?
Ours were lost in the Flood!

6 I don't know who my grandfather was; I am much more concerned to know what his grandson will be.
Abraham Lincoln

See Thrift 2; *see also* Aristocracy, Families, Heredity, Snobbery

Anger

1 He seems to be angry all the time. Last week he went to a fortune-teller to have his fist read.

2 He was so angry he was beside himself – and you've never seen a more repulsive couple!

3 The worst-tempered people I've ever met were people who knew they were wrong.
Wilson Mizner

See Doctors 49

Animals

1 As the mother kangaroo said, 'I just hate it when it's raining and the kids have to play inside!'

2 My uncle Horace is in the dining room now, stuffing a gorilla – up the chimney. It stops the draughts, you know!

3 My uncle was visiting the zoo and the keeper told him the alligator would eat off his hand. So he tried – and it did!

4 There were three bears. One of them married a giraffe. The other two put him up to it.

5 Deep in the jungle, I came face to face with a ferocious lion.
Did it give you a start?
I didn't need one!

6 Do you know, it takes three sheep to make a sweater?
I didn't even know they could knit.

7 How do you get down from an elephant?
You don't. You get down from a swan.

8 I've heard that a tiger won't hurt you if you carry a violin.
It depends on how fast you carry it.

9 What's the difference between a buffalo and a bison?
I don't know.
You can't wash your hands in a buffalo.

10 I opened my refrigerator one morning and found a rabbit sitting in there. I said, 'What are you doing in here?'
He said, 'This is a Westinghouse, right?'
'Yes.'
'So, I'm westing!'

See The Bible 5, 6, City Life 5, England and the English 3, Gambling 7, Limericks 6, Mankind 1; see also Birds, Cats, Cross Jokes, Dogs, Horses

Anniversaries

1 A silver-wedding party is the occasion on which a married couple celebrate the fact that twenty-five years of their marriage is over.

2 The biggest surprise you can give your wife on your anniversary is to remember it.

3 The farmer and his wife were discussing how to celebrate their silver-wedding anniversary.
The wife said, 'Shall I kill a chicken?'
And the farmer replied, 'Why blame a poor bird for something that happened twenty-five years ago?'

See Infidelity 11, Stinginess 32; see also Birthday Parties, Birthdays, New Year, Parties, Thanksgiving

Antiques

1 An antique is something your grandparents bought for five pounds, your parents sold for fifty and you bought again for 500.

2 I got a statue of the Venus de Milo cheap because it was faulty. It had both arms.

3 I own heirlooms, you own antiques, he owns junk.

4 I've got a dining-room suite that goes back to Louis the Fourteenth. Unless I pay Louis by the thirteenth!

5 Most antiques aren't what they're cracked up to be.

6 She was only an antique-dealer's daughter, but she wouldn't allow much on the sofa.

7 When old junk meets new money you've got an antique.

8 My uncle's got a Chippendale chair. That's nothing. My uncle's got an Adam's apple.

9 A crafty old antique-dealer is travelling through rural Somerset when he spots a priceless Chippendale cabinet in a junk shop. He knows he will make tens of thousands of pounds reselling it if he can persuade the shop-owner that it's worthless. He offers the man five pounds, explaining that the only reason he's

interested is that he needs some firewood and the wood should burn well.

So the price is agreed and the dealer explains that he'll return the next day with his van to pick up the cabinet.

The following morning, the dealer drives up and sees a pile of old wood sitting outside the shop. 'What's that?' he says.

'It's the cabinet,' says the shop-owner. 'I felt so guilty charging five pounds for firewood that I've done you a favour and chopped it up for you.'

See Honesty 1; see also Decoration, Furniture

Anxiety

1 I'm not saying she's the nervous type, but it takes two stiff gins to give her the courage to open her bottle of tranquillizers.

2 If my dad wasn't so shy and reserved, I'd be at least four years older than I am.

3 Me worried? I'm telling you, these days I'm sleeping like a baby – I wake up every three hours, crying my eyes out.

4 It requires a great deal of inexperience to be beyond the reach of anxiety.
Anon.

5 There are two days in the week on which I never worry: one is yesterday and the other is tomorrow.
Anon.

See also Fear, Timidity, Worry

Apathy

1 Do you think voters today are apathetic?
Who cares?

Apologies

1 Man is the only member of the animal kingdom that apologizes. Or needs to.

2 Very sorry can't come. Lie follows by post.
Telegram from Charles Beresford

Appearance

1 Does he look ill? He looks like he gave his pallbearers the slip.

2 Ever since I told her she had a nice profile, she walks everywhere sideways.

3 He had so many spots on his face, his friends used to play connect-the-dots on it.

4 He looks like an undertaker started work on him but was suddenly called away.

5 Her measurements were 38, 24, 35 – but not necessarily in that order.

6 My brother takes a bath once a month whether he needs one or not.

7 She had eyes like two limpid pools – and a nose like a diving board.

8 She looked like she got dressed in front of an aeroplane propeller!

9 She spent five hours at the beauty salon – just getting an estimate.

10 She wanted to have her face lifted but it proved impossible. So, for half the price, they lowered her body.

11 She was amazing! That girl had everything a man could want: big muscles, a beard, a moustache . . .

12 The trouble was, she looked a vision in the evening but a sight in the morning.

13 They say some faces are so ugly they could stop a clock. His could stop Switzerland!

14 To look at his face, you'd think his hobby was stepping on rakes.

15 Do you ever file your nails?
No, I just cut them off and throw them away!

16 He's got a good head on his shoulders.
Yes, but it would look a lot better on his neck.

17 So your sister makes up jokes. Is she a humorist?
No, she works in a beauty salon.

18 There was something different about this girl.
How do you mean?
She had a beard.

19 Why don't you wash your face occasionally? I can see what you had for breakfast this morning!
Oh, yeah. What did I have?
Bacon and eggs.
Wrong. That was *yesterday* morning!

20 My uncle and aunt were dawdling round Madame Tussaud's when the commissionaire came up to them and said, 'Can you keep moving, please, we're stocktaking.'

See also Baldness, Beards and Moustaches, Beauty, Clothes, Faces, Figures – Fat, Figures – Thin, Height – Short, Height – Tall, Plastic Surgery, Shaving, Ugliness

Approval

1 Admiration: our polite recognition of another's resemblance to ourselves.
Ambrose Bierce

See also Flattery

Archaeology

1 An archaeologist is someone whose life is in ruins.

Arguments

1 Are we incompatible? We can't even agree on what to argue about!

2 He's so argumentative, he won't even eat food that agrees with him.

3 I may not agree with what you say but I'll defend to the death your right to shut up.

4 I try not to argue with my wife. I might win, and then I'd really be in trouble.

5 I wouldn't mind him having the last word – if only he'd get to it.

6 I'm warning you, I could lick you with both hands tied behind your back!

7 Let me put it this way. Shut up!

8 Look, I'll meet you half-way. I'll admit I'm wrong if you'll admit I'm right.

9 My boss said he would welcome an exchange of opinions. What he meant by that is that I should arrive with mine and go away with his.

10 My husband's a magician. He can turn anything into an argument.

11 My wife always forgives me when she's in the wrong.

12 My wife and I have finally come to terms. Hers!

13 My wife and I started arguing on our wedding day. When I said, 'I do,' she said, 'Oh no you don't!'

14 My wife said to me, 'Can't we ever have a quiet little discussion without you putting your two cents in?'

15 My wife's hobby is making things – like mountains out of molehills.

16 Of course he's inflexible. He won't even listen to both sides of a record!

17 We've been married fifteen years now and we've only had one quarrel. It started on our wedding day and it hasn't finished yet!

18 But you promised to forgive and forget!
Yes, but I don't want you to forget that I've forgiven and forgotten!

19 Come over here!
I *am* over here!

20 I've come to see the head of the household.
You'll have to wait a minute. We're just deciding it!

21 A husband and wife were having a furious row in a restaurant. The wife screamed, 'You disgusting swine! Of all the low-down, low-life skunks you're the lowest, you miserable excuse for a human being!'
The husband suddenly realized, they were being observed from another table. 'Quite right, darling,' he said, 'and what else did you tell him?'

22 A husband and wife had not spoken to each other for hours following a sharp difference of opinion. Finally, the husband decided to surrender. 'I'm sorry,' he told her. 'I've been thinking about it and you're absolutely right.'
'It's too late now,' the wife yelled. 'I've changed my mind!'

23 I am not arguing with you – I am telling you.
James McNeill Whistler

24 My wife was too beautiful for words, but not for arguments.
John Barrymore

26 What part of 'No' don't you understand?
Bumper sticker

26 When people are least sure, they are often most dogmatic.
J. K. Galbraith

See The Army 4, Divorce 25, Hobbies 1, Women – The Male View 3; *see also* Enemies, Fighting, Marriage, Swearing

Aristocracy

1 He's just a crumb from the upper crust.

2 He can trace his family tree right back to when his family used to live in it.

3 His family have been aristocrats for degenerations.

4 She has such an upturned nose that every time she sneezes, she blows her hat off.

5 It's nothing but the best for him. He even has monogrammed tea-bags.

6 He's a member of the effluent society – one of the stinking rich.

7 I come from a hunting family. My mother went out hunting every morning.
Hunting what?
My father.

8 LADY: I'd like twelve dozen roses for my daughter's coming-out party.
FLORIST: If you don't mind me asking, what was she put away for?

See Laziness 3; *see also* Ancestors, Families, Heredity, Snobbery

Army, The

1 He's got an excellent war record: Vera Lynn singing *The White Cliffs of Dover*.

2 I come from an old military family: one of my ancestors fell at Waterloo. Someone pushed him off Platform Nine!

3 I got this medal in the war for saving two women. One for me and one for the general.

4 I had a very distinguished army career. I fought with Mountbatten

13

in Burma. I fought with Alexander in Tunis. I fought with Montgomery at Alamein. I couldn't get on with anybody!

5 I won my sergeant's stripes the hard way. I started as a lieutenant.

6 My father got discharged from the army with back trouble. He kept deserting and they kept bringing him back!

7 My only regret was that I had but one life to give for my country. If I'd had two, I would have felt a lot safer.

8 My platoon was behind me as one man. And that's all there was – one man.

9 Nobody could dig a foxhole like I could. I once dug one so deep, it was just short of desertion.

10 Have you got your gun with you, Private?
Yes.
Yes what, Private?
Yes, indeed!
That's better.

11 Have you heard I'm now in the army?
Did you get a commission?
No, just my salary!

12 I only had one bullet left. So I shot fifty of them.
Fifty of them with one bullet?
Yes, they were coming at me in single file.

13 I proved to the enemy that this was no place for cowards.
How?
I ran like mad.

14 I was decorated for saving the lives of the entire regiment.
What did you do?
I shot the cook.

15 My name's Colonel Henry Davenport, DSO, MC, OBE.

That's a funny way to spell Davenport.

16 Q: What must a man be to be buried with full military honours?
A: Dead.

17 RECRUIT: You don't want me in the army. Look, I've got one leg shorter than the other.
MEDICAL OFFICER: It doesn't matter. Where you're going, the ground's very uneven.

18 SERGEANT: Fire at will!
SOLDIER: Which one is Will?

19 SERGEANT: You failed to turn up for camouflage class!
PRIVATE: How can you be sure?

20 So how does your uniform fit you, Private?
Well, sir, the jacket is all right but the trousers are a little loose around the armpits.

21 What were you in civilian life?
Happy!

22 Where were you wounded?
In the Dardanelles.
How very painful.

See Bores 30, Ethnic Jokes 3, Old Age 26, Scotland and the Scots 5, Strength 1; *see also* The Navy, Victory, War

Art and artists

1 An artist is a man who won't prostitute his art – except for money.

2 An artist is what anyone can claim to be – and no one can prove them wrong.

3 He wanted to paint her in the nude, but she insisted he keep his clothes on.

4 He went to art school but got thrown out of the life class for trying to trace the nudes.

5 He's a complete philistine. The only thing he knows about Art is that it's short for Arthur.

6 He's a terrible artist. He couldn't even draw the curtains!

7 Rembrandt produced roughly 300 paintings – of which nearly 1,000 are in America!

8 You've got to hand it to the Venus de Milo. I mean, how else would she eat?

9 How do you go about carving a statue of an angel?
It's easy. You just get a block of marble and chip away everything that doesn't look like an angel.

10 I'd like to donate my paintings to a worthy charity.
How about the Institute for the Blind?

11 Is that a Constable over the fireplace?
Yes, he's sitting up there because his boots are damp.

12 Is this another of your abstract paintings?
No, it's a mirror!

13 This painting is supposed to be of a man and a woman sitting under a tree.
So why isn't it?

14 VAN GOGH: Take this ear as a token of my affection for you.
WOMAN: Why, thank you!
VAN GOGH: Pardon?

15 The model ascended the ladder
As Titian, the artist, had bade her.
The position, to Titian,
Suggested coition
So he climbed up the ladder and had her!

16 When I was in Italy last year, I bought a painting from a little gallery in Florence. When I got it home, I took it to a dealer in Bond Street and asked him what he thought of it.
He said, 'The good news is it's a genuine Pandino, from his Venice period. The bad news is that Pandino was a plumber.'

17 Abstract art: a product of the untalented, sold by the unprincipled to the utterly bewildered.
Al Capp

18 All art is quite useless.
Oscar Wilde

19 An artist is somebody who produces things that people don't need to have.
Andy Warhol

20 Every time I paint a portrait, I lose a friend.
John Singer Sargent

21 The English public takes no interest in a work of art until it is told that the work in question is immoral.
Oscar Wilde

22 What garlic is to salad, insanity is to art.
Augustus Saint-Gaudens

See Antiques 2; see also Critics

Atheism

1 An atheist is someone with no invisible means of support.

2 There's a new Dial-a-Prayer for atheists. You dial the number and no one answers.

See also Church, God, Heaven, Hell, Religion, Scepticism

Audiences

1 Last night's audience was with him all the way. No matter how fast he ran, he still couldn't shake them off!

2 If my fanny squirms, it's bad. If my fanny doesn't squirm, it's good. It's as simple as that.
Harry Cohn

3 The play was a great success, but the audience was a failure.
Oscar Wilde

See Singing – Insults 17, Speakers and Speeches 9; *see also* Actors and Acting, Circus, Dancing, Films, Opera, Speakers and Speeches, Theatre

Australia and Australians

1 They say a well-balanced Australian is one with a chip on both shoulders.

2 A bushman walked into a pub in the Northern Territories, pulling behind him an enormous crocodile on a leash.
   'What can I get you?' said the barman.
   'Do you serve Pommies?'
   'English people? Sure, we serve them.'
   'Great,' said the bushman, 'I'll have a meat pie for myself and a couple of Pommies for the croc!'

Awards

1 I'm not sure that I deserve an honour such as this, but then, what is my opinion against that of thousands?

2 When they heard he was being honoured, everyone in the hall as one shouted, 'Why?'

3 You'll have to excuse me. I was so surprised at getting this award, I almost dropped my acceptance speech!

4 I can forgive Alfred Nobel for having invented dynamite, but only a fiend in human form could have invented the Nobel Prize.
George Bernard Shaw

See also Actors and Acting, Tributes, Tributes – Responses

Babies

1 A baby is a perfect example of minority rule.

2 A baby is something that gets you down in the daytime and up at night.

3 We call our baby 'Teeny'. We'd call him 'Martini' but he isn't dry enough.

4 They said the baby looked just like me. Then they turned him the right way up!

5 I was a premature baby – my father wasn't expecting me.

6 As babies, we used to share the same nappy. It was the only way to make ends meet.

7 Darling, can you get up and go to see why the baby isn't crying.

8 I was so surprised when I was born that I couldn't talk for a year and a half.

9 It's easy to look after a baby. All you've got to do is keep one end full and the other end empty.

10 One of the first things you learn from a baby is that you should never change nappies in midstream.

11 People who say they sleep like a baby usually don't have one.

12 The baby was christened 'Glug-Glug'. The vicar fell into the font!

13 The baby's father and mother were first cousins. That's why he looks so much alike.

14 There's nothing like having a baby to make you realize it's a changing world.

15 You know what they say: out of the mouths of babes comes ... cereal.

16 But, darling, this isn't our baby!
I know, but it's a much nicer pram!

17 I hear that God has sent you two more brothers.
That's right. And He knows where the money's going to come from, I heard Dad say last night.

18 When the baby cries at night, who gets up?
The whole street!

19 I know a woman who just had triplets.
Heavens. do you know that triplets happen only once in every 15,000 births?
I know. I wonder when she ever had time to do the housework.

20 I've got a baby brother. He's called Onyx.
Why Onyx?
Because he was onyxpected.

21 Is your baby a boy or a girl?
Of course. What else could it be?

22 It must be time to get up, darling.
How do you know?
The baby's fallen asleep.

23 My father was very disappointed when I was born.
Why? Did he want a girl?
No, he wanted a divorce.

24 My sister is expecting a little stranger.
Oh, I'm sure they'll soon get to know each other.

25 PROUD FATHER: My new baby looks just like me!
NURSE: Well, never mind. As long as it's healthy.

26 What's the new baby's name?
I don't know. We can't understand a word he says!

27 Now you've had the baby, you must be worried about getting your figure back.
Not so much as I'm worried about getting the father back!

28 Babies are such a nice way to start people.
Don Herold

See Song Titles 3; *see also* Babysitters, Birth, Children

Babysitters

1 A babysitter is a teenage girl you hire to let your kids do whatever they want.

2 A babysitter is a girl hired to solve the problem of what to do with the leftovers.

3 A babysitter is a girl you hire at two pounds an hour to eat five pounds' worth of food and make ten pounds' worth of telephone calls.

4 We've devised a great new way to make sure the babysitter does her job properly. We keep the baby in the fridge.

See also Babies, Children

Baldness

1 He wears a wig. It makes him look at least ten years sillier.

2 He's very sensitive about his hair. I don't know why. He hasn't got any!

3 I could tell you things about your baldness that would make your hair fall out.

4 I started going bald very early. In fact, in high school I was voted 'Most Likely to Recede'.

5 I'm not bald. I'm just too tall for my hair!

6 I'm not really bald. I've just got a tall face!

7 I've been washing my hair too much – it's shrinking!

8 The great advantage of being bald is that, when someone calls unexpectedly, all you've got to do is straighten your tie.

9 The only way I know to keep your hair from falling out is to knot it from the inside.

10 They're just marketing a new cure for baldness. It doesn't grow hair, it just shrinks your head to fit what hair you've got left.

11 Did you lose your hair by worrying?
Yes, worrying about losing my hair.

12 HAIRDRESSER: Do you find split hair a problem?
CUSTOMER: Yes. Mine split a year ago!

13 How do I avoid falling hair?
Jump out of the way!

14 PATIENT: Have you got anything to keep my hair in?
DOCTOR: How about a shoebox?

15 Your hair's getting thinner.
So who wants fat hair?

16 When you're losing your hair at the front, it means you're a great thinker. And when you're losing your hair at the back, it means you're a great lover.
But I'm losing mine at the front *and* the back.
That means you think you're a great lover!

See Figures – Fat 15; *see also* Appearance, Barbers, Hair

Bankruptcy

1 He certainly had a lot of nerve. He took a taxi to the bankruptcy court, and invited the driver in as a creditor!

2 My friend was facing bankruptcy. In his despair, he turned to the Bible for consolation – and opened it at Chapter 11.

See also Borrowing and Lending, Credit, Credit Cards, Hard Times, Inflation, Money

Banks and banking

1 A bank is a financial institution from which you can borrow money as long as you can provide sufficient evidence to show you don't need it.

2 A banker is someone who lends money to the already affluent.

3 A banker is simply a pawnbroker with a manicure.

4 Banking is just like government – a system of checks and balances. If you want to have a cheque, you have to have a balance.

5 But I can't be overdrawn. I've still got fifteen cheques left!

6 Don't you sometimes wish that the man who writes the bank's advertising was also the man who approves the loans?

7 I don't trust banks to get their figures right. If bankers can count, why do they always have six windows and two cashiers?

8 I'd love to work in a bank. They've got the two things I like best: money and holidays.

9 If money doesn't grow on trees, how come the banks have so many branches?

10 The bank wrote to me yesterday to ask me to return some money I'd borrowed. I told them I can't – I haven't finished with it yet.

11 They turned me down for a loan. And all I wanted was enough to pay for a one-way ticket to South America.

12 How much have you got in your bank?
Hold on, I'll just give it a rattle.

13 What is the name of your bank?
'Piggy'.

14 A man walks into a bank to cash a cheque and the cashier says, 'OK, but you'll have to identify yourself.'
So the man looks into a mirror and says, 'Yes, that's me all right!'

15 LETTER TO AGONY AUNT: I have two brothers. One works in a bank and the other is a convicted serial killer. My father died in the electric chair and my mother is a drug-dealer. I've just met a wonderful girl and I've asked her to marry me. My problem is, should I tell her that I have a brother who is a banker?

16 The bank director was impressed by the young trainee's facility with figures. He said, 'Where did you learn your maths?'
And the trainee said, 'Yale.'
'Yale! And what's your name?'
'Yerry Yackson.'

17 It is easier to rob by setting up a bank than by holding up a bank clerk.
Bertolt Brecht

See Christmas 5; *see also* Accountants, Bankruptcy, Borrowing and Lending, Credit, Credit Cards, Debt, Hard Times, Inflation, Money, Saving, Spending, Thrift, Wealth

Barbers

1 Just give me a shave. I haven't got time to listen to a haircut.

2 BARBER: (*Holding up the mirror*) So how do you like it?
CUSTOMER: Could you make it a little longer in the back?

3 How do you want your hair cut? Off!

4 Now I've started to lose my hair, you should charge me less for a haircut.
On the contrary, I should charge you more for looking for it.

5 BARBER: How was that lotion I gave you for growing hair on your bald patch?
CUSTOMER: Well, you remember telling me to rub it into my scalp every night?
BARBER: Yes.
CUSTOMER: Well, my head's still bald but I have to shave my fingers twice a day!

See also Baldness, Beards and Moustaches, Hair, Talkers

Baseball

1 In our team we have so few hits that if anyone reaches first base, he has to stop and ask the way.

2 My team's lost so many games that when it rains, we have a victory party!

3 The reason I like baseball better than golf is that when you hit the ball in baseball, someone else chases after it.

4 We've got to get a new catcher. The only thing ours has caught this season is tonsillitis.

5 PITCHER: I thought I did pretty good stuff today.
MANAGER: Well, the batters on the other team certainly liked it!

6 The team was in a dreadful batting slump so the coach decided to hold a special practice session, but the way the players hit, or mis-hit, the ball just underlined how bad the problem was. So the coach jumped out of the dug-out, grabbed a bat and said, 'Let me show you guys how it's done.'
The pitcher threw the ball and the coach missed it completely. He tried again, and missed again. After ten swings, he still hadn't managed to hit the ball properly.
When he missed the eleventh, he threw the bat to the ground and said, '*That's* what you've been doing. Now get up there and hit the damned thing!'

7 Baseball has the great advantage over cricket of being sooner ended.
George Bernard Shaw

8 Managing is getting paid for home runs someone else hits.
Casey Stengel

See also Defeat, Losers, Sport, Victory

Beach

1 I got an award for bravery on the beach. I saved a young girl from a lifeguard!

2 I saw a mermaid at the beach. What a figure – 36, 23 and 95p a pound.

3 The beach was so exclusive, even the tide couldn't get in.

4 Ow, a crab's just bitten my toe!
Which one?
I don't know. All crabs look alike to me!

5 What did you do during the summer?
I was a lifeguard.

What did you do?
I saved women.
What for?
The winter.

See Figures – Fat 29, Pollution 2, Pollution – Water 2; *see also* Holidays, The Sea, Summer, The Sun, Weather – Hot

Beards and moustaches

1 Did you know you can't hang a man with a moustache? You have to use a rope.

2 Girls are crazy about my moustache. I can kiss them and brush their teeth at the same time.

3 I put varnish on my moustache. I like to keep a stiff upper lip.

4 I've got a really tough beard. My electric razor has three settings: 'Slow', 'Medium' and 'Timber!'

5 There was a dispute at a school over the suspension of a teacher who, against all the rules, grew a long, black beard. But finally they had to keep her.

6 There's a man at the door with a moustache.
Tell him I've already got one.

See Appearance 11, 18, Manners 10, Teeth 10; *see also* Barbers, Faces, Hair, Shaving

Beauty

1 Did anyone ever tell you how beautiful you are – and mean it?

2 I used to love Marilyn Monroe; she was my favourite member of the opposite sex. In fact, she was about as opposite as you could get.

3 She had a smile that could light up a small town!

4 She had something guaranteed to knock your eye out – a husband.

5 She was wearing a dress so tight I could hardly breathe.

6 She went in for the beauty contest, came second and was bitterly disappointed. She was the only entrant!

7 She's the kind of girl you can take home to mother. Provided, of course, that you can trust your father.

8 What a beauty! She had a smile that could ripen bananas.

9 I was once taken for Miss World.
You may have been taken for Miss World, but I bet they brought you back in a hurry.

11 Any girl can be glamorous. All you have to do is stand still and look stupid.
Hedy Lamarr

12 You'd be surprised how much it costs to look this cheap.
Dolly Parton

See Legs 7; *see also* Appearance, Cosmetics, Plastic Surgery, Ugliness

Begging

1 He said he hadn't had a bite in two days, so I bit him.

2 BEGGAR: I haven't eaten for a week.
PASSER-BY: Well, you must force yourself.

3 BEGGAR: I haven't had food for so long, I've forgotten what it tastes like.
PASSER-BY: Don't worry, it still tastes the same!

4 Can you give me a pound for a cup of coffee?
But you can get a cup of coffee for 50p.
I know, but I thought you might like to join me.

5 Can you spare ninety pounds for a cup of tea?

Ninety pounds for a cup of tea? Why?
Well, I can't go into a restaurant dressed like this, can I?

6 I haven't eaten anything in three days!
I wish I had your will-power!

7 Would you give me 50p for a sandwich?
I don't know. Let's see the sandwich!

See Beverly Hills 3, Business 17, Dogs 10; *see also* Borrowing and Lending, Charity, Hard Times, Poverty

Beverly Hills

1 In Beverly Hills every December, kids sit on Santa's lap and ask him what he wants for Christmas.

2 The richest plumbers in the world are in Beverly Hills. They don't even bother to make housecalls.

3 No one's poor in Beverly Hills. Even the bums live on Skid Drive.

See Exercise 3, Wills 2; *see also* Hollywood, Shopping, Spending, Texas and Texans, Wealth

Bible, The

1 According to the Bible, the lion will lie down with the lamb. But the lamb won't get too much sleep!

2 ADAM TO EVE: Wow, where on earth did you learn to kiss like that?

3 God made Adam and then He rested. But since Adam made Eve, nobody's rested!

4 Noah would have made a great businessman. He managed to float a company when the whole world was in liquidation.

5 All the animals entered the ark in pairs. Except the worms.
What do you mean?
They entered the ark in apples.

6 Finally, Noah managed to land his Ark on Mount Ararat and, when he'd let down the gangplank, the animals started to leave, led by two giraffes. Two lions followed, then two tigers. Then came *four* gnus.
A man standing on the shore said to Noah, 'Why so many?'
And Noah said, 'Well, there's some good gnus and some bad gnus . . .'

7 'The Good Book' – one of the most remarkable euphemisms ever coined.
Ashley Montagu

See Ancestors 5, Bankruptcy 2, Death 15, Films 6, Love 4, Pests 3, Tributes 17; *see also* Catholics, Church, God, Religion

Bigamy

1 A bigamist is someone who makes a second mistake before correcting the first.

2 A bigamist is a man who has loved not wisely but two well.

3 Bigamy is having one wife too many. Monogamy, in certain cases, is the same thing.

4 Bigamy is the only crime on the books where two rites make a wrong.

5 Poor woman – always a bride, never a bridesmaid.

6 If I were to marry two women, would that be bigamy?
It would be very big of you.

7 JUDGE: I find you not guilty of bigamy. You may now go home to your wife.
DEFENDANT: Thank you, but which one?

8 What's the penalty for bigamy?

Two mothers-in-law.

See also Courtroom, Divorce, Infidelity, Marriage, Weddings

Birds

1 A friend of mine crossed a seagull with a parrot. He still does what a seagull does to people on the beach, but now he apologizes for it!

2 He crossed a homing pigeon with a parrot so that if it got lost, it could ask the way.

3 He crossed a carrier pigeon with a woodpecker so that it would not only carry messages but also knock on the door when it arrived.

4 I crossed a woodpecker with a parrot. Now, when the tree starts to fall, it shouts, 'Timber!'

5 Last year I crossed a hen with a parrot. Now, when it lays an egg, it comes over and tells me about it.

6 Two pigeons were flying over a car dealer's and one said, 'Why don't we put a deposit on that Mercedes?'

7 How much is that parrot?
One hundred pounds.
Fine. Send me the bill.
I'm sorry but you have to take the whole bird.

8 What's that noise?
It's an owl.
I know, but 'oo's 'owling?

9 A couple were taking a stroll in the country when a passing pigeon dropped one straight on the man's head. As he tried to clean up the mess, the woman said, 'Hold on, I've got a paper tissue here.'
   And the man said, 'Don't be silly. He'll be miles away by now!'

10 A hen is only an egg's way of making another egg.
Samuel Butler

See Knock Knock Jokes 7, Lawyers 12, Pollution – Air 2, Sex 34; *see also* Animals, Cross Jokes, Pets

Birth

1 Don't ask me why I was in hospital when I was born. Up till then I'd never had a day's illness in my life.

2 I was an unwanted child. After I was born, my father spent a month trying to find a loophole in my birth certificate.

3 I was born on 24 December, I wanted to be home for Christmas!

4 My dad was so delighted when I was born that he rushed out to tell all his friends. We're expecting him back any day now.

5 When he was born he was so ugly that the doctor slapped his mother.

6 How come you were born in Scarborough?
I wanted to be near my mother.

7 I weighed only six ounces when I was born.
Good heavens! Did you live?
I certainly did! You should see me now!

8 MIDWIFE: It's a girl!
FATHER: Oh.
MIDWIFE: Are you disappointed?
FATHER: Not really. A girl *was* my second choice.

9 Should women have children over forty?
No. Forty are quite enough!

10 Tell me, Doctor, is it a boy?
Well, the one in the middle is!

11 Labour pains had started. The anxious father-to-be called the doctor and told him.
   The doctor said, 'How far apart are the pains?'
   And the father-to-be replied, 'I'm

not absolutely sure, but I think they're in the same place.'

See Actors and Acting 5, Hospitals 4, Insults 72, Losers 15; see also Babies, Birth Control, Hospitals, Names

Birth control

1 Birth control is a way of avoiding the issue.

2 They've just invented the most effective birth-control pill ever. It weighs two and a half tons and when you jam it up against your bedroom door, there's no way your husband can get in.

3 We've been married thirty years now. Our idea of birth control is to turn the lights on.

4 But, Doctor, I thought if you did it standing up, you couldn't get pregnant.
Ah yes, a popular misconception.

5 DOCTOR: A glass of water is a cheap and effective contraceptive.
PATIENT: Do I take it before or after intercourse?
DOCTOR: Instead of.

6 What do you call people who use the rhythm method of birth control?
Parents.

See Dating 19; see also Babies, Birth, Sex

Birthday parties

1 By the time we'd lit the last candle on his birthday cake, the first one had gone out.

2 I tried to count the candles on his birthday cake, but the heat drove me back.

See Families 6; see also Age, Birthdays, Middle Age, Old Age, Parties

Birthdays

1 He was born on 2 April – a day too late.

2 I always remember my wife's birthday. It's the day after she reminds me of it.

3 I'm so depressed. My twin brother forgot my birthday!

4 The only thing I want for my birthday is not to be reminded of it.

5 You should have seen the candles on his seventieth birthday cake. It looked like a forest fire!

6 Guess what? It's my birthday!
Congratulations. How old aren't you?

7 WIFE: You forgot my birthday!
HUSBAND: Oh, my God!
WIFE: You forgot it last year too. Why?
HUSBAND: Well, how am I expected to remember your birthday when you never look any older?

8 The President had a birthday party the other day and he was given a birthday cake with candles on it. He closed his eyes and, as he blew out the candles, he made a wish. But when he opened his eyes he was still President.

See Ethnic Jokes 10, Mothers 5; see also Age, Birthday Parties, Middle Age, Old Age

Blind

1 The woman was having a bath when she heard the doorbell ring. She leapt out of the bath stark naked and ran to the front door.
'Who is it?' she shouted.
'Blind man!' came the reply.
So, being of a charitable nature, she opened the door, obviously not bothering to put on a robe to cover herself.

As she opened the door, the man said, 'All right, lady, where do you want me to put these blinds?'

See Art and Artists 10, Religion 18; *see also* Eyes

Boats and ships

1 Excuse me, sir, the Captain invites you to dine at his table.
Certainly not! I didn't come on this cruise to sit with the crew!

2 If the boat should start sinking, who would you save first – me or the children?
Me!

3 Quick! Send an SOS!
How do you spell it?

4 What do you get if you cross the Atlantic with the *Titanic*?
About half-way.

See also The Navy, Sailing, The Sea, Travel

Books

1 They've just launched this great new book club. You send them a cheque for twenty-five pounds, and they leave you alone for the rest of the year!

2 How did you like my book?
It was OK, but a bit too long in the middle.

3 I enjoyed your book immensely. Who wrote it for you?
I'm so glad you liked it. Who read it to you?

4 This book has a great ending.
How about the beginning?
I haven't got to that yet.

5 Books are good enough in their own way, but they are a mighty bloodless substitute for life.
Robert Louis Stevenson

6 When you put down the good things you ought to have done, and leave out the bad things you did do, that's memoirs.
Will Rogers

See Ethnic Jokes 15, Health 8, Sex 5, Television 12, Tidiness 1; *see also* Books – The Critics, Censorship, Libraries, Literature, Literature – The Critics, Poets and Poetry, Writers and Writing

Books – the critics

1 I got a free copy of this book and I still feel cheated.

2 This book provides a rattling good yawn.

3 If you were to be marooned on a desert island and had the whole of Canadian literature to choose from, what would you take?
Poison.

4 It is written without fear and without research.
Dorothy Parker

5 The love affair between Margot Asquith and Margot Asquith will live as one of the prettiest love stories in all literature.
Dorothy Parker

See also Books, Literature, Literature – The Critics, Writers and Writing

Bores

1 A bore is someone who, when you ask him how he is, tells you.

2 A lecturer is someone who talks in other people's sleep.

3 A bore is a man with a glass in one hand and your lapel in the other.

4 Excuse me, but my leg has gone to sleep. Do you mind if I join it?

5 He can be outspoken, but I've never seen anyone do it yet.

6 He can brighten up a room just by leaving it.

7 He can talk for hours on any given subject, and *days* if he knows anything about it.

8 He can talk the whole day through, without stopping once to think.

9 He doesn't have a lot to say. Unfortunately, you have to listen for quite a while to find that out.

10 He never opens his mouth unless he has nothing to say.

11 He was a stupendous bore. Rumour had it he'd had a charisma-bypass.

12 He's a fascinating conversationalist, but only if you happen to be interested in collecting antique matchbox labels.

13 He's a man who brings happiness whenever he goes.

14 He's a man of few words. The trouble is, he keeps repeating them.

15 He's a perfect bore. He finally stops talking long after you've stopped listening.

16 He's got a tongue that only runs when his brain is in neutral.

17 He's got a very effective way of cutting a long story short. He interrupts!

18 He's the sort of person who, if you ask him what time it is, tells you how the watch works.

19 He's the sort of man who can brighten anyone's day – simply by saying goodbye.

20 If you ever see two people together and one of them looks bored, chances are he's the other.

21 Just a few minutes talking to him makes you want to jump for joy – off a tall building.

22 There's never a dull moment with him. It's continuous!

23 What a bore! He simply cannot understand people who only talk when they've got something to say.

24 What a talker! Believe me, I've just given him a good listening-to.

25 What a talker he is! But lately he's developed a slight impediment in his speech. He stops to breathe!

26 Anyway, to cut a long story short . . .
Too late!

27 I can hardly hear myself speak!
Don't worry. You're not missing much!

28 Is your husband outspoken?
Not by many.

29 UNCLE JIM: I must tell you about my terrifying experience with the cannibals. There I was, lost in the middle of the jungle, surrounded by twenty hungry cannibals!
NEPHEW: But the last time you told me, there were only *ten* hungry cannibals!
UNCLE JIM: Ah, but you were too young then to know the whole horrible truth!

30 With his grandson on his knee, the old soldier was well into the second hour of his wartime experiences – how he fought here, how he escaped there, how he marched from here to there and so on. Finally the little boy piped up, 'Grandad, what did you need the rest of the army for?'

31 Bore: someone who talks when you wish him to listen.
Ambrose Bierce

32 He has occasional flashes of silence that make his conversation perfectly delightful.
Sydney Smith of Lord Macaulay

33 He is not only a bore, but he bores for England.
Malcolm Muggeridge of Sir Anthony Eden

See Accountants 10, Church 1, Grandparents 2, Marriage 42; *see also* Conversation, Hecklers, Insults, Small Towns, Speakers and Speeches, Talkers

Borrowing and lending

1 Can you lend me ten pounds till pay day?
When's pay day?
I don't know. *You're* the one who's working!

2 Can you pay me back that ten pounds you borrowed from me?
I can't, I'm afraid. But I can lend you ten if that would help.

3 Have you forgotten that you owe me ten pounds?
No, but give me time and I will.

4 I say, can you lend me a fiver for a week, old man?
It depends which weak old man it's for.

See Optimism 4; *see also* Bankruptcy, Banks and Banking, Begging, Credit, Credit Cards, Debt, Hard Times, Inflation, Spending

Bosses

1 A boss is someone who delegates all the authority, shifts all the blame and takes all the credit.

2 A boss is someone who is early when you're late and late when you're early.

3 He was the most hated man in the company. Every time he called a staff meeting, it started with a strip-search.

4 I told my boss that I went to church and prayed for a raise. He told me never to go over his head again!

5 I've got a very flexible boss. He lets me come in any time I want before nine and leave any time I want after five.

6 If you work hard eight hours a day, you can become the boss and work sixteen hours a day!

7 My boss is so mean, if you get in two minutes late he fines you and if you get in two minutes early he charges you rent.

8 Oh, so you're Jim's boss! He's always mentioning your name, Mr Slavedriver!

9 OK, you can have the job as my assistant. But I don't just want a yes-man. Agreed?

10 Please understand, this is just a suggestion. You don't have to do it unless you want to keep your job.

11 You can't help liking the chairman. If you don't, he fires you!

12 You think it's easy being a boss? Every day I have to get up early to see who comes into work late!

13 BOSS: Please don't tell anyone what I'm paying you.
EMPLOYEE: I certainly won't. I'm as ashamed of my salary as you are!

14 I finally got my boss to laugh out loud.
Did you tell him a joke?
No, I asked for a raise!

15 My boss is really tough on late-comers. One day one of his assistants arrived an hour late, all bruised, bloodied and bandaged. And as he limped over to his desk, the boss came in and said, 'Where do you think you've been? You're an hour late.'
The assistant said, 'I'm sorry, I fell down a flight of stairs.'
And the boss said, 'And that took you a whole hour?'

16 Show me an orchestra that likes its conductor and I'll show you a lousy conductor.
Goddard Lieberson

17 You always knew where you stood with Sam Goldwyn: nowhere.
F. Scott Fitzgerald

See Television 18; *see also* Business, Lateness, The Office, Professions, Unemployment, Work

Boxing

1 After the fight I was presented with a special cup – to keep my teeth in.

2 His trainer called him 'Laundry'. He was always hanging over the ropes!

3 I can lick any man with one hand! Unfortunately, my opponent had two.

4 I had quite a good record in the ring. I fought a hundred fights and won all but ninety-nine of them!

5 I used to be a boxer. I fought Joe Frazier once. In the first round, I really had him worried. He thought he'd killed me.

6 I used to run 5 miles before every fight, but my opponents always managed to catch me and beat me up anyway.

7 I would have won my last fight if the referee hadn't stood on my hand.

8 I wouldn't say he's very confident of winning this fight. He's already sold the advertising space on the soles of his shoes.

9 I'll say this for my opponent: he was a clean fighter. You could tell by the way he kept wiping the floor with me.

10 I'm very superstitious. I keep a horseshoe in my glove for luck!

11 In the first round I had the champ down on one knee. He was bending over to see if I was still breathing!

12 My best punch was a rabbit punch. Trouble was, they wouldn't let me fight rabbits.

13 There was one thing he never got to see in the course of his boxing career – the end of the first round.

14 What a fight! I came out of my corner and I tried a right, then a left jab, then another left jab, then a right uppercut. And then my opponent came out of *his* corner.

15 When I was a boxer, they used to call me Rembrandt. I was always on the canvas!

16 I never see my husband at breakfast. Being a boxer, he never gets up before the stroke of ten.

17 MANAGER: You can beat him hands down!
BOXER: But he doesn't want to keep his hands down!

18 Just before the fight started, my trainer started yelling in my ear. He told me that my opponent beat his wife, kicked his kids and starved his mother. That really made me fighting mad. If there's one thing I can't stand, it's someone shouting in my ear!

19 The boxer struggled to his corner and, gasping for breath, asked his second, 'What round is this?'
And the second said, 'As soon as the bell rings, it'll be the first.'

20 There was an old boxer who was having trouble sleeping. So the doctor told him, 'Just lie down, relax and start counting to 1,000.'
A week later the boxer came back to the surgery. He said, 'It's no good. I keep jumping up at the count of nine!'

21 The hardest thing about prize-fighting is picking up your teeth with a boxing glove on.
Kin Hubbard

See Advertising 3, Ice Hockey 2; *see*

also Defeat, Fighting, Losers, Sport, Victory

Britain and the British

1 At his best the Briton can be diligent, virtuous and high-minded. At his worst he can be diligent, virtuous and high-minded.

2 An Englishman is never happy unless he is miserable; a Scotsman is never at home but when he is abroad; an Irishman is never at peace but when he is fighting.
Anon., nineteenth century

3 The British tourist is always happy abroad as long as the natives are waiters.
Robert Morley

4 There's an old saw to the effect that the sun never sets on the British Empire. While we were there, it never even rose.
Ring Lardner

See also England and the English, The English Language, Ireland and the Irish, Scotland and the Scots

Business

1 A businessman can't win these days. If he does something wrong, he's fined; if he does something right, he's taxed.

2 A customer called the store and asked, 'What time do you open?' and the manager replied, 'What time can you get here?'

3 A rich kid asked his father for a Mickey Mouse outfit, so his father gave him an advertising agency.

4 A successful manager is one who believes in sharing the credit with the man who did the work.

5 An executive is someone who can take three hours for lunch without hindering production.

6 Business is what, when you don't have any, you get out of.

7 CHAIRMAN: Right, let's vote on the recommendation. All those against, raise their hands and say, 'I resign.'

8 He's the world's worst businessman. If he was a florist, he'd close on Mother's Day.

9 I started this business on a shoestring and after six months I'd tripled my investment. Now I just want to know what to do with the spare shoestring.

10 If this company appoints any more executives, there'll be nobody left to do the work.

11 To sell something you have to someone who wants it – that is not business. But to sell something you don't have to someone who doesn't want it – that's business.

12 We're a non-profit-making organization. We don't mean to be, but we are.

13 How do you make money selling your watches so cheaply?
Easy. We make a fortune repairing them.

14 How's business?
Terrible. The month before last I lost 10,000. Last month I lost 20,000 . . .
So why don't you shut up shop?
But how would I make a living?

15 I made a million pounds' profit last year!
Honestly?
Well, let's not go into that!

16 Still working for the same old outfit?
That's right – the wife and kids.

17 It was six o'clock in the morning when the beggar started knocking on the rich man's door. There was

no answer, so he knocked again. And again.

Finally, the rich man appeared at his bedroom window. 'How dare you wake me up at this time!' he shouted.

And the beggar replied, 'Look, I don't tell you how to run your business, so don't you tell me how to run mine!'

18 The directors decided to award an annual prize of fifty pounds for the best idea for saving the company money. It was won by a young executive who suggested that in future the prize money be reduced to ten pounds.

19 Corporation: an ingenious device for obtaining individual profit without individual responsibility.
Ambrose Bierce

See The Bible 4; *see also* Accountants, Bosses, Consultants, The Office, Professions, Work

Butchers

1 Did you hear about the butcher who backed into the bacon slicer and got a little behind in his orders?

See Inflation 7; *see also* Food

C

California

1 Living in California adds ten years to a man's life. And those extra ten years I'd like to spend in New York.

2 San Francisco is like muesli: take away the fruits and the nuts and all you have left is the flakes.

3 It's a scientific fact that if you stay in California, you lose one point of IQ every year.

4 There's nothing wrong with southern California that a rise in the ocean level wouldn't cure.
Ross MacDonald

See Light-bulb Jokes 1; *see also* America and the Americans, Beach, Beverly Hills, Hollywood, Los Angeles

Cannibals

1 He was a very ambitious cannibal – always trying to get ahead.

2 My great-great-grandfather was a missionary who was eaten by cannibals. At least he died in the knowledge that he was giving them their first taste of Christianity.

3 My uncle converted these cannibals to Roman Catholicism. Now on Fridays they only eat fishermen.

4 This poor cannibal was really sick. I think he'd eaten someone who disagreed with him.

5 What is a cannibal?
A man who goes into a restaurant and orders the waiter.

6 Deep in the jungle we were captured by cannibals, but they were very nice to us. They had us for dinner!

See Bores 29; *see also* Travel

Capitalism

1 Isn't capitalism wonderful! Under what other system could the ordinary man in the street owe so much?

2 Under capitalism, it's dog eat dog. Under Communism, it's just the opposite.

See also Banks and Banking, Business, Conservatives, Money, Stock Market, Wealth

Cars

1 A car is a four-wheeled vehicle that runs up hills and down pedestrians.

2 Ever since 1965 I've dreamt of having a BMW and last week my dream finally came true, I bought a 1965 BMW!

3 He had a car so long, it took him five minutes to drive it through the one-minute carwash.

4 He promised to buy me a foreign convertible – and all I got was a rickshaw!

5 He told me the car was very economical. It only used petrol when the engine was running!

6 His new car has three speeds: Fast, Very Fast and Guilty, M'lud.

7 I call my car Flattery. It gets me nowhere!

8 I drive a '75 Chevy. That's not the year – it's the resale value!

9 I know they must have turned back the clock on the car – it was in Roman numerals!

10 I once drove cross-country in just two weeks – that's ten days to drive and four days to refold the maps.

11 I took my old car in for an oil change. The mechanic took one look and suggested I keep the oil and change the car.

12 I've got to do something with my car. Everything makes a noise except the horn!

13 I've got terrible car trouble. The engine won't start and the payments won't stop.

14 My car is for four people – one driving and three pushing.

15 My garage has a wonderful rescue service. They think nothing of coming out in the middle of the week.

16 My new car has got something that will last a lifetime – the monthly payments!

17 So all right, these small cars can stop on a dime. But when they try to drive *over* the dime, that's when the trouble starts.

18 The traffic's so bad in the city these days, the only way to change lanes is to buy the car next to you.

19 There are only two types of motorway in this country – those that are under construction and those that are under repair.

20 We stand behind every car we sell. Just in case it needs a push!

21 You say you've run out of petrol? That's right. Tell me, will it damage the car if I drive on an empty tank?

22 Can I borrow your foot pump? Why?

Why do you think. I've got flat feet!

23 Do you know how to make your own anti-freeze? Take away her nightie!

24 DRIVER: What do I do if the brakes suddenly fail? MECHANIC: Hit something cheap.

25 How did you get your puncture? I didn't see the fork in the road!

26 MECHANIC: Your trouble is the battery. It's flat! DRIVER: Oh dear, what shape should it be?

27 SON: Dad, I'm afraid the car's got water in the carburettor. DAD: Where *is* the car? SON: In the lake.

28 This car is sound in every department! Yes, I can hear!

29 What do you expect to get out of your new convertible? My teenage son.

30 When I got home last night, I found my car in the kitchen.
I asked my wife how it got there and she said, 'It was easy – I just turned left at the dining room.'

31 Get in, sit down, shut up and hold on.
Bumper sticker

32 There are no liberals behind steering wheels.
Russell Baker

Catholics

1 We were discussing the Pope outside the Vatican when he drove past.

I said, 'Talk of the devil!'

2 The Mother Superior was asking the girls at the convent school about their ambitions for the future.

'And how about you, Imelda, what do you want to be?'

'I want to be a prostitute,' replied Imelda.

'You want to be a *what*?' shrieked the Mother Superior.

'A prostitute.'

'Oh, God be thanked! I thought for one terrible moment you said a *Protestant*.'

3 The newly ordained young priest asked an older colleague if he would listen in while he was taking confession and give him his honest opinion of the way he handled it.

The older priest agreed and, at the end of the day, the young priest asked him what he thought.

'Well,' said the older man, 'you were quite good, I thought, but on the whole I'd like to have heard more "Tsk, tsk, tsks" and slightly fewer "Oh, wows".'

4 Why should we take advice on sex from the Pope? If he knows anything about it, he shouldn't.
George Bernard Shaw

See Cannibals 3, Dating – Chat-up Lines 1, Laziness 8, Stupidity 23; *see also* The Bible, Church, God, Religion

Cats

1 I came home late one night and the wife complained that the cat had upset her. It was her own fault for eating it.

2 We've got a cat called Ben Hur. We called it Ben till it had kittens.

3 CUSTOMER: Have you got a cod's head for the cat?

FISHMONGER: Why, are you doing a transplant?

4 Did you know there's a black cat in the dining room?
Don't worry, they're supposed to be lucky.
Well this one certainly is. He's eating your dinner!

5 The clever cat eats cheese, then breathes down rat holes with baited breath.
W. C. Fields

See Childhood 1, Death 17, Doctors 48, 52, Poverty 4; *see also* Animals, Birds, Dogs, Pets

Censorship

1 What you don't know can hurt you.

2 Censorship, like charity, should begin at home; but, unlike charity, it should end there.
Clare Boothe Luce

3 Censorship is when we stop people reading or seeing what we do not want to read or see ourselves.
Lord Diplock

See also Books, Morality, Nudity, Prudery

Charity

1 All the money raised tonight will go towards an old people's charity. It may not actually get there, but it *will* be going towards it . . .

2 Remember, the organizer's bank account is entirely supported by voluntary contributions.

3 He's done a lot for the Jews – just by not being one.

4 The big difference between charity and philanthropy is that charity can't afford a press agent.

5 We started this charity just three weeks ago and already we've raised nearly 100,000 pounds – and we haven't even got a disease yet!

6 When it comes to giving to charity, some people stop at nothing.

7 Would you like to buy a ticket for the Policeman's Ball?
Sure, I love a dance.
This isn't a dance, it's a raffle!

See also Begging, Money, Philanthropy, Poverty

Childhood

1 I can honestly say that I was never kept late after school. Mainly because I never went.

2 I first saw the light of day in Exeter. I was actually born two years earlier in Manchester!

3 One day a man came to our door and said he was collecting for the children's home. So my Dad gave him five of us.

4 We were all great singers in our house. We had to be.
Why?
There was no lock on the lavatory door.

5 It's never too late to have a happy childhood.
Bumper sticker

See Circus 8, Crime 11, Dancing 4, Faces 5, Music 16, 26, Television 17, Trades Unions 3; *see also* Babies, Children, Fathers, Mothers, Parents, Poverty

Children

1 After she'd had fifteen of his children, she got a divorce on the grounds of compatibility.

2 At the age of four I was left an orphan. I ask you, what could I do with an orphan?

3 Children can be a great comfort in your old age – and they can help you reach it faster too!

4 Children just can't win: if they're too noisy, they're punished; if they're too quiet, they have their temperature taken.

5 Children never put off till tomorrow what will keep them from going to bed tonight.

6 Children should be seen and not had.

7 Do your children a favour – don't have any.

8 Even when he joined the Boy Scouts, he was still a little devil. He used to walk old ladies half-way across the road.

9 I always wanted to spend more time with my kids. Then one day I did!

10 I used to be the sort of kid my parents told me not to play with.

11 I'd have been divorced years ago if it wasn't for the children. I didn't want them and neither did the wife!

12 I've got three kids – one of each.

13 If your parents didn't have any children, the chances are you won't either.

14 Most kids today, when asked to name the four seasons, can only name two: football and cricket.

15 My brother was a real wild child. My parents had to feed him with a whip and a chair!

16 My children really brighten up the house. They never turn off the lights!

17 My mother went to the doctor's and asked if she could have an abortion. The doctor replied, 'It's too late. Your kid's just started school!'

18 My parents hated me so much that they got another kid to play me in our home movies.

19 One day my parents challenged me to a game of hide-and-seek. Ten years later I found them in a town 200 miles away.

20 Our kids make us want to jump for joy – off a tall building.

21 The hardest thing in the world to raise is a child — especially in the mornings.

22 The only thing my kids ever did to earn money was to lose their baby teeth.

23 The rule in our house is never hit the children except in self-defence.

24 There were always lots of happy children around our house – which used to really annoy me, because I was an only child.

25 There's only one way to bring up kids right – but nobody knows what it is.

26 When I was a kid I was pretty stupid. In fact, I didn't realize I was twelve until I was fourteen!

27 Did you have a happy childhood?
I don't remember. I was only a kid at the time!

28 FATHER: I think it's about time we talked about the facts of life.
CHILD: Certainly. What do you want to know?

29 FIRST KID: I found some contraceptives on the patio.
SECOND KID: What's a patio?

30 How do you like children?
Boiled.

31 How old are you?
Seven.
You should be ashamed of yourself. When I was your age I was ten!

32 I finally got my little boy to stop biting his nails.

What did you do?
I made him put on his shoes.

33 When I was a kid, I ran away from home. It took them six months to find me.
Six months? Why?
They didn't look.

34 My little boy came in the other day with a serious look on his face and said, 'Dad, can I ask you a question? Where do I come from?'

It was a question I'd been dreading, but I sat him down and told him, as gently as I could, all about the birds and the bees. When I finished he was very quiet and he got up, said, 'Thank you, Dad,' and headed for the door.

I said, 'So what made you ask me?'

And he turned around and said, 'I just wanted to know because Bobby next door says *he* comes from Manchester.'

35 The child didn't say a word until he was eight years old. Doctors, psychiatrists, speech therapists – they'd all tried to help, but to no avail

Then, one lunchtime, he suddenly looked up and said, 'These french fries are freezing cold!'

His mother was amazed. She said, 'I didn't know you could talk! Why haven't you spoken before?'

And the boy said, 'Everything's been all right until now!'

36 Two aunts were watching their four-year-old niece sitting in front of the television.

'What a shame she isn't very P-R-E-T-T-Y,' said one.

And the four-year-old turned round and said, 'But it doesn't matter as long as I'm C-L-E-V-E-R.'

37 Two little boys were talking together in the playground when a little girl walked past.

And one of the boys said, 'You know, when I stop hating girls, that's the one I'm going to stop hating first!'

38 Any kid will run any errand for you, if you ask at bedtime.
Red Skelton

39 Before I was married, I had six theories about bringing up children. Now I have six children – and no theories.
Earl of Rochester

40 Children should neither be seen nor heard from – ever again.
W. C. Fields

41 Don't have any children. It makes divorce so much more complicated.
Albert Einstein

42 I must have been an insufferable child; all children are.
George Bernard Shaw

See Clothes 1, Consultants 7, Drink 14, Gambling 1, Games 5, Holidays 4, Insanity 1, Losers 19, Stinginess 4, Television 9, Weddings 35; see also Babies, Childhood, Families, Fathers, Mothers, Parents

China and the Chinese

1 So what do you think of Red China?
I think it looks lovely on a blue table-cloth.

See Food 10, Restaurants 1, 5, 8

Christmas

1 At Christmas I bought my son a train set for me to play with.

2 Christmas, when we exchange lots of things we'd like to keep for lots of things we don't want.

3 Christmas is the time when you buy this year's presents with next year's money.

4 Christmas, when people get emotional over their family ties – especially if they have to wear them.

5 Christmas? That's when your bank account is seasonally adjusted.

6 Have you seen the new aluminium Christmas trees? You really can't tell them from the real plastic ones.

7 I asked the boss what he wanted for Christmas and he said, 'Just the usual – gold, frankincense and myrrh.'

8 I got a surprise present from my wife last Christmas – a pair of socks. I was expecting a set of golf clubs.

9 I had a fantastic Christmas. I got lots of terrific presents I can't wait to exchange!

10 I'm giving my kids some very unusual presents this Christmas. Batteries, toys not included!

11 I'm trying to think of what to give my brother for Christmas. What do you give a man who's had everyone?

12 It's Christmas and time again to start asking the question: where to go to pay how much for how many of which kind of what to give to whom?

13 Most people go through three Santa Claus stages. First, you believe in Santa Claus. Then, you don't believe in Santa Claus. Finally, you *are* Santa Claus.

14 My wife has very simple tastes. For Christmas all she wants is a five-pound box of money.

15 Tell me, why does Christmas come just when the stores are so crowded?

16 The only thing I don't like about office Christmas parties is looking for a new job afterwards.

17 This year I'm giving money for

Christmas presents. It's the cheapest
thing I can find.

18 We had my mother-in-law for
lunch on Christmas Day. I prefer
chicken myself, but times are
hard.

19 You know what Christmas is like in
the middle of a recession? It's when
your family looks on greedily as
you carve the Big Mac.

20 Are you having the usual for Christmas?
That's right – relatives!

21 Let's exchange presents this Christmas.
Why not. I always exchange yours!

22 Merry Christmas, sir. I'm the one
who empties your dustbin.
Merry Christmas to *you*. I'm the
one who fills it!

23 My uncle did his Christmas shop-
ping early.
What did he get?
Six months.

24 SHOPPER: That's a terrific train set.
I'll take it!
SALES ASSISTANT: I'm sure your son
will just love playing with it.
SHOPPER: You may be right. I'll
take two.

25 I had a terrible row with my wife
on Christmas morning.
She said, 'You've done absolutely
nothing to help with Christmas
dinner!'
I said, 'What do you mean? Look
at the turkey – I've plucked it and
I've stuffed it. And all you've got to
do now is kill it and put it in the
oven!'
See Beverly Hills 1, Birth 3, Crime
7, 20, Cross Jokes 1, Divorce 23,
Poverty 6; *see also* Church, Gifts, Parties

Church

1 He was a marvellous preacher. At

the end of his sermon, there was a
tremendous awakening.

2 I go to a church that's so liberal it's
only open on Tuesdays.

3 If all the people who sleep in church
were laid end to end, they'd be a lot
more comfortable.

4 PRIEST: We all know that you can't
take it with you, so if you put it in
the collection plate, I'll see that it's
sent on ahead.

5 What a preacher! His sermons were
like water to a drowning man.

6 The minister finished his sermon by
telling the congregation that the following week he would be preaching
on the subject of the sin of lying,
and, to prepare themselves, they
should all read St Luke, Chapter
25.
On the next Sunday, the minister
began his sermon by asking for a
show of hands. Who had read St
Luke, Chapter 25?
All hands went up and the minister said, 'Well, there are only
twenty-four chapters in St Luke, so
I will now proceed with my sermon
on the sin of lying.'

7 The minister was troubled because
every Sunday an increasing number
of his congregation started leaving
the church during his sermon. Then
one day he had an idea . . .
The next Sunday he began his
sermon with these words, 'The first
half of my sermon today will be for
the sinners amongst you. The second
half will be for the saints . . .'

8 The priest was about to baptize the
little baby at the font. Turning to
the father, he said, 'And what's her
name?'
The father said, 'Emily Jessica
Katherine Laura Alice Frances
Phoebe Eleanor Daisy Poppy.'
And the priest turned to his curate

and said, 'I'll have a little more water, please!'

9 Pray: to ask that the laws of the universe be annulled on behalf of a single petitioner confessedly unworthy.
Ambrose Bierce
See Bosses 4, Drink 45, Old Age 14; see also The Bible, Catholics, Funerals, God, Religion, Weddings

Circus

1 A friend of mine worked in the circus. He was engaged to a lady contortionist. But she broke it off.

2 Following an accident at the circus, the lion-tamer is looking for a tamer lion.

3 I had got a job in the circus, being shot from a cannon. I got 10p a mile plus travelling expenses.

4 I used to work in a circus, being shot from a cannon into a net. Then, after a year or so, came my big break – I missed the net.

5 Ladies and gentlemen, I'm afraid we do not have a complete show tonight. We have fired the human cannonball, and have been unable to find another man of his calibre.

6 One night, the tightrope walker had a terrible accident. He was tight but the rope wasn't.

7 She used to be married to a trapeze artist. But she caught him in the act.

8 When I was eight I ran away with a circus. When I was nine they made me bring it back again.

9 My brother's with the circus – he gets 500 pounds a week for swallowing a 4-foot sword.
What's so good about swallowing a 4-foot sword?
He's only 3 feet tall.

See also Animals, Show Business

City life

1 A hurricane swept through the inner city last week and did millions of pounds' worth of improvements!

2 Dimsby's an awful town. I spent a month there one night!

3 I don't understand. Why do they call it the 'rush hour' when everything is at a standstill?

4 I lived in a really tough neighbourhood. If you didn't get home by ten, they declared you legally dead.

5 In the city zoo the animals are kept behind bars – for their own safety.

6 It's so tough where I live that nobody bothers to ask the time. They just steal your watch!

7 Most people in the city have come up from the country to make enough money to leave the city and live in the country.

8 The crime is so bad down town, even the muggers travel around in pairs.

9 The town is a real dump. It isn't actually twinned with anywhere – it's just got a suicide pact with Scunthorpe.

10 The underground is so crowded these days that even the men are standing.

11 What's the best thing to come out of Manchester?
The M62.

See Flying 8, Summer 4; see also Hard Times, Modern Times, New York, Poverty, Small Towns

Cleanliness

1 I've devised a way of keeping all my pots and pans and dishes abso-

lutely sparkling clean. I never use them!

2 What I'm looking for is a spot-remover that'll remove the spots left by other spot-removers.

See also Appearance, Homes, Homes – Squalid, Housework, Tidiness

Clothes

1 A sweater is a garment worn by a child when its mother feels cold.

2 He said he bought his suit for a ridiculous price. The truth is, he bought it for an absurd figure.

3 He said I'd look just perfect in something long and flowing – like a river.

4 He was wearing his Italian-style suit – spaghetti bolognese all down the front.

5 He's discovered a new use for old clothes. He wears them!

6 Last week my wife cut out her dress pattern on the living-room floor. She ended up with two dresses – one silk and one Axminster.

7 I have a suit for every day of the year. And this is it.

8 I thought my shirt had shrunk in the wash until I realized I was trying to get my head through a button-hole.

9 I told my wife she should wear her dresses longer – about three years longer.

10 I'm trying to do a deal with my laundry. I'll give them back all their pins if they give me back all my buttons.

11 I've got these boots that are absolutely waterproof. When it rains, not a drop comes out!

12 I've just bought this new type of shirt you can wear in the rain. It gets absolutely soaking wet but you can wear it in the rain.

13 Let's face it – nothing can replace the old-fashioned one-piece cover-all swimsuit. And it practically has.

14 Miniskirts are getting shorter and shorter. No one knows what they'll be up to next.

15 My wife gave me a smoking-jacket for my birthday. It took me nearly an hour to put it out.

16 My wife has just two complaints: first, she's got absolutely nothing to wear. And second, she's run out of wardrobe space to keep it in.

17 My wife has two wardrobes jam-packed with nothing to wear.

18 She looked sensational! She was wearing a gownless evening strap.

19 She looked as if she'd thrown something on – and missed!

20 She looked as if she was poured into her dress and forgot to say when.

21 She says she hasn't got a thing to wear. I'm telling you, her wardrobe is packed so tight there are moths in there that haven't learned to fly yet!

22 She says she made her dress out of odds and ends. Well, it's certainly odd where it ends.

23 She was wearing one of those dresses that holds on tight going round curves.

24 She was wearing a swimsuit that looked as if it hadn't been delivered yet.

25 She was wearing a miniskirt. If it was any shorter, it would be a collar.

26 She's got a dress in her wardrobe so skimpy the moths have to stand on one leg.

27 He had his dinner jacket on – with his dinner still on it.

28 We've got one advantage over the

Victorians. To find out if a lady was knock-kneed, they had to listen.

29 How d'you like this new suit? Made to measure in three days for only forty pounds.
But what's that lump on the back?
That's not a lump, it's the tailor. He hasn't quite finished yet.

30 HUSBAND: I hate to say this but your swimming costume is very tight and very revealing.
WIFE: If you don't like it, you don't have to wear it.

31 Now, sir, how would you like a belt in the back?
How would *you* like a kick in the teeth?

32 Oh yes, sir, that suit fits you like a glove.
Fair enough, but could you show me one that fits me like a *suit*?

33 She opened the door in her nightie.
That's a funny place to have a door.

34 That's a pretty loud suit, isn't it?
Yes, but I've got a muffler to go with it.

35 That's a strange pair of shoes you're wearing, one black and one white. They must be unique.
Not at all. I've got another pair just like them at home.

36 Was that suit made-to-measure?
Yes.
Where were you at the time?

37 What do you think would go well with these new purple, yellow and green socks?
Thigh-length boots.

38 Whenever I'm down in the dumps, I get myself a new dress.
So *that's* where you get them.

39 Why are you wearing only one glove? Did you lose one?
No, I found one!

40 You smell good. What have you got on?
Clean socks.

41 As she watched her mother trying on her new fur coat, the daughter said, 'Mother, don't you realize that some poor, dumb beast suffered so that you could have that coat?'
And the mother looked at her and said, 'Don't you dare talk about your father that way!'

45 She's terrific, my great-aunt Gertrude. It doesn't matter how freezing it is, she still goes out to get the coal in her nightie. I even bought her a shovel but she says she can hold more in her nightie.

See The Army 20, Beauty 5, Christmas 4, Courtroom 13, Driving – Police 1, Figures – Thin 1, 5, 8, 10, Funerals 1, Hard Times 27, Infidelity 15, Men and Women 13, Police 11, Show Business 1, Travel 3, Weddings 4, 5, Work 30; *see also* Appearance, Fashion, Hats, Shopping

Coffee

1 I don't have the energy in the mornings to make myself real coffee. I just sprinkle the grounds over my moustache and drink a cup of hot water.

2 The coffee they serve here is a special blend – of yesterday's and today's.

3 I drink about fifty cups of coffee a day.
Good heavens, doesn't that keep you awake?
It certainly helps.

4 What are you drinking – tea or coffee?
They didn't say.

See Begging 4, Flying 14, Laziness 14, Work 5; *see also* Drink, Food, Restaurants, Restaurants – Waiters

Coincidences

1 I met a man just now I haven't seen in twenty years.
That's nothing. I met a man just now I've never seen before in my life!

2 Would you believe it! Forty years ago, while sunbathing in her garden, Mrs Edna Grimshaw of Shepton Mallet lost her engagement ring. Yesterday, while digging in the very same garden, her son Rodney ruptured himself.

See Speakers and Speeches 1

Comedians

1 A comedian is someone who knows a good joke when he steals one.

2 He had them rolling in the aisles – towards the exits.

See Insults 49; *see also* Humour, Introductions, Jokes, Laughter, Speakers and Speeches

Computers

1 Abandon all hope, you who press ENTER here.

2 My new computer printer can produce 200 pages a minute. It certainly cuts down on the paperwork!

3 One micro-computer maker was so successful, he had to move to smaller premises.

4 Software can never replace greyware.

5 The computer is a great invention. There are as many mistakes as ever but now it's nobody's fault.

6 They sacked a guy at the office because they found a computer that could do everything he could do. Sadly, when he told his wife, she went out and bought the same computer.

7 They've invented the perfect computer. If it makes a mistake it blames another computer!

8 To err is human, but to *really* screw things up you need a computer.

9 We had a terrible day at the office. The computers went down and everybody had to learn to think all over again.

10 BOSS: Why is it that every time I come into your office, you're playing video games on your computer?
PROGRAMMER: It must be that the carpeting in the hall muffles your footsteps.

11 This computer will cut your workload by 50 per cent.
I'll take two of them!

12 If you put tomfoolery into a computer, nothing comes out but tomfoolery. But this tomfoolery, having passed through a very expensive machine, is somehow ennobled and no one dares criticize it.
Pierre Gallois

See Consultants 9; *see also* Business, Gadgets, Modern Life, The Office

Confidence

1 I have no self-confidence at all. If a woman says 'yes', I tell her to think it over.

2 I never had any self-confidence. Even when I worked as a lift attendant I used to keep stopping every couple of floors to ask the way.

See also Success, Vanity, Victory

Congress

1 You don't have to join the navy to see the world. You just become a Congressman.

2 Congress consists of one third, more or less, scoundrels; two thirds, more

or less, idiots; and three thirds, more or less, poltroons.
H. L. Mencken

3 It could probably be shown by facts and figures that there is no distinctly native American criminal class except Congress.
Mark Twain

4 Senate office hours are from twelve to one with an hour off for lunch.
George S. Kaufman

5 There are two periods when Congress does no business: one is before the holidays, and the other after.
George D. Prentice

See also Conservatives, Democracy, Government, Politics and Politicians, Ronald Reagan, Republicans

Conservatives

1 A conservative is someone who believes that nothing should be done for the first time.

2 A conservative is someone who admires radicals a century after they're dead.

3 The Conservative Party stands for progress, change and innovation. But not yet.

4 A tourist engaged an old man in conversation in the main street. 'Well, you must have seen a lot of changes over the years,' he said.

'Sure have,' replied the pensioner, 'and I've been against every one of them!'

5 Conservative: a statesman who is enamoured of existing evils, as distinguished from the liberal, who wishes to replace them with others.
Ambrose Bierce

See also Capitalism, Government, Politics and Politicians, Ronald Reagan, Republicans

Consultants

1 A consultant is someone who's called in at the last minute to share the blame.

2 A consultant is someone who takes the watch off your wrist and tells you what time it is.

3 A consultant is simply an executive who can't find a job.

4 A consultant is a man who's smart enough to tell you how to run your own business and too smart to start one of his own.

5 A consultant is someone who saves his client almost enough to pay his fee.

6 A consultant is a man who knows 100 ways of making love but can't get a girl.

7 An efficiency expert taught his child to say his prayers once a year on New Year's Day. The rest of the time, the child just jumped into bed and said, 'Ditto.'

8 Those that can do. Those that could, but now don't, consult.

9 A mainframe computer on which everyone in the office depended suddenly went down. They tried everything but it still wouldn't work. Finally, they decided to call in a high-powered computer consultant.

He arrived, looked at the computer, took out a small hammer and tapped it on the side. Instantly the computer leapt into life. Two days later the office manager received a bill from the consultant for 1,000 pounds.

Immediately he called the consultant and said, 'One thousand pounds for fixing that computer? You were only here five minutes! I want that bill itemized!'

The next day the new bill arrived. It read, 'Tapping computer with hammer: one pound. Knowing where to tap: 999 pounds.'

10 Consult: to seek another's approval of a course already decided upon.
Ambrose Bierce

See also Accountants, Business

Conversation

1 If other people are going to talk, conversation becomes impossible.
James McNeill Whistler

2 No man would listen to you talk if he didn't know it was his turn next.
Ed Howe

See also Bores, Gossip, Speakers and Speeches, Talkers

Cooking

1 Everything I cook turns out tough. Can anyone lend me a soup knife?

2 He's the only man I know who can spoil cornflakes. He boils them in the bag!

3 Her cooking is really something to write home about – for your mother's recipes.

4 Her cooking was not so much cordon bleu as cordon noir.

5 Hi, honey, I'm home! Mmmmm, what's thawing?

6 I always have a problem when I cook for friends. I never know what kind of wine goes with heartburn!

7 I cast my bread upon the waters tonight. Of course, my wife said it was soup.

8 I get a lump in my throat when I think of my wife's rock cakes. In fact, I get a lump in my throat when I *eat* my wife's rock cakes.

9 I hate outdoor barbecues. I wouldn't have one in the house!

10 I make my soup so thick that when I stir it, the room goes round.

11 I said to my wife, 'Where am I when you serve those great meals from which we always have the leftovers?'

12 I'll never forget the first time she cooked for me. She passed the cakes and told me to take my pick. I didn't need a pick, I needed a hammer and chisel.

13 I've got this wonderful new idea for leftovers. I throw them out!

14 In my opinion, the best way to serve spinach is to someone else.

15 The secret to cooking rice so it doesn't stick together is to boil each grain separately.

16 The other day my wife cooked me a Mexican meal. It was so authentic, you couldn't even drink the water.

17 I've just bought this new juicer and I'm trying it out on everything. Have you ever tried toast juice?

18 In our house we always throw out the leftovers. Ideally, we should also throw out the originals!

19 It took me three hours yesterday to stuff a turkey. I was so angry at the end, I could have killed it!

20 Mmm, my wife's chicken really tickles the palate. She leaves the feathers on.

21 My wife cooks for fun. For food we go out to a restaurant!

22 My wife doesn't need to call us when dinner is ready. We just listen out for the smoke alarm!

23 My wife feeds me so much fish I'm breathing through my cheeks.

24 My wife is a hopeless cook. Last week *Gourmet* magazine tried to buy back her subscription!

25 Once I made a rhubarb tart 3 feet

long. I couldn't find any shorter rhubarb!

26 She cooked food like my mother used to make – just before they took my father to hospital.

27 The trouble with young wives today is that all they've learned how to do is defrost frozen food. Why can't they learn to open tins like their mothers used to do?

28 Where there's smoke, there's toast.

29 Do you know how to make a Swiss roll?
Push him down an alp!

30 What do you call someone who's eaten one of my wife's 'specialities'?
An ambulance.

31 WIFE: I've got some good news and some bad news. First, I've burned your supper.
HUSBAND: And what's the bad news?

32 Be content to remember that those who can make omelettes properly can do nothing else.
Hilaire Belloc

See The Army 14, Christmas 25, Holiday Camps 4, Husbands and Wives 35; *see also* Cooking – Insults, Diets, Drink, Food, Restaurants, Restaurants – Waiters

Cooking – insults

1 Any of her leftovers we give straight to the dog. And the dog gives them straight to the cat.

2 Her cheesecake melts in your mouth. True, it may take a day or two, but eventually it melts in your mouth.

3 I miss my wife's cooking – as often as I can.

4 My wife can't cook. She uses a smoke alarm as a timer!

See also Cooking, Drink, Food

Corruption

1 A bribe is when the giver says, 'Thanks', and the receiver says, 'Don't mention it.'

2 Can we trust our public figures any more? I mean, one week they're on the cover of *Time*, the next week they're doing it.

See Politics and Politicians 11, 13; *see also* Crime, The Law, Lawyers, Mafia

Cosmetics

1 I've always thought beauty comes from within – within jars, tubes, compacts, sprays . . .

2 Make-up is used by teenagers to make them feel older sooner and by their mothers to make them feel younger longer.

3 People criticize her for wearing too much make-up, but it saved her the other day. She tripped and fell, but she was OK because she landed on her eyelashes!

4 Some of today's pop singers don't shrink from using make-up. If they did, they'd be midgets by now.

See also Appearance, Beauty, Fashion

Country life

1 I love being out here in the country, where there's nothing doing every minute.

2 They've got a lovely place in the country. It's just twenty minutes from London – by phone.

See City Life 7, Summer 4; *see also* Farming, Gardening

Courtroom

1 He threw himself on the mercy of the court – and missed.

2 I don't recognize this court! You must have had it decorated.

3 The jury wanted to add a rider. So the judge got on his high horse.

4 DEFENDANT: I was drunk as a judge.
JUDGE: Surely you mean drunk as a lord?
DEFENDANT: Yes, my lord.

5 I'm sending you to prison for three months.
What's the charge?
There's no charge. Everything's free!

6 JUDGE: Are you trying to show contempt for this court?
DEFENDANT: No, I'm trying to hide it!

7 JUDGE: Crime doesn't pay.
DEFENDANT: I know, but the hours are good.

8 JUDGE: For this appalling crime I have no option but to sentence you to fifty years in jail.
DEFENDANT: But your honour, I'm sixty-five years old. I'll never live long enough to serve that sentence!
JUDGE: Well, just do the best you can.

9 JUDGE: I find you innocent of the charge of robbery.
DEFENDANT: Thank you. Does that mean I can keep the money?

10 JUDGE: Is this the first time you've been up before me?
DEFENDANT: I don't know. What time do you normally get up?

11 JUDGE: What were you doing when the police caught you in the back of the shop?
LOCKSMITH: I was making a bolt for the door.

12 JUDGE: What possible reason could you have for acquitting this villain?
FOREMAN OF THE JURY: Insanity.
JUDGE: What? All twelve of you?

13 You stand accused of stealing a petticoat.
I'm sorry, but it was my first slip!

14 You're charged with driving at eighty miles per hour on a motorway.
But I wasn't going at anything like that speed!
Were you doing sixty?
No!
Thirty?
No!
Twenty?
No!
OK, fined 300 pounds for parking on a motorway!

15 Jury: a group of twelve men who, having lied to the judge about their hearing, health and business engagements, have failed to fool him.
H. L. Mencken

See Cars 6, Writers and Writing 7; *see also* Crime, The Law, Lawyers, Murder, Prison

Credit

1 I bought this car on hire purchase – 10 per cent down and the balance to be paid on receipt of several threatening letters.

2 Preferential creditor: the first person to be told there's no money left.

3 There's only one problem with buying something on credit. By the time you're really sick of something, you finally own it.

4 What a shopper! She's got everything credit can buy.

5 My credit is so bad, they won't even take my cash!

See also Banks and Banking, Borrowing and Lending, Credit Cards, Debt, Money

Credit cards

1 Credit cards are what people use after they discover that money can't buy everything.

2 Life was simpler before credit cards. You didn't have to wait until the end of the month to find out how poor you were.

3 Money can't buy happiness. That's why we have credit cards!

4 The great advantage of having a credit card is that it saves you from having to count your change.

See also Banks and Banking, Borrowing and Lending, Credit, Debt, Money, Shopping, Spending

Cricket

1 I used to play under the worst captain ever. He always used to put me into bat in the middle of a hat-trick!

2 Our wicket-keeper is absolutely hopeless. The only thing he caught all season was whooping cough.

3 How do you mean, you had to explain the cricket match to your wife?
She found out I hadn't gone to it.

4 What happens to a cricketer when his eyesight starts to fail?
He applies to be an umpire.

5 His wife was in full flow: 'Cricket, cricket, cricket – that's all you think about. What about us? I bet you couldn't even tell me what day we were married!'
'Yes I could,' replied the husband. 'It was the day Botham scored 147 against the Australians!'

6 Cricket: casting the ball at three straight sticks and defending the same with a fourth.
Rudyard Kipling

7 I bowl so slow that if after I have delivered the ball and don't like the look of it, I can run after it and bring it back.
J. M. Barrie

See Baseball 7; *see also* Defeat, Losers, Sport, Victory

Crime

1 He comes from a family of criminals and now he's following in his father's fingerprints.

2 He wanted me to join him in his racket, but there were strings attached.

3 He was arrested for stealing a calendar. He got twelve months!

4 I saw a sign in this restaurant which read: 'Watch Your Hat and Coat!' So I did – and somebody stole my dinner!

5 It was three hours before I realized my bedroom had been burgled. I just thought my husband had been looking for some clean socks.

6 My uncle makes money the old-fashioned way. He steals it!

7 My uncle was put in jail for doing his Christmas shopping early. They found him in Selfridges at 4 a.m.

8 Scotland Yard was baffled. Interpol was baffled. The FBI was baffled. But with one brilliant masterstroke I solved the crime. I confessed!

9 Smash and grab robbers have come up with answer to the problem of double-glazing. They use two bricks!

10 There's a permanent crime wave where I live. It's the only place I know that, when you buy a pair of

nylon stockings, they ask you for your head size.

11 When I look back on my life, I think, hey, I haven't done too badly. I started off as an unwanted child and today I'm wanted by at least six police forces.

12 Can you see a policeman around here?
I'm afraid I can't.
Right then! Stick 'em up!

13 Doctor, I can't stop stealing things.
Take these tablets for two weeks. If that doesn't work, get me a colour telly!

14 Ever since I was a baby, I've been blackmailed.
Blackmail? That's a very ugly word.
I was a very ugly baby.

15 Excuse me, I'm doing a survey on self-defence. Would you know how to defend yourself against a karate attack?
No, I wouldn't.
Good! Give me your wallet!

16 He had a gun in his hand and a knife in his back. Who do you think poisoned him?
Who?
Nobody. He'd been strangled.

17 I knew one thing – the murderer was ruthless!
How did you know?
I had Ruth with me.

18 Why did you shoot your husband with a bow and arrow?
I didn't want to wake up the kids.

19 WIFE: I think I hear burglars. Are you awake?
HUSBAND: No.

20 You're charged with stealing a Christmas turkey.
I'm sorry, sir, I took it for a lark.
There's no resemblance whatsoever.
Fined twenty pounds.

21 A couple were walking down Bond Street in London when they stopped to look in a jeweller's window. The woman said, 'I'd love those ruby earrings.'
So the man took a brick out of his pocket, smashed the window, grabbed the earrings and gave them to the woman.
A little further down the street they stopped to look in another jeweller's window. 'Oh, look at that lovely diamond ring!' said the woman. 'I'd just love it!'
So the man took another brick from his pocket, smashed a hole in the window, grabbed the ring and handed it to the woman.
A few moments later they found themselves outside yet another jeweller's window. The woman said, 'I'd really love to have that pearl necklace.'
And the man said, 'That's enough. You must think I'm made of bricks!'

22 A woman was in the supermarket when a friend rushed in and said, 'There's someone stealing your car!' The woman rushed out but was soon back.
Her friend said, 'Did you catch him?'
And the woman said, 'No, he was too quick. But I got his number!'

23 I was walking home the other day when this man emerged from the shadows.
'Sir,' he said, 'could you please spare me the price of a meal? I've no money, I've no home, I've no job. All I have in the world is this switchblade knife.'

24 The Carters got a surprise in the post one morning – two tickets to a top West End show, along with a

note that read: 'Guess who these are from!'

By the time they went off to see the show, they still had no idea who could have sent them. When they got home they discovered that the house had been ransacked – the TV, video, hi-fi, computer all gone.

And there on the kitchen table was another note that read: 'Now you know!'

25 The head of a rich Italian family was kidnapped on his way to work and soon the first demand – for billions of lire – arrived, along with a fingertip of his which the ruthless gang of kidnappers had cut off.

When the family refused to pay the ransom, a piece of the victim's ear was sent to them, then a little toe, then a tooth. After some weeks of this grisly correspondence, the family suddenly announced that they were not interested in talking to the gang any more.

The next day they got an urgent phone call from the gang leader, anxious to know why they would no longer negotiate for the victim's release.

And the family replied, 'Because now we've got more of him than you've got.'

26 This guy said, 'I'm terrified of those people. They're planning to shoot me and stab me and poison me and put me in a bucket of cement and throw me in the river and it worries me.'

I said, 'Why?'

And he said, 'Because I can't swim.'

27 A man who has never gone to school may steal from a freight car, but if he has a university education he may steal the whole railroad.
Franklin D. Roosevelt

See Advertising 7, Beards and Moustaches 1, City Life 8, Doctors 44, Fear 3, Gifts 4, 8, Insurance 13, Stock Market 5; see also Courtroom, Driving – Police, The Law, Lawyers, Murder, Police, Prison, Robbery

Critics

1 Any fool can criticize – and many of them do.

2 It's a terrific show! Don't miss it if you can!

3 Some people think this is the worst, most banal, most puerile piece of playwriting ever inflicted on a paying audience. Others don't think it's as good as that.

4 ARTIST: So what's your opinion of my painting?
CRITIC: It's worthless.
ARTIST: I know, but I'd like to hear it anyway.

5 A critic is a gong at a railroad crossing clanging loudly and vainly as the train goes by.
Christopher Morley

6 Criticism is the art wherewith a critic tries to guess himself into a share of the artist's fame.
George Jean Nathan

7 I love every bone in their heads.
Eugene O'Neill

8 I never read bad reviews about myself, because my friends invariably tell me about them.
Oscar Levant

9 Nature fits all her children with something to do,
He who would write and can't write, can surely review.
James Russell Lowell

10 Unless the bastards have the courage to give you unqualified praise, I say ignore them.
John Steinbeck

Cross jokes

1 At Christmas, my father crossed a turkey with a centipede so everyone could have a drumstick.

2 He crossed a cow with a zebra and got striped milk.

3 He crossed a hyena with a parrot so that it could tell him what it was laughing about.

4 He crossed a parrot with a centipede and got a walkie-talkie.

5 He crossed a kangaroo with a sheep and got a woolly jumper.

6 He crossed a bridge with a car and got to the other side.

7 He crossed a road with a chicken and got the answer we've all been looking for.

8 If a man could be crossed with a cat, it would improve man, but it would deteriorate the cat.
Mark Twain

See Boats and Ships 4, Sociology 2; *see also* Birds, Knock-knock Jokes, Light-bulb Jokes, Tom Swifties

Dancing

1 Ballroom dancing is the art of getting your feet out of the way faster than your partner can step on them.

2 Dancers run in my family. It's just a pity they don't dance!

3 Have you seen what goes on in discos today? In most clubs in my town, they've had to ban premarital dancing.

4 How did I learn to dance? Simple – when I grew up there were six kids and only one bathroom.

5 I enjoyed the ballet but I couldn't understand why they all danced on their toes. Why don't they just get taller people?

6 I used to be a tap-dancer but I had to give it up. I kept falling in the sink.

7 My husband does a terrific tango – no matter what the band is playing.

8 Our next performer was told by doctors twenty years ago that he would never dance properly again. And he hasn't!

9 She'd be a great dancer if it weren't for two things – her feet!

10 The great thing about disco-dancing today is that nobody knows when you make a mistake.

11 You have seen nothing until you've seen this man dance. *Then* you've seen nothing.

12 GIRL: Ouch! That's the third time you've stepped on my toes!

BOY: I'm sorry. I've never danced so badly before.
GIRL: So you *have* danced before?

13 I took my girlfriend into the middle of the floor and performed the best Highland Fling you've ever seen.
I bet she was amazed.
Amazed? She was petrified. The band was playing a waltz!

14 MAN: I'm afraid my dancing's not so good. I'm a little stiff from badminton.
WOMAN: I don't care where you're from. You won't dance with me again!

15 So how did you learn to limbo-dance?
Trying to get into pay toilets.

See Charity 7, Drink 7, Feminism 11. Husbands and Wives 52, Religion 15, Romance 24, Scotland and the Scots 2; *see also* Exercise, Show Business, Theatre

Dating

1 Girls are mad about me. They throw flowers at my feet. They fall at my feet. They worship my feet. They don't think much of my face, but my feet are having a wonderful time.

2 Girls go out with him by the dozen. It's safer than going out with him alone.

3 His girlfriend treated him like dirt. She always hid him under the bed!

4 I asked her for her phone number and all she would give me was her dialling code.

5 I asked if I could see her home, so she showed me a picture of it.

6 I said to her, 'Would you mind if I took a lock of your hair – I'm trying to stuff a mattress.'

7 I took her home, she invited me in and I told her to get into something cooler. So she went and sat in the fridge.

8 I went out on this blind date. I was hoping for a vision but she turned out to be a sight.

9 I'm sorry but I can't go out with you on Saturday. I'm expecting a headache.

10 I've got bad luck in relationships. Every time I meet a nice girl, either she's married or I am.

11 It was a magical night. The moon was out, and so were her parents.

12 My ambition is to be the last man on earth – so that I can find out if all those girls were telling me the truth.

13 My computer-dating bureau came up with the perfect gentleman. Still, I've got another three goes.

14 Our courtship was fast and furious. I was fast and she was furious.

15 She's a little tired this morning. She went out last night on a double date and the other girl didn't turn up.

16 She's got boyfriends by the score – and most of them do.

17 There's nothing more expensive than a girl who's free for the evening.

18 When they first met, they were rough and ready – he was rough and she was ready.

19 Young people should be careful while parking because, remember, accidents cause people.

20 Her father said to me, 'Are your intentions honourable or dishonourable?'
I said, 'D'you mean to say I've got a choice?'

21 Are you married?
No, just practising.

22 BOY: Do you know what virgins have for breakfast?
GIRL: No, what?
BOY: Mmmm, just as I thought!

23 BOY: Do you want to get in the back seat?
GIRL: Can't I stay in the front seat with you?

24 BOY: I'd like to see more of you.
GIRL: There isn't any more of me.

25 BOY: I'm not feeling myself to-night.
GIRL: You're telling me!

26 BOY: May I hold your hand?
GIRL: I'll manage, thank you very much. It's not very heavy!

27 BOY: So how about it?
GIRL: Your place or mine?
BOY: If it's going to be a hassle, forget it!

28 Don't you love driving?
Well, I usually stop first.

29 GIRL: I said some foolish things to you last night.
BOY: Yes.
GIRL: And that was one of them.

30 How would you like to go out for a meal next Thursday?
Well, I don't know if I'm going to be hungry next Thursday.

31 I was planning to marry her, but her family objected.
Her family?
Yes, her husband and four kids.

32 I went out with a pair of twins last night.
Did you have a good time?
Yes and no.

33 LANDLADY: Have you got a lady in your room?
LODGER: Hang on, I'll ask her!

34 SHE: Would you like to see where I was vaccinated?
HE: You bet!
SHE: OK, we'll drive past it in a minute.

35 So what did your blind date look like?
Well, he looked a lot better over the telephone.

36 Sorry, I can't go out with you to-night – I'm getting married.
So how about tomorrow night?

37 Who was that lady I seen you with last night?
You mean, 'I *saw*.'
Sorry, who was that eyesore I seen you with last night?

38 You're just my type, and you know why? Gentlemen prefer blondes.
But I'm no blonde.
And I'm no gentleman.

39 BOY: Come out for a meal with me.
GIRL: I can't.
BOY: But I don't want to eat on my own.
GIRL: I can't.
BOY: And I'd love to talk to you.
GIRL: I can't.
BOY: I'm going to the Ritz.
GIRL: I can.

40 BOY: Darling, we're going to have a wonderful time tonight. I've got three tickets for the theatre.
GIRL: But why do we need three tickets?
BOY: They're for your mother, your father and your little sister!

41 Harry was waiting on the corner for his blind date to arrive. Suddenly, this girl walked up to him.
Harry said, 'Are you Jane?'
She said, 'Are you Harry?'
Harry said, 'Yes.'
She said, 'I'm not Jane.'

42 My fiancée told me she was going to break off our engagement. She said her feelings towards me had changed. So I asked her for the ring back and she said that while her feelings towards *me* had changed, she still felt the same towards the ring.

43 He's not good enough for you!
Sign above mirror in women's room, Ed Debevic's diner, Beverly Hills

44 I'm not playing hard to get, I *am* hard to get.
Bumper sticker

See Confidence 1, Gifts 9, Hair 15, Losers 18, School 16; *see also* Dating – Chat-up Lines, Engagements, Gold-diggers, Kissing, Proposals, Romance, Sex, Sexual Attraction, The Single Life

Dating – chat-up lines

1 Excuse me, I don't normally talk to strange women in the street but I'm on my way to confession and I'm a bit short of material.

2 Excuse me, I'm a stranger here. Can you direct me to your house?

3 Pardon me, but I'm writing a telephone book. May I have your number?

4 You're just my type – you're a girl.

5 Would you like to come up to my room and help me write my will?

6 BOY: Hi, where have you been all my life?
GIRL: Out of it, thank goodness!

7 BOY: I'd go to the ends of the world for you!
GIRL: Yes, but would you stay there?

8 If you believe in the hereafter, you'll give me a kiss.

What's the hereafter got to do with a kiss?

A kiss is what I'm here after.

9 MAN: Where have you been all my life?

WOMAN: Well, for the first half of it, I wasn't even born.

10 Tell me, where did you get those big, blue eyes?

They came with my face.

11 WOMAN: How strange. You look like my fourth husband.

MAN: My God! How many have you had?

WOMAN: Three!

12 Improve your image – be seen with me.

Bumper sticker

13 Tell me about yourself – your struggles, your dreams, your telephone number.

Peter Arno

See also Dating, Romance, Sex, Sexual Attraction, The Single Life

Death

1 Death is just another way of saying, 'Yesterday was the last day of the rest of your life.'

2 Death is nature's way of telling you to slow down.

3 My uncle fell into a vat of cold cream – and softened to death.

4 Strange, isn't it? Everyone wants to go to heaven but no one wants to die.

5 Undertakers have put up the cost of funerals by more than 15 per cent in the last year. They say it's to do with the high cost of living!

6 They say you shouldn't say anything about the dead unless it's good.

He's dead? Good!

7 Drowned in varnish! What a horrible way to go!

On the contrary. They say he had a beautiful finish!

8 How much did your uncle leave when he died?

Everything!

9 I almost got killed twice today!

Once would have been enough!

10 I hate you. I can hardly wait till you're dead so I can dance on your grave!

In that case, I'll tell them I want to be buried at sea!

11 It's no good, I've got one foot in the grate.

You mean 'grave'?

No, I mean 'grate'. I want to be cremated.

12 My uncle died and all he left was an old clock.

Shouldn't be much trouble winding up his estate!

13 My uncle Jack died the other day.

Oh dear, what did he die of?

I don't know, but it wasn't anything serious.

14 What's the death rate around here?

Same as it's always been – one per person!

15 Why does Granny read the Bible so much?

I think she's cramming for her finals.

16 WIFE: I've been thinking things over and I've decided I'd like to be cremated.

HUSBAND: OK, love, get your coat on.

17 A man goes off on a business trip, leaving his cat in the care of a neighbour. A few days later he phones the neighbour to ask about his pet and the neighbour says, 'The cat has died.'

The poor man is distraught and

says to his friend, 'Couldn't you have broken it to me more gently? The first time I called you could have told me that the cat was on the roof, the next time that the cat had fallen off the roof and wasn't looking too well, and so on.'

When he returned he got a new cat and, a few weeks later, set off on another trip, leaving the new pet with the same neighbour. After a few days he called. 'How's the cat?'

'The cat is just fine, but I think you should know, your mother's on the roof.'

18 Eric had just read the news that the richest man in the county had died. He sat at the bar and cried into his beer. His friend Derek tried to comfort him.

'But Eric, you weren't even related to him.'

'I know. That's why I'm crying!'

19 Old Robin Hood was lying in bed in his cottage deep in the heart of Sherwood Forest. Knowing that he didn't have much longer to live, he called in Little John and said, 'Bring me my bow and arrow and open the window. I will fire the arrow and I want you to bury me wherever it lands.'

So Little John fetched the bow and arrow and Robin Hood fired it. Just two days later, Little John and the rest of the Merry Men, in accordance with Robin's dying wish, buried him on top of the wardrobe.

20 Dying is a very dull, dreary affair. And my advice to you is to have nothing whatever to do with it.
W. Somerset Maugham

21 Dying is the most hellishly boresome experience in the world! Particularly when it entails dying of 'natural causes'.
W. Somerset Maugham

22 I cannot forgive my friends for dying; I do not find these vanishing acts of theirs at all amusing.
Logan Pearsall Smith

23 If I could drop dead right now, I'd be the happiest man alive.
Sam Goldwyn

24 Oh well, no matter what happens, there's always death.
Napoleon Bonaparte

See Advertising 6, Dogs 35, Golf 28, 29, Hecklers 28, Insults 16, 73, Newspapers 4, Patriotism 1, Politics and Politicians 45; *see also* Funerals, Heaven, Murder, Reincarnation, Wills

Debt

1 A deficit is what you have when you haven't as much as you had when you had nothing.

2 America has the highest standard of living in the world. It's just a pity we can't afford it.

3 Bankruptcy is a legal proceeding whereby you put your money in your trouser pockets and give your jacket to your creditors.

4 I lost control of my car the other day. I forgot to keep up the payments!

5 I'm determined to stay out of debt – even if I have to borrow money to do so.

6 I've got a great way of putting off my creditors. I send them a postcard saying, 'Cheque enclosed.'

7 I've tried paying my debts with a smile, but they still want money.

8 If you lend five pounds to a friend and you never see him again, it's worth it.

9 My dad had a problem. He was always running into things – like debt!

10 Of course I'm broke, I owe money that hasn't been minted yet!

11 The country's national debt totals billions of pounds. Which raises the interesting question, how do you repossess a country?

12 Times are tough, I'm ten pounds short of having 25p!

13 When he borrowed money from me, he said, 'I'll be eternally indebted to you.' And he meant it!

14 With all the loans and credit cards and mortgages available these days, anyone who isn't hopelessly in debt just isn't trying.

15 You're looking at a success story. I started off with nothing and look at me now – 10,000 pounds in debt.

16 I've got this great idea for keeping my bills down.
What is it?
A paperweight!

17 There's a man outside who says you owe him money.
What does he look like?
He looks like you better pay him!

18 There's a man at the door to see you.
With a bill?
No, just a nose like anybody else's.

19 A worker went to see his boss to ask for a raise on the grounds that there were three companies after him.
    The boss asked which three and the worker said, 'The gas company, the phone company and the finance company.'

See Dentists 8, Funerals 7, History 2, Success 11; *see also* Bankruptcy, Banks and Banking, Borrowing and Lending, Credit, Credit Cards, Inflation, Money, Poverty, Spending

Decisions

1 When I was a junior executive, the directors would always try to involve me in the decision-making process. Sometimes they even let me toss the coin.

2 I have no plans and no plans to have plans.
Mario Cuomo

See also Business, Decisiveness

Decisiveness

1 Any fool knows that and I'm no exception.

2 Are you sure?
I'm positive.
Only a fool is positive.
Are you sure?
I'm positive.

See also Business, Decisions

Decoration

1 Do you know how to make a Venetian blind?
How?
Poke your finger in his eye.

2 I bought a second-hand carpet in mint condition.
You mean good as new?
No, I mean it's got a hole in the middle.

See Stinginess 30; *see also* Antiques, Do It Yourself, Furniture, Home, Homes, Homes – Squalid, Houses

Defeat

1 I took my defeat like a man. I blamed it on my wife!

2 As always, victory finds 100 fathers, but defeat is an orphan.
Count Galeazzo Ciano

See also Losers, Victory

Democracy

1 Democracy is a state of mind in which every man is as good as every other man, provided he really is.

2 The great thing about living in a democracy is that you can say what you think without thinking.

3 Democracy is a form of government by popular ignorance.
Elbert Hubbard

4 Democracy gives every man the right to be his own oppressor.
James Russell Lowell

5 Democracy: a government of bullies tempered by editors.
Ralph Waldo Emerson

6 One fifth of the people are against everything all the time.
Robert F. Kennedy

See also Congress, Government, Houses of Parliament, Politics and Politicians

Dentists

1 I said to my dentist, 'Do you promise to pull the tooth, the whole tooth and nothing but the tooth?'

2 I think my dentist is in trouble. Last week he took out all my gold fillings and put in IOUs.

3 I see my dentist twice a year – once for each tooth.

4 He's got so many cavities, he talks with an echo.

5 She's got so much bridgework, if you want to kiss her, you have to pay a toll.

6 My dentist found such a big cavity, he sent me to a chiropodist.

7 I'm changing to a new dentist. The old one got on my nerves.

8 Nothing gets an old dental bill paid like a new toothache.

9 The first thing you learn from orthodontists is that buck teeth is the condition, not the price.

10 How much will it cost to pull this tooth?
Twenty-five pounds.
What, for five minutes' work?
I'll work slower if you want.

11 PATIENT: So what's the verdict?
DENTIST: Well, your teeth are fine, but your gums have got to come out.

12 So how did you get on at the dentist's?
It was a scream!

13 So the dentist didn't hurt a bit?
Not until I saw the bill.

See Eyes 18; *see also* Health, Illness, Mouths, Teeth

Diet

1 Her idea of a balanced diet is to have a bacon sandwich in each hand.

2 The most difficult part of a diet isn't watching what you eat. It's watching what other people eat.

3 The only good thing to be said for dieting is that it definitely sharpens your appetite.

4 Advice to thin men – Don't eat fast. Advice to fat men – Don't eat ... fast.

5 All these diet experts are living off the fat of the land.

6 Diets are for people who are thick and tired of it!

7 DOCTOR: I'm going to give you a diet sheet and some slimming pills. In three months I want half of you to come back for a check-up.

8 Don't be fooled by appearances. A banana is a cream cake disguised as a fruit!

9 Eat, drink and be merry, for tomorrow we diet!

10 Have you heard of the new 'Jungle diet'? All you eat are bananas, coconuts and palm oil. You don't lose any weight but you can certainly climb trees.

11 I went on this special 'fourteen-day diet' – and all I lost was two weeks.

12 I'm on the new 'skipping diet'. I'm skipping lunch, I'm skipping dinner . . .

13 I'm putting myself on this strict diet. I'm not going to eat between snacks.

14 I've got to go on a diet. This morning I tightened my belt and got 3 inches taller!

15 It took a lot of will-power, but I finally managed to give up dieting!

16 It wasn't till I went on a diet that I realized I was a bad loser.

17 It's not the minutes you spend at the table that make you put on weight, it's the seconds.

18 Most diets can be summed up with this advice: if it tastes good, spit it out.

19 My sister has a great new idea for a diet. You can eat as much as you like – you just don't swallow it.

20 No matter what kind of diet you're on, you can normally eat as much as you want of anything you don't like.

21 Obesity is the mother of invention.

22 On his latest diet, my husband is losing five pounds a week. In a year and a half, I'll be rid of him completely.

23 On my new diet, I'm starving myself to death just so that I can live a little longer.

24 One of the best reducing exercises I know consists of putting both hands against the table edge and pushing back.

25 Talk about desperate – my husband even shaves before standing on the bathroom scales!

26 The best thing for a person on a diet to eat is less.

27 The best way to lose weight is by skipping – chocolates and desserts.

28 The day I decided to go on a diet was when I got short of breath going *down* the stairs.

29 The great thing about a diet is that it helps you gain weight more slowly.

30 The trouble with a diet is that you don't eat what you like and you don't like what you eat.

31 I'll have a banana split made with two bananas, three scoops of vanilla ice-cream, chocolate-chip sauce, chopped nuts and a big dollop of whipped cream.
Would you like a cherry on top?
No thanks. I'm on a diet!

32 Wait a minute! I thought you were on a diet?
I am. But I've had my diet and now I'm having my dinner!

33 Your stomach is enormous! You should diet.
What colour?

34 The second day of a diet is always easier than the first. By the second day, you're off it.
Jackie Gleason

See Begging 6, Hard Times 11; *see also* Cooking, Drink, Exercise, Figures – Fat, Figures – Thin, Food

Diplomacy

1 A diplomat is someone who is appointed to avert situations which would never occur if there were no diplomats.

2 Diplomacy is the art of making others believe that you believe what you don't believe.

3 A diplomat is someone who thinks twice before saying nothing.

4 As a US diplomat, he was hopeless. He even called the ruler of one of America's closest allies 'Queenie'. And that was the first time he'd met him!

5 Diplomacy is the art of skating on thin ice without getting into deep water.

6 A diplomat is someone who acts disarming when his country is not.

7 If a diplomat says yes, he means perhaps; if he says perhaps, he means no; and if he says no, it means he's not a diplomat.

8 The art of diplomacy is to say nothing – especially when you're speaking.

9 A diplomat is a man who always remembers a woman's birthday but never remembers her age.
Robert Frost

10 To say nothing, especially when speaking, is half the art of diplomacy.
Will Durant

See Age 10; *see also* Manners, Politics and Politicians

Divorce

1 A couple I know in Hollywood have just ironed out their divorce settlement. Now, at last, they can go ahead with the wedding.

2 Divorces are arranged so that lawyers can live happily ever after.

3 I belong to a support group called Divorcees Anonymous. Whenever I feel like leaving my wife, they send over an accountant to talk me out of it.

4 I got married because I was tired of going to the launderette, eating take-away food all the time and always having holes in my socks. I got divorced for the same reasons!

5 I hear you're getting a divorce. Who's the lucky man?

6 If we didn't have divorce, where would we get waitresses?

7 Let me tell you a fairy-story adapted for the times we live in. Once upon a time there was a Mummy Bear, a Daddy Bear and a Baby Bear from a previous marriage . . .

8 My ex-wife was fanatically tidy. She divorced me because I had one little hair out of place. It was blonde and it was on my jacket!

9 My wife and I were considering a divorce. But when we looked at the cost of the lawyers, we decided to put in a new swimming pool instead.

10 My wife would divorce me if she could think of a way of doing it without making me happy.

11 Nowadays, a divorce costs more than a wedding – but it's worth it.

12 Our divorce was so amicable, I proposed to her again.

13 People today seem to be marrying more and enjoying it less.

14 She got a divorce on the grounds that her husband had only spoken to her three times in the course of seven years of marriage. She also got custody of the three children.

15 She's very sentimental. She got divorced in the same dress her mother got divorced in.

16 I'm afraid my wife and I are incompatible. I want a divorce and she doesn't.

17 The only thing my husband and I

had in common was that we were married on the same day.

18 There's a new chain of jewellery stores just opened in America. They rent out wedding rings!

19 To be truthful, you could split the blame for the failure of our marriage – between my wife and her mother.

20 We married for better or for worse, but not for good.

21 When her divorce came through, it made her feel like a new man.

22 Can you remember your first kiss?
I can't even remember my first husband!

23 HUSBAND: What would you like for Christmas?
WIFE: A divorce.
HUSBAND: I wasn't thinking of spending that much!

24 My wife's been missing now for over a week and I do so want her back.
Because your heart is so full of love?
No, because the sink is so full of dishes.

25 Why did you agree on a divorce?
Because we couldn't agree on anything else.

26 An old couple who'd been married more than sixty years got divorced in their nineties. When asked why they had left it so late, the wife replied, 'We wanted to wait until the children were dead.'

27 She'd only been married six weeks when the young bride started divorce proceedings.
'You've been married just six weeks,' said the judge, 'and you're tired of him already?'
'No, but by the time the divorce comes through, I will be.'

See Babies 23, Children 11, Honeymoons 4; see also Alimony, Bigamy, Infidelity, Marriage, Separation

Do it yourself

1 My husband is absolutely no good at fixing things. So everything in the house works.

2 Put a hammer in my husband's hand and you've put together two things of roughly equal intelligence.

3 Can I put this wallpaper on myself? Certainly, but it'll probably look better on a wall.

4 PLUMBER: Where's the drip?
HOUSEWIFE: He's in the bathroom, trying to fix the leak!

See Accidents 17, Arguments 15, Cars 23, Dogs 33, Hospitals 13, School 32; see also Decoration, Hobbies, Home, Homes, Houses

Doctors

1 A specialist is a doctor with a smaller practice but a bigger home.

2 An apple a day keeps the doctor away. And so does not paying your bills.

3 Fortunately, my doctor doesn't believe in unnecessary surgery. Which means he won't operate unless he really needs the money.

4 I finally found a way to get my doctor to make house calls. I've bought a home on the golf course!

5 I think my doctor's more interested in my money than in my health. When I went to him this morning he said, 'I wonder what's wrong with you. Let me feel your purse.'

6 I went to the doctor's this morning. I couldn't go last week – I was sick.

7 I've got a truly dedicated doctor. He thinks nothing of coming out in the middle of the week!

8 Is a paediatrician a man with little patients?

9 Is the doctor expensive? I swallowed a 10p piece and he made me cough up five pounds.

10 Some doctors prefer to tell you the bad news face to face. Others prefer to send you the bill by post.

11 The doctor said he'd have me on my feet in no time and he was right. I had to sell my car to pay his bill!

12 The doctor has given me three days to live – but not consecutively.

13 Doctor, I want to undergo a sex-change operation.
From what?

14 Doctor, can I get a second opinion?
Of course you can. Come back to-morrow.

15 Doctor, every bone in my body hurts.
Well, just be glad you're not a herring!

16 DOCTOR: Your pulse is as steady as a clock.
PATIENT: Maybe that's because you're feeling my wrist watch!

17 Doctor, I get this stabbing pain in my eye every time I have a cup of tea.
Try taking the spoon out.

18 Doctor, I think I've broken my neck.
Really? Well, keep your chin up!

19 Doctor, I keep thinking I'm a pair of curtains.
For heaven's sake, pull yourself together!

20 Doctor, I'm in great pain from my wooden leg.
How can a wooden leg cause you pain?
My wife keeps hitting me over the head with it.

21 Doctor, I've broken my arm in two places.
Don't go back to either of them!

22 Doctor, my son has just swallowed my pen! What shall I do?
Use a pencil.

23 Doctor, my irregular heartbeat is bothering me.
Don't worry. We'll soon put a stop to it.

24 Doctor, my hands won't stop shaking!
Tell me, do you drink a lot?
No, I spill most of it!

25 Doctor, you've got to help me. Everyone thinks I'm a liar.
I find that hard to believe.

26 DOCTOR: Did that medicine I gave your uncle straighten him out?
PATIENT: It certainly did. They buried him yesterday!

27 DOCTOR: Have you ever been troubled by appendicitis?
PATIENT: Only when I've tried to spell it.

28 DOCTOR: I can't tell what's wrong with you. I think it's drink.
PATIENT: OK, I'll come back when you're sober.

29 DOCTOR: I'm afraid you've got a dodgy ticker.
PATIENT: Thank goodness. I was afraid there might be something wrong with my heart.

30 DOCTOR: I'm afraid you're anaemic.
PATIENT: I'd like a second opinion.
DOCTOR: OK, you're ugly too.

31 DOCTOR: I'm afraid I've got bad news for you. You could go at any time.
PATIENT: But that's *good* news. I haven't been for six days.

32 DOCTOR: If I find the operation necessary, would you have the money to pay for it?
PATIENT: If I didn't have the money,

would you find the operation necessary?

33 DOCTOR: So how are your broken ribs coming along?
PATIENT: Well, I keep getting this stitch in my side.
DOCTOR: Good, that shows the bones are knitting.

34 DOCTOR: That's a nasty cough you've got there. Have you had it before?
PATIENT: Yes.
DOCTOR: Well, you've got it again.

35 DOCTOR: The best thing for you to do is to give up drinking, smoking and wild women.
PATIENT: What's the second best?

36 DOCTOR: When you get up in the morning do you have a furry tongue and a pain in the middle of your shoulders and feel terribly depressed?
PATIENT: Yes, I do.
DOCTOR: So do I. I wonder what it is.

37 DOCTOR: You have acute appendicitis.
FEMALE PATIENT: I came here to be examined, not admired.

38 DOCTOR: You've burnt both your ears! How did it happen?
PATIENT: I was ironing when the telephone rang.
DOCTOR: But how did you burn both of them?
PATIENT: Well, just as soon as I put the phone down, it rang again.

39 DOCTOR: You've got six months to live.
PATIENT: But what if I can't pay your bill in that time?
DOCTOR: Then I'll give you another six months.

40 Does the doctor still believe in house calls?
Certainly. What time can you get to his house?

41 I went to his evening surgery, I always do.
Why's that?
Well, I like to give him time for his hands to warm up.

42 I'm off to the doctor's. I feel a bit dizzy.
Vertigo?
No, just round the corner.

43 PATIENT: Doctor, I can't sleep at night.
DOCTOR: Well, I advise you to eat something before you go to bed.
PATIENT: But two months ago you advised me never to eat anything before going to bed.
DOCTOR: But that was two months ago. Medical science has made enormous strides since then.

44 DOCTOR: I've decided that you're a kleptomaniac.
PATIENT: You mean I help myself because I can't help myself?

45 PATIENT: My wife is going out of her mind. She spends the whole day blowing smoke rings.
DOCTOR: There's nothing wrong with that. I like blowing smoke rings myself.
PATIENT: But my wife doesn't smoke.

46 So, Doctor, do you think I'm going to live?
Yes, but I don't advise it!

47 Tell me, Doctor, when my finger heals will I be able to play the piano?
Of course you will.
That's marvellous, I never could before.

48 The doctor told me to take two tablespoonfuls of Persian cat's milk.
How do you get milk from a Persian cat?
Take his saucer away.

49 The trouble is, Doctor, I seem to

lose my temper very easily these days.
I beg your pardon?
I told you once, you blithering idiot!

50 DOCTOR: Stick your tongue out and say 'Ahh!'
PATIENT: Ahh!
DOCTOR: Well, your tongue looks all right, but why the postage stamp?
PATIENT: So that's where I left it!

51 A man walks into a doctor's surgery with a duck on his head.
The doctor says, 'What can I do for you?'
And the duck says, 'I want this wart on my foot removed!'

52 A woman rang the doctor in a panic, 'Doctor, what can I do? My husband has just swallowed a mouse!'
The doctor said, 'I'll be right over, but while you're waiting, wave a piece of cheese in front of his mouth.'
When the doctor arrived, he discovered the woman waving a mackerel in front of her husband's mouth.
'I said a piece of cheese, not a mackerel!' he cried.
And the woman said, 'But I had to get the cat out first!'

53 Eating in a fish restaurant, a diner began to choke on a bone. As his face grew redder and redder, the waiters stood there, not knowing what to do.
Finally, another diner rushed over and said, 'I'm a doctor. Let me at him.'
The doctor put his arms round the man and suddenly pulled them tight. The bone shot out and a grateful diner turned to the doctor.
'Thank you, thank you,' he said.

'Now tell me, how much do I owe you?'
And the doctor said, 'I'll settle for half of what you would have paid me while you were choking.'

54 I was having a complete medical examination. The doctor pointed to a jar on the shelf and said, 'I want you to fill that.'
I replied, 'What! From here?'

55 The doctor said, 'Go over to the window and put your tongue out.'
I said, 'Why?'
He said, 'Because I don't like the chap who lives opposite.'

56 The doctor didn't stay long with the patient. As he left the house, he told the patient's wife, 'There's nothing wrong with your husband. He just thinks he's sick.'
A few days later the doctor rang to check if his diagnosis had been correct.
'How's your husband today?' he asked the wife.
'He's worse,' said the wife. 'Now he thinks he's dead.'

57 The patient entered the doctor's consulting room and sat down wearily. He said, 'The thing is, Doctor, I just feel generally under the weather.'
And the doctor said, 'Maybe it's your diet. What sort of things do you eat?'
'Well, my favourite food is snooker balls. I can't eat enough of them. For breakfast I have a couple of red ones. I have a brown and a black one mid-morning, then for lunch I have a couple of yellows, and for supper some pinks and some more yellows.'
'Well, you know what your trouble is,' said the doctor. 'You're not getting enough greens.'

58 Doctors are just the same as lawyers; the only difference is that lawyers

merely rob you, whereas doctors rob you and kill you too.
Anton Chekhov

59 Physician: one upon whom we set our hopes when ill and our dogs when well.
Ambrose Bierce

See Crime 13, Drink 28, 41, 49, Eyes 11, Golf 22, Husbands and Wives 50, Loneliness 2, Memory 6, Music 18, Newlyweds 4, Pessimism 4, Sex 26, Sleep 12, Soccer 6, Weddings 13; *see also* Amnesia, Health, Hospitals, Hypochondria, Illness, Medicine, Plastic Surgery, Psychiatry

Dogs

1 Buy 'Woof', the pet food dogs ask for by name!

2 Every day my dog and I go for a tramp in the woods. The dog loves it. But the tramp is getting a bit fed up.

3 I bought a watchdog last week and you can't say he doesn't do what he's told. Last night he watched a burglar steal half the contents of the house.

4 I call my dog Isaiah.
Why?
Because one eye's 'igher than the other.

5 I got myself a Dobermann pinscher. He goes round all day pinching Dobermanns.

6 I got that dog when he was a puppy, and in no time at all I had him eating out of my leg.

7 I took my dog to a flea circus, and he stole the show.

8 I sent my dog to an obedience school. He still bites me, but at least he says grace first.

9 I'd send my dog to one of these new pet psychiatrists – except he knows he's not allowed on the couch.

10 I've been teaching my dog to beg. Last night he came home with £1.27.

11 I've got a watchdog. Trouble is, all he watches is television.

12 I've got a miniature poodle. The miniature turn your back, he does a poodle.

13 My dog saw a seat in the park with a notice on it saying WET PAINT. So he did.

14 My dog's just like one of the family. I wouldn't like to say which.

15 Remember the film *Lassie Come Home*? I was in that. I played the lead!

16 Remember, a barking dog never bites – while barking.

17 The dog I've got now is so clever. When we go to obedience classes, I'm the one on the lead.

18 There's only one way to stop a dog barking in August. Shoot it in July!

19 We call our dog Hickory, because he's got such a rough bark.

20 CUSTOMER: Have you any dogs going cheap?
PET-SHOP MANAGER: No, I'm afraid all our dogs go 'Woof!'

21 CUSTOMER: Does this dog have a pedigree?
PET-SHOP OWNER: A pedigree? Listen, if this dog could talk, he wouldn't be speaking to either of us.

22 Do you realize that your dog barked all night long?
Yes, but don't worry. He sleeps all day!

23 Don't worry. A barking dog never bites!
Yes, but does the dog know that?

24 Hey, your dog's just eaten my hat!
Don't worry. He likes hats.
But it was my best hat!
It doesn't matter. All hats are the same to him.
Are you trying to annoy me?
What makes you say that?
It's your attitude.
It's not my 'at 'ee chewed, it's *your* 'at 'ee chewed!

25 I play chess with my dog nearly every day.
Your dog plays chess? That's fantastic!
Not really. I beat him two times out of three.

26 Keep that dog out of my house. It's full of fleas!
Rex, keep out of that house. It's full of fleas!

27 My dog bit my leg last night.
Did you put anything on it?
No, he liked it just as it was.

28 My dog plays poker with me.
That's fantastic! He must be very intelligent.
Not really. Every time he gets a good hand, he wags his tail.

29 My dog took first prize in the cat show.
How was that?
He took the cat.

30 My dog's a blacksmith.
How's that?
Just give him a kick and he makes a bolt for the door.

31 We've just had our dog put down.
Was he mad?
He was furious!

32 Why did you buy a dachshund?
So all the kids could pet him at the same time.

33 Why do you call your dog Handyman?
Because he does odd jobs around the house.

34 WORRIED DOG OWNER: My dog chases everyone he sees on a bike. What should I do?
VET: Take the bike away from him immediately.

35 I just heard about this woman who decided to take her dog to Israel. She put him in a special bag and flew direct to Tel Aviv. But when she landed and went to the luggage carousel, there was no sign of the bag.

So she complained and the airline officials started a search of all the luggage in the airport. Sure enough, they found the bag. But when they opened it, the dog was dead.

'What are we going to do?' they cried. 'She'll be furious! She'll sue us!'

'I've got an idea,' said one. 'It's a cocker spaniel and there's a pet shop just down the road. I'll go and get another cocker spaniel, put it in the bag and she'll never know the difference.'

Twenty minutes later, they went up to the woman, apologized for the delay and handed her the bag.

The woman was so relieved. She opened the bag and the dog jumped out.

'This isn't my dog!' she cried.

'How do you know?' they asked her.

'Because he died two days ago,' she said. 'I was bringing him to Israel to bury him!'

36 I loathe people who keep dogs. They are cowards who haven't got the guts to bite people themselves.
August Strindberg

37 To his dog, every man is Napoleon; hence the constant popularity of dogs.
Aldous Huxley

See Mankind 3, Pests 1, Psychiatry 21, Psychology 3, Wealth 6; *see also* Animals, Cats, Pets

Drink

1 A drunk is someone who goes into a bar optimistically and comes out misty optically.

2 Absinthe makes the heart grow fonder.

3 After four martinis my husband turns into a disgusting beast and after the fifth, I pass out altogether.

4 For the perfect pick-me-up, take the juice from a bottle of whisky.

5 Frankly, I'd rather have a case of the measles than a case of this wine.

6 He couldn't make both ends meet because he made one end drink.

7 He drinks so much, when you dance with him you can hear him slosh.

8 He may have had a little too much to drink last night. Two hours after the bar closed he was still out in the car-park, doing his imitation of a speed bump.

9 He's very particular about what he drinks. It has to be liquid.

10 I don't drink to be sociable. I drink to get drunk.

11 As always, my husband went out fit as a fiddle and came home tight as a drum.

12 I drink to steady my nerves. Last night I got so steady I couldn't move.

13 I know I'm drunk when I feel sophisticated but can't pronounce it.

14 I never consume alcohol. You see, I don't think it's right to drink in front of my children. And when I'm away from my children, I don't need to drink.

15 I took her home from the party. I placed her head on my shoulder. Someone else was carrying her feet.

16 I wasn't that drunk. I could still lie on the floor without holding on.

17 I wouldn't call him a steady drinker – his hands shake too much.

18 Dignity is the one thing that alcohol doesn't preserve.

19 I've decided I've got to stop drinking. I don't think I'm an alcoholic yet, but I *am* beginning to see the writing on the floor.

20 I've invented a new cocktail called a Card Table. When you've had a couple, your legs fold up right under you.

21 I've just joined the AAAA. It's for people who're being driven to drink.

22 I've ruined my health by drinking to everyone else's.

23 Me, drunk? But I've only had tee martoonies!

24 Tho' I might be slightly under the affluence of incohol, I'm not so think as you drunk I am.

25 I'm not drunk though some thinkle peep I am.

26 And anyway, I've got all day sober to Sunday up in.

27 My uncle used to go round drinking champagne from ladies' slippers. He wound up with athlete's tongue.

28 My uncle was feeling under the weather so he went to the doctor for a check-up. They found the problem. There was a small amount of blood in his alcoholic system.

29 Our new pub has got three barmaids – two for serving and one for listening.

30 The beer's so flat at this pub, they serve it on a plate.

31 The police said I was drunk but I don't think that's fair. It's just the way I react to an excess of alcohol.

32 There's a local bar that employs only midget waiters – to make the drinks look bigger.

33 There's nothing wrong with drinking like a fish as long as you drink what a fish drinks.

34 They say that liquor improves with age and I think they're right. The older I get, the more I like it.

35 Why do I drink so much? Because I recently donated my body to science and I'm preserving it in alcohol until they can use it.

36 Do you drink?
No.
Then hold this bottle while I tie my shoelaces.

37 Do you know a way you could sell more beer?
No, how could I sell more beer?
Just fill the glasses properly.

38 DRUNK: Take me to 150 Church Lane.
TAXI DRIVER: You're already at 150 Church Lane.
DRUNK: All right, but next time don't drive so damned fast!

39 Every time I get drunk I see rabbits with red spots.
Have you seen your doctor?
No, just rabbits with red spots.

40 I fell down the stairs with two pints of whisky.
Heavens, did you spill any?
No, I managed to keep my mouth shut.

41 I'm going to give you a bottle of whisky for your birthday.
Please don't, my doctor has forbidden me to drink liquor.
All right, I'll give you something else you'll appreciate.
What's that?
The name of a new doctor.

42 My wife drives me to drink.
You're lucky. I have to walk!

43 POLICEMAN: And where do you think you might be going at this time of night, sir?

DRUNK: To a lecture, Officer.
OFFICER: And tell me, sir, who on earth would be giving a lecture at this time of night?
DRUNK: My wife.

44 This brandy is 100 years old.
Really? It tastes just like new!

45 VICAR: Drunk again, eh?
DRINKER: Really? So am I.

46 Where's the nearest boozer?
You're talking to him!

47 Whisky is slow poison.
I'm in no hurry.

48 Why do you call your local the Stradivarius?
Because it's a vile inn.

49 DOCTOR: Do you drink to excess?
PATIENT: I'll drink to anything!

50 A drinker rolled home late on a Friday night and, as he walked in, he found his wife with her hand outstretched.
She said, 'OK, hand over your pay-packet!'
With a guilty look on his face, he pulled it out of his pocket, handed it to her and said, 'It's not all there. I spent half of it on something for the house.'
And she said, 'Oh, that was nice. What was it?'
And he said, 'A round of drinks!'

51 A drunk was weaving his way home one night with a bottle of whisky in each coat pocket when he stepped off the curb and was hit by a passing car.
As he lay groaning in the gutter, the poor car driver ran back, noticed an ever-growing pool of liquid spreading across the road and shrieked, 'Oh, my God!'
'What is it?' cried the drunk.
'It's blood!'
'Thank God for that,' said the drunk. 'I thought it was the whisky!'

52 A friend of mine drank so much on a trip to Europe that when he got to Italy he was the only one in the party who couldn't see anything wrong with the Tower of Pisa.

And he was so drunk when he came back that they had to pay duty on him to get him through Customs.

53 A man who has obviously had a little too much to drink staggers into an Alcoholics Anonymous meeting and is met at the door by a member who says, 'So, you've obviously come here to join.'

'No,' says the man, 'I've come here to resign!'

54 Do you know, in this town there are more than 300 pubs. And I'm proud to say that I haven't been in one of them.

I forget which one it is, but there's one of them I definitely haven't been in.

55 I've invented this marvellous new tonic wine containing iron, glucose and rum. The iron gives you strength, the glucose gives you energy and the rum? The rum gives you ideas of what to do with all that strength and energy.

56 On the chest of a barmaid in Sale
Were tattooed the prices of ale,
And on her behind,
For the sake of the blind,
Was the same information in Braille.

57 Two friends arrived home after spending the night in several bars. The first one took the key from his pocket and tried unsuccessfully to put it into the lock.

After several failed attempts, his friend said, 'Do you want me to try and steady your hand?'

'No, my hand's OK. You try and hold the house!'

58 I'm not saying he's a world-champion drinker, but he'd got an entry in the Record Book of Guinnesses.
Frederick Oliver

See Courtroom 4, Doctors 28, Figures – Fat 1, Graffiti 4, Health 13, Husbands and Wives 5, Introductions 1, Life 7, Music 11, Old Age 20, Parties 9, Railways 13, Stinginess 2, 3, 12, 27, 29, 34; *see also* Addiction, Alcoholism, Coffee, Food, Parties

Driving

1 He's a very careful driver. He always looks both ways before hitting something.

2 I'm a very careful driver. I always slow down when going through a red light.

3 If you don't like the way I drive, get off the pavement!

4 If your wife wants to drive, don't stand in her way.

5 My driving is definitely getting better. Now, when I park, it's just a short walk to the pavement.

6 Technology has transformed the experience of driving. When I first started, you had to wind down your window to shout at another driver. Now you just call him on your car phone!

7 The really careful driver watches the car behind the car in front of him.

8 Then there was the woman who said to her husband, 'Be an angel and let me drive.' So he did – and now he is.

9 You should have seen me back the car out of the garage this morning. Problem was, I forgot I'd backed it *into* the garage last night!

10 Didn't you notice the thirty-miles-per-hour sign?

No, officer, I must have been driving too fast to see it!

11 Hello, is that the police? Look, I've just crashed into three cars, knocked down a street light, wrecked a bus shelter and gone through a shop window.
I see, sir. And where are you now?
Wouldn't you like to know!

12 HUSBAND: That's the third time I've had to replace the clutch.
WIFE: Well don't blame me. I never use it!

13 I'm sorry, Officer. Was I driving too fast?
Either that, or flying too low!

14 Sorry I'm late. I got held up by the traffic lights.
D'you mean they were stuck on red?
Oh no. They kept changing colour, but they didn't have one I liked.

15 Why do you always drive with your brakes on?
I want to be ready in case there's an emergency!

16 I couldn't keep my eyes off this young couple in the car in front of me on the motorway today. They were snogging passionately for about twenty miles.
So what's so unusual about that?
They were in separate cars!

17 I think the traffic's getting worse. I was trying to cross the high street yesterday. After five minutes a policeman came up to me and said, 'There's a zebra crossing just round the corner.'
So I said, 'Well, I hope he's having better luck than I am!'

18 All those in favor of conserving gasoline, please raise your right foot!
Sign on New York freeway

19 As a matter of fact, I *do* own the road.
Bumper sticker

See Drink 21, The Environment 3, Farming 9, History 4, Husbands and Wives 39, Railways 2, Vanity 18, Wind 1; *see also* Accidents, Cars, Driving – Police, Insurance, Parking, Travel

Driving – police

1 POLICEMAN: What gear were you in at the time of the accident?
DRIVER: Jeans, T-shirt and a pair of trainers.

2 POLICEMAN: Why is one side of your car painted red and the other side blue?
DRIVER: I like to hear the witnesses contradict each other.

3 POLICEMAN: Can you explain why you were doing fifty-three miles an hour in a thirty-five-miles-an-hour zone?
DRIVER: Certainly. I'm dyslexic.

See Law 17; *see also* Cars, Crime, Driving, The Law, Lawyers, Police

Drought

1 The cattle are now so thin, they brand them two at a time using carbon paper.

2 Have you heard the latest idea for saving water? You dilute it.

3 The drought round here is getting worse. Last week, the house next door caught fire and the fireman had to blow it out.

4 The drought is so bad in the West Country that the prisoners in the punishment cells at Dartmoor are on a strict bread and bread diet.

5 Things were so tough during our last drought that the management

had to close two lanes of the local swimming pool.

6 I got a letter from my cousin in Africa. Apparently there's a terrible water shortage out there.
But there's *always* a water shortage out there!
No, but this time it's serious.
How do you know?
The stamp is stuck on with a pin.

See also Rain, Summer, The Sun, Water, Weather, Weather – Hot

Drugs

1 Grass is nature's way of saying, 'High!'

2 Blow your mind. Smoke gunpowder.

3 One good turn-on deserves another.

4 If you can remember the seventies, you weren't there.

5 Just say 'No' to drugs. If only to drive the prices down!

See also Addiction

E

Earthquakes

1 How strong was our last earth-quake?
Well, let's just say that my zip code changed three times in a minute and a half.

2 If you're in Los Angeles and you feel a quake starting, there are two things to remember. One: run to a doorway for protection. And two: make sure the doorway is in New York.

3 The experts say you can predict an earthquake by observing the behaviour of your pets.
They're right. The night before our last quake, our cat and our cocker spaniel packed their bags and headed off for two weeks in Acapulco.

See Marriage 27; *see also* Los Angeles

Economics

1 A recession is what takes the wind out of your sales.

2 An economist is an expert who will know tomorrow why the things he predicted yesterday didn't happen today.

3 If the economy is really bouncing back, why are our customers' cheques doing the same?

4 Is there going to be a devaluation? That's the $63,000 question.

5 Prosperity is something that business-men create for politicians to take the credit for.

6 The economy is now on a solid foundation – it's on the rocks!

7 An economist was sent to an idyllic Caribbean island to try to introduce the inhabitants to some twentieth-century ideas of efficiency and good management.
On his first day there, he met a man sitting on his porch in the middle of the day with a bottle of beer in his hand. He explained to him that life would be so much better if got himself a regular job.
'Why?'
'Because then you could make some money.'
'Why do I need to make money?'
'Because when you've made enough, you can retire and you won't have to work any more.'
'But I don't work *now!*'

8 Economists are people who see some-thing work in practice and wonder if it would work in theory.
Ronald Reagan

9 Give me a one-handed economist! All my economists say, 'On the one hand . . . on the other'.
Harry S. Truman

See Accountants 15; *see also* Bank-ruptcy, Banks and Banking, Borrow-ing and Lending, Debt, Govern-ment, Hard Times, Inflation, Money, Politics and Politicians, Poverty, Spending, Thrift

Education

1 Education is the ability to quote Shakespeare without attributing it to the Bible.

2 Education today is teaching a child how to talk and then teaching it how to keep quiet.

3 It's still possible to get a good high school education. You just have to go to college to get it.

4 My son is following in the footsteps of some really great men. He just went down in history!

5 When your son finishes his education, what will he be?
About forty!

6 'Whom are you?' said he, for he had been to night school.
George Ade

7 Sixty years ago I knew everything; now I know nothing. Education is a progressive discovery of our own ignorance.
Will Durant

See Gardening 13, Scepticism 1, Television 12; see also Children, School, Teachers, University

Egotists

1 An egotist is a man who plays too big a part in his own life.

2 Be careful what you say about me. You're talking about the man I love!

3 I'm not saying he thinks he's God, but he always listens when he spakes unto himself.

See also Actors and Acting, Bores, Vanity

Elections

1 Elections consist of two sides and a fence.

2 My election result reminded me of the earth – I was flattened at the polls.

3 In elections, when all is said and done, a lot more is said than will ever be done.

4 You can campaign in poetry. You govern in prose.
Mario Cuomo

See Gambling 5, Graffiti 9; see also Congress, Defeat, Democracy, Houses of Parliament, Losers, Politics and Politicians, Victory

Electricity

1 An electrician is a man who wires homes for money.

2 WIFE: Wire you insulate?
ELECTRICIAN: I couldn't get ohm earlier.

See also Gadgets, Home, Homes, Houses, Modern Times

Embarrassment

1 I won't tell you what he did, but even my shock-proof watch was embarrassed!

See also Manners

Enemies

1 He keeps telling me he's on my side – but then, so is appendicitis!

2 I have no enemies at all. I have lots of friends who dislike me. But no enemies.

3 Love your enemies. It makes them so damn mad.

4 The perfect enemy is a man who stabs you in the back, then gets you arrested for carrying a concealed weapon.

5 He's his own worst enemy.
Not while I'm around!

6 I am free of all prejudice. I hate everyone equally.
W. C. Fields

See also Arguments, Fighting, Friends, War

Engagements

1 I hear you're engaged. So who's the lucky woman?
Her mother!

2 What will your father say when we tell him we're engaged?
Oh, he'll be delighted. He always is!

See also Dating, Marriage, Proposals, Romance, Weddings

England and the English

1 In England, saving for a rainy day and saving for a holiday are usually the same thing.

2 Not only is England an island but every Englishman as well.

3 The Englishman is very fond of animals – especially roasted with two veg.

See Art and Artists 21; *See also* Britain and the British, The English Language

English language, The

1 One thing I was taught at school is that double negatives are a complete no-no.

2 Don't you know the Queen's English?
Of course I do. And so's the King.

3 I'm suffering from an 'orrible 'eadache.
What you need is a couple of aspirates.

4 Is there a word in the English language which contains all the vowels?
Unquestionably.

5 A man was on his way to a pet shop when he bumped into a friend.

'I'm going to buy a mongoose,' he explained.
'Can you get one for me?' said the friend.
'I would but I don't know the plural of mongoose,' said the man. 'Is it "mongooses"? Is it "mongeese"? I'd be embarrassed if I said the wrong word.'
'No problem,' replied the friend. 'Just say "I'd like a mongoose, please. And, while you're at it, I'll have another one."'

See Gardening 12, Professions 4, Radio 8; *see also* England and the English, Languages, School, Swearing

Entertaining

1 After dinner last night, our hostess suggested we adjourn to the library for coffee. But when we drove over there, it was closed.

2 I thought I invited you to come after dinner.
But that's what I *have* come after.

See Losers 10; *see also* Cooking, Diets, Drink, Food, Hospitality, Restaurants, Restaurants – Waiters

Enthusiasm

1 Zeal: a certain nervous disorder afflicting the young and inexperienced.
Ambrose Bierce

See also Excess

Environment, The

1 Have you seen the latest environmentally sound product in the shops? It's a mouthwash for people who drink tap water.

2 KLEENY-KLEEN PLUS is phosphate-free, CFC-free, completely

biodegradable and approved by environmentalists everywhere. Unfortunately, it doesn't clean clothes.

3 The government is finally doing something about energy conservation. They're asking motorists to remember to turn off their windscreen wipers whenever they drive under a bridge.

4 Whenever he thought about the environment he felt absolutely terrible. So at last he came to a fateful decision. He decided not to think about it.

5 If sunbeams were weapons of war, we would have had solar energy long ago.
George Porter

6 The earth is like a spaceship that didn't come with an operating manual.
R. Buckminster Fuller

See Driving 18; *see also* City Life, Country Life, Farming, Pollution, Pollution – Air, Pollution – Water, Water

Equality

1 What makes equality such a difficult business is that we only want it with our superiors.
Henry Becque

See France and the French 3; *see also* Democracy, Feminism, Politics and Politicians

Eskimos

1 Have you heard the Eskimo national anthem? It's 'Freeze a Jolly Good Fellow'.

2 I went to visit an Eskimo friend for a couple of months – and then I decided to stay all night.

3 The Eskimos call themselves God's frozen people.

4 Is it true that Eskimos eat whalemeat and blubber?
Yes, but then you'd blubber too if you had to eat whalemeat!

5 What is the song that Eskimos sing before they sit down to eat?
'Whale Meat Again'.

6 An Eskimo was on trial in a court in northernmost Alaska. The judge turned to him and said, 'Where were you on the night of October to April?'

See also Weather – Cold

Espionage

1 Did you hear about the secret agent who had to spend a whole weekend rewriting his report because he hadn't realized he'd run out of invisible ink?

2 You know what they say: variety is the life of spies.

See also Diplomacy, Government, War

Ethnic jokes

1 A Udopian won his country's first ever gold medal at the Olympics. He was so proud of it, he had it bronzed.

2 Last week they had to shut down Udopian Airlines. They'd run out of coal!

3 The Udopian general was taken to the psychiatrist to be treated for delusions of grandeur. He thought he was a British Army private.

4 They don't have ice cubes any more in Udopia. The inventor died and took the recipe with him.

5 They held a Miss Udopia Contest and the winner came in third.

6 A car dealer in Udopia got caught turning back all the fuel gauges.

7 A Udopian heard that most car accidents take place within 2 miles of home. So he moved.

8 You can always tell a Udopian Airlines plane when it's snowing. It's the one with chains around the propeller.

9 A Udopian was cutting a block of ice into little cubes – so they would fit into his icetray.

10 CENSUS TAKER: When's your birthday?
UDOPIAN: 16 December.
CENSUS TAKER: Which year?
UDOPIAN: Every year!

11 FIRST UDOPIAN: Hello, Sam!
SECOND UDOPIAN: Hello!
FIRST UDOPIAN: Hey, you've got an answer for everything!

12 Have you heard the latest Udopian joke?
Careful – I come from Udopia!
That's all right. I'll tell it slowly!

13 How does a Udopian spell 'farm'?
E-I-E-I-O!

14 What's smarter than two Udopians?
One Udopian.

15 Why does a Udopian dictionary cost so little?
Because it's not in alphabetical order.

16 FIRST UDOPIAN: Do you know that man only uses one quarter of his brain?
SECOND UDOPIAN: So what does he do with the other quarter?

17 Why does the new Udopian Navy have glass-bottomed boats?
So they can see the old Udopian Navy!

18 UDOPIAN CHILD: Why have you gone on the pill, Grannie?
UDOPIAN GRANDMOTHER: I don't want to have any more grandchildren.

19 A Udopian was walking past a factory late at night when he noticed a bell with a sign that read: PRESS BELL FOR NIGHT WATCHMAN. So he pressed the bell and eventually he heard a door opening on the other side of the yard and the footsteps of the night watchman making his way towards the gate.

The night watchman then opened an inner gate, disabled the alarm and finally opened the outer gate.

'Yes,' he said. 'What do you want?'

And the Udopian said, 'I just wanted to know why you couldn't press the bell yourself.'

See also Hecklers, Insults, Losers, Stupidity

Excess

1 Too much of a good thing can be wonderful.
Mae West

2 Moderation is a fatal thing . . . Nothing succeeds like excess.
Oscar Wilde

See also Enthusiasm, Moderation, Wealth

Exercise

1 And now for your morning exercises. Ready? Up, down, up, down, up, down, up, down. And now the other eyelid.

2 Fit? The only exercise she gets is jumping to conclusions.

3 Heard the latest service for health-conscious people in Beverly Hills? Valet jogging.

4 I can't believe it. This morning I

jogged backwards for a mile and put on six pounds!

5 I love jogging, except for the part after you put on your trainers.

6 My doctor told me that exercise could add years to my life. He was right. I feel ten years older already!

7 No, I don't exercise. The way I see it, if God had meant for us to touch our toes, he would have put them further up our body.

8 The advantage of exercising every day is that you die healthier.

9 The trouble with jogging is that, by the time you realize you're fit enough to do it, it's too far to walk back.

10 Walking is a pleasure only when you can afford to drive if you want to.

11 Can you stand on your head?
No, it's too high.

12 Do you take exercise after your bath?
Yes. I usually step on the soap as I get out!

13 Does your husband do any exercise?
Well, he was out last week four nights running.

14 Exercise is bunk. If you are healthy, you don't need it; if you are sick you shouldn't take it.
Henry Ford.

15 I get all my exercise acting as a pallbearer to my friends who exercise.
Chauncey Depew

16 It is a fact that not once in all my life have I gone out for a walk. I have been taken out for walks; but that is another matter.
Max Beerbohm

See also Diets, Figures – Fat, Figures – Thin, Sport, Strength

Experience

1 Experience is the comb life gives you after you lose your hair.

2 The trouble with experience is that you never have it until after you need it.

3 We learn from experience that men never learn anything from experience.
George Bernard Shaw

4 What a man knows at fifty which he didn't know at twenty is, for the most part, incommunicable.
Adlai Stevenson

See also Age

Eyes

1 He was so cross-eyed, he went south-east to join the North-West Mounted Police.

2 He was so near-sighted, he couldn't even see his contact lenses.

3 He's lost his glasses and he can't look for them until he's found them.

4 I've got three pairs of spectacles: one for short-sightedness, one for long-sightedness and one to look for the other two.

5 My doctor told me my eyes were weak. That's ridiculous. On a clear day I can see my glasses.

6 My eyes are so bad, I've got to wear contact lenses just to see my glasses.

7 My sight's so bad, I need glasses to find my glasses.

8 She had romantic eyes. I could tell from the way they snuggled up to each other.

9 She's stopped wearing glasses. She looks better but she doesn't see as well.

10 You can't miss him. He's the only man I know who's got handlebar eyebrows!

11 DOCTOR: You need glasses.
PATIENT: But how do you know?
DOCTOR: I could tell the moment you walked through that window.

12 My uncle's got a glass eye.
Did he tell you?
No, it just came out in the conversation.

13 Tell me, have your eyes ever been checked?
No, they've always been blue.

14 Tell me, why do you wear those glasses?
I've got spots before my eyes.
And do the glasses help?
Yes, the spots are much bigger now.

15 WOMAN: I've just broken my glasses. Do I have to be examined all over again?

OPTICIAN: No, madam, just your eyes.

16 You look terrible. Have you been in a fight?
No, I just dropped my contact lens in a revolving door.

17 You need glasses!
But I'm already wearing glasses!
In that case, *I* need glasses.

18 Not many people realize, but bad eyesight can be responsible for the loss of perfectly good teeth. I'm a dentist and one day one of my patients came to me with a dreadful headache. I had to extract seventeen teeth before I cured it.
This would never have happened if I'd had good eyesight.

19 Your eyes shine like the pants of my blue serge suit.
Groucho Marx and Morrie Ryskind for Groucho Marx in *The Cocoanuts*

See Cricket 4, Dating – Chat-up Lines 10, Police 9, 10, Religion 7, Television 6; *see also* Blind, Faces

F

Faces

1 He says he can't believe his ears. I can't either!

2 Of course she smiles a lot. Her teeth are the only thing she has that aren't wrinkled.

3 She has a peach-like complexion – all yellow and fuzzy.

4 She was so pleased with her pretty chin that she added three more.

5 When I was a kid I had acne so bad my dog called me Spot.

6 With a face like yours, you should be in radio.

7 Your face is familiar – I might even say commonplace.

8 Pardon me, but haven't I seen your face somewhere else?
No, it's always been right here between my ears.

See also Appearance, Beards and Moustaches, Eyes, Hair, Mouths, Plastic Surgery, Shaving, Ugliness

Failure

1 Did you hear about the man who shot an arrow into the air – and missed.

2 For years I thought I was a failure. Then they told me to be positive and it worked. Now I'm positive I'm a failure!

3 This is a man who started out as an underweight, inexperienced, unselfconfident dishwasher in Grimsby. Unfortunately, he never lived up to his early promise.

4 You're not going to get anywhere if you think you're already there.

5 Failure is the condiment that gives success its flavor.
Truman Capote

6 I don't know the key to success but the key to failure is trying to please everybody.
Bill Cosby

7 No one is completely unhappy at the failure of his best friend.
Groucho Marx

8 Show me a good and gracious loser and I'll show you a failure.
Knute Rockne

See also Defeat, Losers, Mistakes, Success, Tributes, Victory

Fame

1 A celebrity is simply an actor with a publicity agent.

2 A celebrity is someone who works all his life to become well known, then starts wearing dark glasses to avoid being recognized.

3 He was the toast of the town. That's why everyone wanted to butter him up.

4 I couldn't believe I'd been invited to this dinner. I was the only person I hadn't heard of!

5 I heard of a well-known actor who used to carry a note in his wallet which read, 'I am a famous celebrity. In case of an accident, please call a reporter.'

6 Let me introduce a man world-famous in Wolverhampton.

7 Me, famous? These days I'm not even a household name in my own household.

8 Being a star has made it possible for me to get insulted in places where the average Negro could never hope to get insulted.
Sammy Davis Jnr

9 A celebrity is one who is known to many persons he is glad he doesn't know.
H. L. Mencken

See Losers 4; *see also* Hollywood, Popularity, Success

Families

1 A much married wife rushed up to her much married husband. 'Come quickly,' she cried, 'your kids and my kids are beating up our kids!'

2 A family is just like a bath. At first it's OK but later on it's not so hot.

3 I came from a big family. I was the fourteenth of thirteen children.

4 I come from a big family. There were nineteen of us. I didn't know what it was like to sleep on my own until I got married.

5 I got married so I could have a big family. And I got one – hers!

6 My brother ate nearly all my birthday cake. I call that the most unbrotherly act since the Beverley Sisters.

7 My salary goes into five figures – my wife and four kids.

8 They treated the au pair like one of the family – so she left.

9 This watch I'm wearing is a family heirloom. I value it so much because my grandfather – on his deathbed – sold it to me.

10 You can see why grandparents and grandchildren get on well with each other. They have a common enemy.

11 DOCTOR: Is there any insanity in your family?
WIFE: Yes, my husband thinks he's the boss.

12 What did your daughter do last weekend?
Her hair and her nails.

13 I'm ashamed to be your father. You're a disgrace to our family name of Wagstaff, if such a thing is possible.
Bert Kalmar, Harry Ruby, S. J. Perelman and Will B. Johnstone for Groucho Marx in *Horse Feathers*.

See Christmas 4, Crime 1, Proposals 12, Success 8; *see also* Children, Fathers, Grandparents, Mothers, Nepotism, Parents,

Farewells

1 And now, in response to numerous requests, Goodnight!

2 I'm leaving now. If I should return during my absence please wait until I get back.

3 I've had a most enjoyable evening – but not tonight.

4 That's it – goodbye! And if the phone doesn't ring, it's me!

5 Please don't bother showing me to the door.
It's no bother. In fact, it's a pleasure.

See also Absence, Departures, Retirement, Tributes, Unemployment

Farming

1 A farmer is a man who's outstanding in his field.

2 He's bought a farm 10 miles long and 3 inches wide. He's planning to grow spaghetti!

3 I used to work on a farm as a pilot. I used to pilot here, pilot there . . .

4 I've got a chicken that lays eggs so big, it only takes six of them to make a dozen!

5 Milking a cow is the easiest thing in the world. Any jerk can do it.

6 Owning a farm is what a city dweller dreams of at 5 p.m., never at 5 a.m.

7 The farmer's new scarecrow is so intimidating that not only have the crows stopped stealing his corn, they're even bringing back the stuff they stole last year.

8 Today's farmer hasn't just got to remember what crops he hasn't grown, but which fields he hasn't grown them in.

9 CAR DRIVER: Did you realize that six of your chickens are no longer laying?
FARMER: How do you know?
CAR DRIVER: Because I've just run over them!

10 I used to work on a farm but I soon left. It was the same old story – the farmer's daughter.
So the farmer had a daughter?
No, he didn't. That's why I left!

11 TOURIST: Hey, is that bull safe?
FARMER: Well, he's a darn sight safer than you are!

12 A farmer once called his cow Zephyr,
She seemed such an amiable hephyr.
But when he drew near
She bit off his ear,
Which made him considerably dephyr.

13 The farmer's boy was late for school and he explained to the teacher that he'd had to take the bull over to the cow.
The teacher said, 'But couldn't your father do that?'

'No, miss, you've got to have a bull,' the boy replied.

14 This fat farmhand was walking along with a duck in his arms when he passed a stranger.
'What are you doing with that pig?' said the stranger.
'It isn't a pig,' replied the farmhand. 'It's a duck.'
And the stranger said, 'I was talking to the duck!'

See Anniversaries 3, Drought 1, History 3, Hunting 5, Jokes 3, Post Office 6, Weather – Cold 1, Wind 2; see also Country Life, Environment, Gardening

Fashion

1 That's an interesting outfit you're wearing. Do you think that style will ever come back?

2 Fashion is a form of ugliness so intolerable that we have to alter it every six months.
Oscar Wilde

3 Fashion: a despot whom the wise ridicule and obey.
Ambrose Bierce

See also Appearance, Clothes, Cosmetics, Hats, Jewellery

Fathers

1 Last year on Father's Day, my son gave me something I've always wanted: the keys to my car.

2 My dad used to play games with me as a kid. He used to throw me in the air – and walk away.

3 FATHER: When I was your age I worked sixteen hours a day in this business, seven days a week!
SON: I really appreciate it, Dad. If it wasn't for all your ambition,

determination and hard work, I might have had to do that myself.

4 I'll never forget Father's Day last year. I called my Dad on the phone, wished him Happy Father's Day and had a really good conversation that went on for ages, all about Mum and when I was a kid and playing in the park and going for rides in the car. It was great.

As we were finally saying good-bye, there was a catch in his voice and he said three words which, as long as I live, I'll never forget.

He said, 'Who are you?'

5 My father was not a failure. After all, he was the father of a President of the United States.
Harry S. Truman

See Anxiety 2, Business 16, Losers 11; *see also* Children, Families, Grandparents, Mothers, Parents, Teenagers

Fear

1 He was as nervous as a long-tailed cat in a room full of rocking chairs.

2 Aren't you going to shake hands? They're already shaking.

3 When you heard the burglar outside your window, did you play it cool? You bet. In fact, I was so cool I was shivering!

4 You're shaking like a leaf! How do you want me to shake?

5 Coward: one who in a perilous emergency thinks with his legs.
Ambrose Bierce

See The Army 13; *see also* Anxiety, Flying – Fear of, Timidity

Feet

1 His feet were so big, he was taller lying down than standing up.

2 Your shoes are on the wrong feet! But these are the only feet I've got!

See Dancing 9, Dating 1, Memory 3, Stupidity 30

Feminism

1 Funny, isn't it? You never hear of a man being asked how he combines marriage with a career.

2 I know I'm old-fashioned but I believe my wife shouldn't work. She should just stay at home and do the cooking, the washing, the ironing, the cleaning . . .

3 I'm glad my wife's become a feminist. Now she complains about *all* men – not just me.

4 If women are so much smarter than men, how come they wear shirts that button down the back?

5 The odd thing about feminists is that they want to get ahead in the office but they resist advances.

6 Women who seek to be equal with men lack ambition.

7 What's the best thing about women's lib? It gives you girls something to do in your spare time!

8 People call me a feminist whenever I express sentiments that differentiate me from a doormat . . .
Rebecca West

9 A man can be called ruthless if he bombs a country to oblivion. A woman can be called ruthless if she puts you on hold.
Gloria Steinem

10 God made man. Then he stepped back, looked and said, 'I can do better than that!'
Dr Joyce Brothers

11 Remember Ginger Rogers did everything Fred Astaire did, but she did it backwards and in high heels.
Ann Richards

12 Women will never be as successful as men because they have no wives to advise them.
Dick Van Dyke

13 WOMEN'S RIGHTS NOW!
Yes, dear.
Graffiti

See also Equality, Women, Women – The Male View

Fighting

1 Then we started to fight – and we went at it hammer and tongs. I won in the end, though. I had the hammer.

2 One young man was sitting on another's chest outside a pub, with his fist upraised. Just then a woman came out of the pub.
'Wait!' she cried. 'You wouldn't hit a man when he was down, would you?'
And the man on top said, 'What do you think I got him down for?'

See Marriage 25, Soccer 1, Weddings 18; *see also* Arguments, The Army, Boxing, Defeat, Enemies, Victory

Figures – fat

1 All this drinking gives me a terrific hangover. You can see it when I stand sideways.

2 He certainly watches his weight. He has it right out in front of him, where he can see it.

3 He'd be the right weight for his height if he was 8 feet 7.

4 He's got so many double chins, you'd think he was looking at you over a stack of pancakes.

5 He's so fat that when he walks down the road, he looks like two boys fighting under a blanket.

6 He's so fat it takes him two trips to go through a revolving door.

7 He's too fat to play golf any more. If he puts the ball where he can hit it, he can't see it – and if he puts the ball where he can see it, he can't hit it.

8 I knew it was time to go on a diet when they made me pay excess baggage on my own body.

9 I suppose I must be overweight – my appendix scar is now 6 inches wide.

10 I think it's time for me to go on a diet. I've just had to put my full-length mirror sideways.

11 I used to be quite an athlete in my time – big chest, firm stomach, etc. But that's all behind me now.

12 I wouldn't say she was fat, but when she was walking down the street yesterday, a couple of policemen came over and told her to break it up.

13 I wouldn't say he was fat, but the other day on the bus he got up and offered his seat to three women.

14 I wouldn't say she's fat, but she gets fan letters from Captain Ahab.

15 It's depressing the only thing about me that's getting thinner is my hair.

16 I'm not saying he's fat, but he can sit around a table all by himself.

17 I'm not saying my husband is fat, but we've been married six years and I still haven't seen all of him.

18 I'm not saying she's fat, but she's got more chins than a Chinese telephone directory.

19 I'm not saying she's big, but her last picture had to be taken by satellite.

20 My wife was so fat when we got married that she needed three relatives to give her away. And when I

carried her across the threshold, I had to make two trips.

21 She's got a million-dollar figure. The trouble is, it's all in loose change.

22 She's got an hourglass figure – but it's later than she thinks.

23 She's not only kept her girlish figure. She's doubled it!

24 She's so fat that when she bought a housecoat, it fitted the house as well.

25 The bride and groom were so fat they had to get married in adjoining churches.

26 They say there are six million fat people in the UK – in round figures.

27 You know you're overweight when you can't get you and the water into the bath at the same time.

28 FAT WOMAN: Officer, could you see me across the street?
POLICEMAN: Madam, I could see you a mile off.

29 She was big! She was sunbathing on the beach at Blackpool when a policeman came along.
He said, 'You'll have to move on, madam, the tide is waiting to come in.'

30 This man came in the room – he must have weighed at least 18 stone.
I said, 'How much do you weigh exactly?'
He said, 'I tip the scales at 9 stone 3 pounds.'
He didn't tip them, he *bribed* them!

See Age 15, Clothes 2, Middle Age 1; see also Appearance, Diets, Exercise, Figures – Thin, Ugliness

Figures – thin

1 He's so skinny that when he's wearing a black suit, he looks like a rolled umbrella.

2 He's so thin, it's only his Adam's apple that gives him any shape at all.

3 He's so thin, he can put his shorts on from either end.

4 Is he thin? I've seen more meat on a butcher's apron!

5 My brothers were so thin, they walked about in the same pair of trousers.

6 My wife's so thin that when she swallows an olive, she looks like she's pregnant.

7 She's so skinny, she has to keep jumping around in the shower to get wet.

8 She's so thin, when she puts on a fur coat, she looks like a pipe-cleaner.

9 She's so thin when she drinks a tomato juice, she looks like a thermometer.

10 She's so thin, when she wears a striped dress, there's only one stripe.

11 She's so thin, when she closes one eye, she looks like a needle.

12 Thirteen is unlucky for her – it's her bust size.

See also Appearance, Diets, Exercise, Figures – Fat, Ugliness

Films

1 A friend of mine married an usherette. At their wedding, she walked down the aisle backwards.

2 I just finished a film last week. I'll get it back from Boots tomorrow morning.

3 I met a writer last week who got the

idea for his second novel from the screen version of his first one.

4 My uncle's crazy about cowboy films. He's the only man I know with spurs on his slippers.

Last night he spent three hours in front of the mirror trying to beat himself to the draw.

5 The film was so bad, we had to sit through it four times to get our money's worth.

6 They're making a new film of *Moses*. They haven't finished it yet, but the word is the baby looks great in the rushes.

7 BOY: Can you see the screen all right?
GIRL: Yes.
BOY: You're not sitting in a draught?
GIRL: No.
BOY: Comfortable seat?
GIRL: Yes, fine!
BOY: Mind changing places?

8 The actor was being asked to jump from a 60-foot cliff into a river. He told the director, 'I'm not going to do it. That river is only 2 feet deep!'

And the director said, 'Of course it is. Do you think I want you to drown?'

9 A wide screen just makes a bad film twice as bad.
Samuel Goldwyn

See Dogs 15, Flying 4, Flying – Economy 2, Nudity 6; *see also* Actors and Actresses, Audiences, Fame, Hollywood, Photography, Show Business, Television

Fish

1 Just how intelligent are dolphins? Well, within just a few weeks of captivity they can train a human being to stand on the side of the pool throwing them fish at least three times a day.

2 We ate in a seafood restaurant last night. The fish was so fresh, it was still chewing the bait.

3 Name two crustaceans.
King's Crustacean and Charing Crustacean!

4 I love eating salmon – salmon soup, salmon steaks, salmon fish-cakes – but I'm beginning to get worried. This spring I had this terrible urge to go north and spawn.

See Beach 2, Drink 33, Lawyers 13, Pollution – Water 3, 4, 5, 7, Smoking 9, Timidity 3; *see also* Cooking, Fishing, Food, Restaurants, The Sea

Fishing

1 Fishing is a jerk on one end of the line waiting for another jerk at the other.

2 Good fishing is just a matter of timing. You have to get there yesterday.

3 Last week I caught a fish so big I nearly dislocated my shoulders just describing it.

4 The great thing about fishing is that it gives you something to do while you're not doing anything.

5 There are two types of fishermen: those who fish for sport and those who catch something.

6 FIRST FISHERMAN: Remember, it's a secret.
SECOND FISHERMAN: OK, I won't tell a sole.
FIRST FISHERMAN: I don't want you to tell any fish.
SECOND FISHERMAN: OK, I won't tell a shoal.

7 Hey, can't you read? That notice says: PRIVATE – NO FISHING.

But I wouldn't be so rude as to read a private notice.

8 Hey, you're not allowed to fish here!
But I'm not fishing. I'm teaching my worm to swim.

9 How many fish have you caught so far?
Well, when I've caught another, I'll have one.

10 You've been watching me fish for three hours now. Why don't you try fishing yourself?
I couldn't. I haven't got the patience.

See also Fish, Pollution – Water, Sport

Flattery

1 Flattery is telling other people exactly what they think of themselves.

2 Flattery is the art of saying the right things for the wrong reasons.

3 Flattery is all right as long so you don't inhale.
Adlai Stevenson

4 I can live for two months on a good compliment.
Mark Twain

5 What really flatters a man is that you think him worth flattering.
George Bernard Shaw

See Age 3; *see also* Approval, Awards, Tributes

Flying

1 A friend of mine married an air hostess. When they got married, she walked down the aisle backwards. And what was worse, when she got to the top of the aisle, she sat on the vicar's lap.

2 Air travel is a way of seeing less and less of more and more.

3 It's amazing how fast these planes get around the world. Last week my brother got on a 747 in New York and in just twelve hours he was in Calcutta. Only trouble was, he was trying to get to Chicago.

4 No matter how bad the in-flight movie, you still shouldn't walk out on it.

5 One hundred years ago they said flying was impossible. Most of us would still say so.

6 Our local airport is so busy these days that all the air traffic controllers can do when a plane takes off is shout, 'Fore!'

7 The plane we were in ran out of fuel, so we all got out and pushed.

8 The speed of travel these days is just amazing. I mean, you can be at Heathrow just three and·a half hours after leaving central London.

9 The stewardess handed out some chewing gum – it was supposed to stop our ears popping during the flight. It worked fine. It was just a bit difficult to get it *out* of our ears when we landed.

10 Can you telephone from an aeroplane?
Certainly. *Anyone* can tell a phone from an aeroplane!

11 CONTROL TOWER: Please report your height and position.
PILOT: I'm 5 feet 11 and I'm in the cockpit.

12 Hello, is that Channel Airways? Can you tell me how long it takes to fly to Paris?
Just a minute.
Thank you very much.

13 How high would you say that jumbo jet is?
Oh, about 6,000 feet.
Really? And how wide?

14 Q: How can you tell when the plane is about to hit turbulence?

A: It's when the stewardess starts to serve coffee.

15 The most amazing flying story I've ever heard happened about five years ago on a flight somewhere in South America. A hijacker smashed his way into the cockpit, killed both pilots and then turned the gun on himself.

So now you had a 150-seat passenger jet, screaming through the air at 70,000 feet and nobody on board capable of landing the thing. But then this eight-year-old kid calmly got up from his seat, walked into the cockpit and offered to take over. He said he'd always been keen on aircraft – he'd read lots of books and even had a jumbo-jet computer game.

So what else could they do? They pulled the bodies of the pilots out of the cockpit, sat the kid at the controls and, above all the hysterical screaming, he managed to get in touch with ground control.

He told them he didn't want to know how to fly the plane, he just wanted them to tell him where the nearest airfield was and what the conditions were.

Then he took the plane off automatic pilot, ordered everybody out of the cockpit and, with incredible self-possession for an eight-year-old, managed to guide that plane – and its 150 terrified passengers – straight into the side of a mountain.

16 For the learner pilot, this was the first time he'd flown a 747 and he found it a real struggle to land, stopping just short of the end of the runway, narrowly avoiding a serious accident. 'I've never seen such a short runway!' he told his co-pilot. 'Not only that, but it's incredibly wide!'

17 In April 1879 he strapped on a pair of wings and leapt from the top of the Eiffel Tower. That day a new word was added to aviation history: compound fracture.

18 This man sitting next to me pointed out of the window and said, 'Look at those people down there. They look like ants.'

And I said, 'They *are* ants. We haven't taken off yet!'

19 We were 5 miles up over Manchester when the pilot came running down the aisle, putting on his parachute.

He said, 'Don't worry. We're having a bit of trouble with the landing gear so I'm going to go on ahead and warn them at the airport.'

See Advertising 11, Ethnic Jokes 2, 8, Farming 3, Figures – Fat 8, Lateness 2, Nudity 5, Optimism and Pessimism 4, Psychiatry 32; *see also* Flying – Economy, Flying – Fear of, Holidays, Travel

Flying – economy

1 I flew in on one of those budget flights. Trouble was, you had to have the exact change to get on board.

2 It was a really cheap airline. Instead of a movie, the pilot flew low over drive-in theatres.

3 Last week I flew on one of those new budget airlines. Before we took off, the stewardess reminded us to fasten our Sellotape.

4 This plane was so old, it had an outside toilet.

See also Flying, Flying – Fear of, Holidays, Stinginess, Thrift, Travel

Flying – fear of

1 A friend of mine was afraid of flying. So he went by boat – and a plane fell on it.

2 Don't worry. Remember, in the case of an accident, the pilot is always first on the scene.

3 I get nothing but rudeness from the stewardesses. It makes you wonder if the adjective from 'hostess' isn't 'hostile'.

4 I have this terrible fear of heights. Whenever I fly, I ask the pilot to stay on the runway as long as possible.

5 I like to stick to terra firma. For me, the firma the ground the lessa the terra.

6 I'm a nervous flyer and it doesn't make it any easier when I get to the airport and see the sign TERMINAL.

7 I'm not a natural flyer. In fact, I get air-sick just licking an airmail stamp.

8 I'm not going up in a plane again until they repeal the law of gravity.

9 My view is, flying may be making the world smaller and smaller – but you still can't fall and miss it.

10 When I'm up in the air, I suffer this sort of groundless fear.

11 How often do jumbo jets crash? Just the once!

12 PASSENGER: You will bring us down safely, won't you?
PILOT: Don't worry, I've never left anyone up there yet.

13 I was sitting next to this guy in the departure lounge. He turned to me and he said, 'God, I hate flying. Hate it! I can't think of a single reason why the plane should stay up in the air. I mean, if something goes wrong, that's it – you've had it. If God had wanted us to fly, he would have given us wings.'
I said, 'So why are you flying, then?'
He said, 'I've got to, I'm the pilot.'

See Religion 17; see also Anxiety, Fear, Flying, Flying – Economy, Holidays, Timidity, Travel

Food

1 Appetizers are little things you eat until you lose your appetite.

2 Bananas are expensive for what they are. After you've skinned them and thrown the bone away, there's nothing left.

3 Every morning I have coffee with two lumps – my wife and her mother.

4 Food is an essential part of any balanced diet.

5 Hors-d'oeuvre: a ham sandwich cut into twenty pieces.

6 I knew he was a bit of a gourmet when I invited him over for an evening of wine, women and song and he asked me what type of wine.

7 I went into this fish and chip shop and I said, 'Fish and chips twice, please!' And he said, 'I heard you the first time.'

8 A refrigerator is the place where you keep leftovers until they are ready to be thrown out.

9 I've eaten so much lettuce recently that the doctor is treating me for greenfly.

10 Is my brother greedy? I tell you, if he was Chinese, he'd use three chopsticks!

11 My doctor says I've got to stop eating so many cornflakes. The trouble is I'm going soggy in the bath.

12 My family was made up of big eaters – after every meal we had to remember to count the children.

13 Never forget: an egg is a whole day's work for a chicken.

14 She's such a noisy eater that when she started on the soup, six people got up and started doing the polka.

15 Would you mind not leaning on the bacon slicer? We're getting a little behind with our orders.

16 BUTCHER: This is the best bacon we've had for years.
CUSTOMER: Then I'd like to see some you've had more recently.

17 CUSTOMER: Is this meat tender?
BUTCHER: As tender as a woman's heart, sir.
CUSTOMER: Then give me a pound of sausages.

18 CUSTOMER: Look here, those sausages you sold me last week had meat in one end and bread in the other!
BUTCHER: Sorry, sir, but these days it's hard to make both ends meat.

19 CUSTOMER: I brought these bacon rashers back. They're bad.
BUTCHER: That's impossible, the bacon was cured only last week.
CUSTOMER: Then it must have had a relapse.

20 Four nice chops please, butcher – and make them lean.
Certainly, madam. Which way?

21 Has a gooseberry got legs?
No.
Then I must have just swallowed a caterpillar.

22 I don't like cabbage and I'm glad I don't like it.
Why's that?
Because if I did like it, I'd eat it – and I hate the stuff!

23 Is this milk fresh?
You bet. Just three hours ago, it was grass!

24 SHOPPER: I don't like the look of that mackerel.
FISHMONGER: If it's looks you want, buy a goldfish!

25 What have you got in your sandwiches?
Let's see – it looks like cheese again.
It's cheese, cheese, cheese every day.
It's driving me mad! Why does it always have to be cheese?
So why don't you ask your wife to make you something different?
I'm not married. I make my own.

26 Could you cut the pizza into just three pieces?
Why's that?
I could never eat six!

27 Why do people eat fish on Friday?
Because it won't keep till Monday.

28 Why don't you ever eat breakfast?
I don't like to eat on an empty stomach!

29 One morning a man came into a baker's shop and ordered a special cake to be made in the shape of the name Cynthia and covered in pink icing.

So the baker got a special cake tin made and baked a beautiful cake in it with the finest ingredients. And when the customer arrived to pick it up, although he liked it, he decided it should read 'For Cynthia'.

So the baker sent the tin away to be altered, then baked another beautiful cake.

But when the customer came in to pick it up he didn't like the shade of pink, so he asked the baker to try again.

Finally the customer came back and was delighted with the whole thing – everything was perfect.

The baker said, 'Where shall we send it, sir?'

And the customer replied, 'Don't bother, I'll eat it here.'

30 Two friends took their sandwiches into a pub and sat down to eat them.

The barman came up and said,

Fortune-telling

'I'm sorry, but you're not allowed to eat your own food in here.'

'No problem,' said one of the men, 'we'll just swap our sandwiches.'

31 Getting enough to eat, and then getting rid of it, are two of the great problems of life.
Ed Howe

See Appearance 19, Doctors 57, Eskimos 4, 5, Gardening 9, Hard Times 23, 24, Heaven 5, Manners 7, Poverty 14, Speakers and Speeches 1, Thanksgiving 1, 3; *see also* Coffee, Cooking, Diets, Drink, Greed, Restaurants

Fortune-telling

1 At the Annual General Meeting of the Clairvoyants' Association, they read out the minutes of next year's meeting.

2 I'm a great fortune-teller. My predictions have proved 100 per cent accurate – 14 per cent of the time.

3 I went to see a spiritualist last night. Was he any good?
Just medium.

4 The other night I looked at a lady's hand and one glance told me she was going to be really lucky.
How could you tell?
She had four aces.

See Anger 1; *see also* Luck

France and the French

1 What does a Frenchman eat for breakfast?
Huit heures bix!

2 What's a *pièce de résistance*?
A French virgin.

3 Every Frenchman wants to enjoy one or more privileges; that's the way he shows his passion for equality.
Charles de Gaulle

See History 5, Politics and Politicians 25; *see also* Languages, Travel

Friends

1 A friend is someone who dislikes the same people you do.

2 A friend is someone who goes round saying nice things about you behind your back.

3 Be nice to your friends. If it wasn't for them, you'd be a total stranger.

4 He's the sort of friend who's always around when he needs me.

5 It's surprising how many friends a man has until he needs one.

6 FIRST WOMAN: Don't talk to me about Susan. She's vain, she's foul-tempered, she's selfish and she's very, very boring. And what's more, she's a mean and spiteful little shrew.
SECOND WOMAN: How can you say those things about her?
FIRST WOMAN: Why not? I'm her best friend!

7 Acquaintance: a person whom we know well enough to borrow from, but not well enough to lend to.
Ambrose Bierce

8 Friends are God's apology for relations.
Hugh Kingsmill

See Debt 8, Failure 7, Success 1; *see also* Enemies, Families

Funerals

1 My grandfather's funeral has cost us 5,000 pounds so far – we buried him in a rented suit.

2 My sister is going out with an undertaker. She's sure he only wants her for her body!

3 My uncle was a chainsmoker. They buried him in a flip-top coffin!

4 Our local undertaker is having a special sale this week. For just five pounds extra, you can take a friend.

5 Remember, all men are cremated equal.

6 The man who first said, 'You can't take it with you', must have been thinking about the cost of funerals.

7 You still haven't paid for your auntie's funeral. If you don't pay by tomorrow, up she comes.

See Golf 27; *see also* Church, Death, Tributes, Wills

Furniture

1 Not all our furniture is antique. But by the time I've paid for it, it will be.

2 Our house has a combination of three types of furniture: antique, modern and comfortable.

3 This clock goes for ten days without winding it.
How long will it go for if you wind it?

See also Antiques, Decoration, Do It Yourself, Home, Homes, Houses

Gadgets

1 The bad news is I accidentally left my electric toothbrush on all night. The good news is I've never seen the bathroom looking so clean.

2 These modern electric toothbrushes are having an effect on tooth care. In fact, my dentist was telling me that in Great Britain today, the major cause of tooth decay is weak batteries.

See also Electricity, Modern Times

Gambling

1 A gambler was determined to introduce his young son to the delights of card games. By the time he was just two years old, the kid could count all the way from one to king.

2 Gambling is a great way of getting nothing for something.

3 I backed this horse at twenty to one – and it came in at twenty-five past four.

4 I had a good day at the races, I didn't go.

5 I made so much money betting on the Labour Party that I became a Conservative!

6 I'm going to Reno this weekend. I hope I break even – I need the money.

7 My brother loves sick animals. Mind you, he doesn't know they're sick when he backs them.

8 My horse came in so late, the jockey was wearing pyjamas.

9 My horse was so slow, the jockey kept a diary of the trip.

10 You can't get away from gambling in Las Vegas. I was in the laundromat, stepped outside for a minute and when I got back, someone had won my wash.

11 The best throw of the dice is to throw them away.
Austin O'Malley

12 The safest way to double your money is to fold it over once and put it in your pocket.
Kin Hubbard

See also Games, Horse-racing, Las Vegas

Games

1 He caught himself cheating while playing patience – and never spoke to himself again.

2 So he threw the first dart and hit a double right off – just as this bloke was putting it to his lips.

3 We played a great game at the party last night. One person left the room and then the rest of us had to guess who it was.

4 Let's play a friendly game of cards! No, let's play bridge!

5 I saw a fascinating story in the paper yesterday. There was this seven-year-old girl playing in a chess tournament in Moscow against twenty world-champion chess players – all at the same time.

And would you believe it – she lost every game!

6 Chess is as elaborate a waste of human intelligence as you can find outside an advertising agency.
Raymond Chandler

See Dogs 25, 28; *see also* Exercise, Gambling, Hobbies, Sport

Gardening

1 A garden is a thing of beauty and a job for ever.

2 A garden is something that dies if you don't water it and rots if you do.

3 Don't throw away your empty seed packets. They are often just the right size for storing your crop.

4 Gardening is man's effort to improve his lot.

5 He's a terrible gardener. Last week his artificial lawn died!

6 Old gardeners never die, they just spade away.

7 The family that rakes together, aches together.

8 The only thing I grow in the garden is tired.

9 What are you going to do with that manure?
I'm going to put it on my rhubarb.
That's a change. We have custard on ours!

10 What are you doing up my tree, young man?
Well … one of your apples fell down and I'm putting it back.

11 A burglar was sent to prison for robbing a stately home but he refused to tell the police where he'd hidden the loot.
A few months later, his wife wrote to him and said, 'Now that you're in jail, there's no one to dig the back garden. I suppose I'll have to do it myself.'

So the robber wrote back to her, saying, 'Don't you dare dig up the back garden! That's where I buried the stuff from the stately home!'
And he handed the letter to a warder to post.
A week later he got another letter from his wife. It said, 'You'll never believe it – yesterday thirty policemen came round and dug up the entire back garden!'
And the robber wrote back, 'Now plant the potatoes!'

12 At the Annual Flower Show, George won nearly every prize for his potatoes, carrots, tomatoes and beans, and as he presented George with his prizes, the Lord Mayor asked him for the secret of his success.
'Manure,' said George. 'Manure, more manure and then even more manure!'
The Mayor's wife turned to George's wife and said, 'You must be very proud of him, but couldn't you just try to get him to use a word other than "manure". It sounds so awful, you know, on vegetables.'
And George's wife replied, 'I doubt it. It's taken me twenty years to get him to say "manure".'

13 Training is everything. The peach was once a bitter almond; cauliflower is nothing but cabbage with a college education.
Mark Twain

14 What is a weed? A plant whose virtues have not yet been discovered.
Ralph Waldo Emerson

See Coincidences 2; *see also* Country Life, Farming, Food

Gifts

1 I'm a man of rare gifts. I haven't given one in years!

2 Last year I gave my little boy one of

these educational toys that are supposed to help prepare you for life. No matter how you put it together, it's wrong!

3 My husband is so thoughtful. For my birthday, he gave me exactly what I needed to exchange for what I really want.

4 On her birthday I told her to go to Bond Street and pick something nice – but just don't get caught.

5 When it comes to giving, some people stop at nothing.

6 HE: I'm going to give you a book for Christmas.
SHE: But I've already got one!

7 I want to get him something he's never had before.
How about a job?

8 What do you give a man who has everything?
A burglar alarm!

9 What do you give a girl who has everything?
Encouragement.

See also Birthday Parties, Birthdays, Charity, Christmas, Philanthropy

God

1 God isn't dead. He just doesn't want to get involved.

2 Is there a God? God only knows.

3 How can we be certain that God is dead? We're not even sure about Elvis.

4 What do you say when you meet God and he sneezes?

5 God's plan had a hopeful beginning,
But man spoiled it all just by sinning.
We trust that this story
Will bring back God's glory,
But at the moment, the other side's winning.

6 The bishop called all the priests from the diocese to the cathedral.
He told them, 'I've got some good news and some bad news. The good news is that I spoke to God today and everything is OK. The bad news is she called from Salt Lake City.'

7 Creator: a comedian whose audience is afraid to laugh.
H. L. Mencken

8 God give me the strength not to trust in God.
Sinclair Lewis

9 God is not a cosmic bellboy for whom one can press a button to get things.
Harry Emerson Fosdick

10 God will provide – ah, if only He would till He does!
Yiddish proverb

11 God, as some cynic has said, is always on the side which has the best football coach.
Heywood Broun

12 I cannot believe in a God who wants to be praised all the time.
F. W. Nietzsche

13 When God invented men, she was only testing.
Graffiti

14 You must believe in God in spite of what the clergy say.
Benjamin Jowett

See Egotists 3, Vanity 21; *see also* Atheism, Catholics, Church, Heaven, Hell, Religion

Gold-diggers

1 A fool and his money are soon popular.

2 Don't marry for money. You can borrow it cheaper!

3 I love her so much, I worship the ground her father found oil on.

4 I married my wife for her money – and believe me, I've earned it.

5 I'm sure she married him for his money. The wedding ceremony was conducted by an accountant!

6 My ambition is to marry a rich girl who's too proud to let her husband work.

7 My girlfriend's got everything. What I want to know is, how do I get it back?

8 Her motto is, 'Every man for myself.'

9 She doesn't mind if he leaves her – as long as he leaves her enough.

10 She earned her Mercedes the hard way. She bought it!

11 She may be good for nothing but she's never bad for nothing.

12 She said, 'I adore men who make things. How much do you make?'

13 She says she's looking for a nice generous man she can take to – and from.

14 She's an uncomplicated girl. She likes him for what he is: rich.

15 The most popular labour-saving device is still a husband with money.

16 You've got to feel sorry for him. He took her for better or for worse and she took him for everything.

17 Daddy, you'll love my new boyfriend. He's so nice and polite.
But does he have any money?
Honestly, you men are all alike. He asked me the same question about you!

See Dating – Chat-up lines 11; *see also* Dating, Marriage, Money, Newlyweds, Romance

Golf

1 At least I hit two good balls today. I stepped on a rake.

2 He couldn't help cheating at golf. One day, when he got a hole in one, he wrote a zero on his card.

3 He plays a fair game of golf – if you watch him.

4 His doctor told him to play thirty-six holes a day, so he went out and bought a harmonica.

5 I love golf. I live golf. I dream golf. If only I could *play* golf!

6 I love playing golf. My only problem is that I stand too close to the ball after I've hit it.

7 I've advised my friend to seek psychological help. He treats golf as if it were a game!

8 Last week I missed a spectacular hole in one – by only five strokes.

9 He's hopeless. He's the only golfer I know who shouts 'Fore!' when he putts.

10 My golf is improving. Yesterday I hit the ball in one.

11 My golf is definitely improving. I'm missing the ball much closer than I used to.

12 NOTICE IN GOLF CLUB: Members are requested not to pick up lost balls until they have stopped running.

13 Sunday is the day all of us bow our heads. Some are praying and some are putting.

14 You can always tell the golfer who's winning. He's the one who keeps telling his opponent that it's only a game.

15 GOLFER: Caddie, will you please stop looking at your watch all the time? It's very distracting!
CADDIE: It's not my watch, sir, it's my compass.

16 GOLFER: I've never played this badly before.
CADDY: You've played before?

17 GOLFER: OK, caddie, can you count?
CADDIE: Certainly, sir.
GOLFER: And can you add up?
CADDIE: Of course.
GOLFER: So what is four plus five plus three?
CADDIE: Nine, sir.
GOLFER: Come on, you'll do!

18 GOLFER: So what's my score?
CADDIE: Fifteen, sir.
GOLFER: Fifteen, eh? Not bad! Let's try the second hole.

19 GOLFER: This is a terrible golf course. I've never played on a worse one.
CADDIE: But this *isn't* the course! We left that more than an hour ago.

20 GOLFER: What a disastrous round. You must be the worst caddie in the world!
CADDIE: I doubt it, sir. That would be too much of a coincidence!

21 Is it a sin to play golf on Sunday?
No, but the way you play it any day is a crime.

22 My doctor has told me I can't play golf.
So *he's* played with you too, has he?

23 My wife says if I don't give up golf she'll leave me.
That's bad luck.
I know, I'm really going to miss her.

24 Well, caddy, how do you like my game?
It's terrific, sir. Mind you, I still prefer golf.

25 A keen golfer goes to his priest and asks him if there are any golf courses in heaven. The priest says he'll find out for him. The next day, the priest calls the golfer and says, 'I've done some checking up and I've got some good news and some bad news. The good news is that there *are* golf courses in heaven and they're far better than any golf courses we have down here.'
The golfer says, 'So what's the *bad* news?'
And the priest says, 'The bad news is that you've got a teeing-off time for next Monday afternoon.'

26 As they left the church on the way to the reception, the groom turned to the bride and said, 'I've got a confession to make: I love golf. I sleep, eat and breathe golf. I'm obsessed with golf. You must realize that it completely dominates my life.'
And the bride turned to the groom and said, 'Thank you for being so honest. Now I have something to tell you: I'm a hooker.'
'No problem,' the groom said, taking her wrists. 'You hold your left hand just a little higher than the right, with your thumb down here . . .'

27 I was playing golf with a friend the other day and, just as we were about to tee off, a funeral procession went by.
My friend put his club down, took off his cap and bowed his head as the cortège passed us.
I said, 'That was a very decent gesture.'
And he said, 'It was the least I could do. She was a damned good wife to me.'

28 Old Harry is dead. And to think that he was going to play golf with us tomorrow.
It's awful!
It's tragic! But wait a minute . . . Maybe we can get Bob to fill in for him!

29 When her husband arrived home from the golf course several hours late, his wife demanded an explanation.

'We had a problem,' he said. 'Frank collapsed and died on the second hole and from then on it was play the ball, drag Frank, play the ball, drag Frank . . .'

30 Why aren't you playing golf with the Colonel any more?

What! Would you play with a man who swears and curses with every shot, who cheats in the bunkers, who alters his scorecard when you're not looking and who never buys a drink in the bar afterwards?

Certainly not!

Well, neither will the Colonel.

31 Give me my golf clubs, the fresh air and a beautiful woman as a partner – and you can have the golf clubs and the fresh air.
George Burns

32 Golf is a game whose aim is to hit a very small ball into an even smaller hole, with weapons singularly ill-designed for the purpose.
Winston Churchill

33 If I had my way, any man guilty of golf would be ineligible for any office of trust in the United States.
H. L. Mencken

See Addiction 1, Doctors 4, Figures – Fat 7, Flying 6, Husbands and Wives 49; see also Defeat, Exercise, Losers, Sport, Victory

Gossip

1 As you know, I never repeat gossip – so please listen carefully the first time.

2 Gossip is a form of malicious talk indulged in by other people.

3 Gossip is what goes in one ear and in another.

4 I hate repeating gossip – but really, what else can you do with it?

5 Did you tell her what I said was in the strictest confidence?
No, I didn't want her to think it was important enough to repeat!

6 Confidant: one entrusted by A with the secrets of B, confided by him to C.
Ambrose Bierce

7 Don't talk about yourself; it will be done when you leave.
Wilson Mizner

8 No one gossips about other people's secret virtues.
Bertrand Russell

See Opera 6, Theatre 5; see also Conversation, Secrets, Talkers

Government

1 If you think there's too much government now, just think what it would be like if we got as much as we're paying for.

2 Just tell me one thing: why is there only one Monopolies Commission?

3 Standing at the top of Whitehall, a visitor to London asked a policeman, 'Can you tell me which side the Foreign Office is on?'
And the policeman replied, 'Ours, I think.'

4 At the very heart of British government there is a luxuriant and voluntary exclusion of talent.
Brian Chapman

5 I learned in business that you had to be very careful when you told somebody that's working for you to do something, because the chances were very high he'd do it. In government, you don't have to worry about that.
George Shultz

6 Never believe anything until it has been officially denied.
Claud Cockburn

7 Reading about one's failings in the daily papers is one of the privileges of high office in this free country of ours.
Nelson A. Rockefeller

8 The single most exciting thing you encounter in government is competence, because it's so rare.
Daniel Patrick Moynihan

9 Working for a federal agency was like trying to dislodge a prune skin from the roof of the mouth. More enterprise went into the job than could be justified by the result.
Caskie Stinnet

See Graffiti 2; *see also* Congress, Economics, Houses of Parliament, Politics and Politicians, The Presidency, Taxes

Graffiti

1 Is there life after birth?

2 Is the UK ready for self-government?

3 Is there intelligent life on Earth?

4 Avoid the Christmas rush – drink now.

5 Jesus Saves. But Moses Invests.

6 Repeal the law of gravity!

7 Support peace or I'll kill you.

8 I'd give my right arm to be ambidextrous.

9 If voting could change anything, it would be illegal.

10 Edith Sitwell is a transvestite.
She's dead, you dope.
OK, Edith Sitwell is a *dead* transvestite.

Grandparents

1 Isn't it great being a grandfather? I love it! The only part I don't like is that you have to sleep with a grandmother.

2 Did I ever tell you about my grandchildren?
No, you didn't – and I really appreciate it!

See also Children, Families, Old Age, Parents

Greed

1 He eats so fast, he's got a water-cooled knife and fork!

2 I'll say he's greedy. His favourite food is thirds!

3 I've never seen anyone eat so fast in my life! I'm telling you, she had starting blocks on her elbows. And it's the first time I've ever seen racing colours on a knife and fork.

4 My doctor has advised me to give up those intimate little dinners for four unless I have three other people eating with me.

5 My trouble is, I don't believe in eating on an empty stomach.

6 My uncle's got an incredible appetite. We went out to a Chinese restaurant the other night and they had to send out for more rice!

7 My wife is very particular about her food. There has to be lots of it!

8 She says she's a light eater. The minute it gets light, she starts!

9 What an appetite the girl has! The only thing she won't have for lunch is dinner!

See also Food

Guests

1 A good host is someone who makes his guests feel at home even when he wishes they were.

2 I passed your house yesterday. Thanks!

3 I must be off now. Don't trouble to see me to the door.
It's no trouble. In fact, it's a pleasure.

Guns

1 They're right. Guns don't kill people. Bullets do.

See Britain and the British 2, Infidelity 3; *see also* Hunting, War

Hair

1 I really take my hat off to my barber. He wouldn't be able to cut my hair if I didn't.

2 Just because he prefers blondes doesn't make him a gentleman.

3 Many a blonde dyes by her own hand.

4 No, he doesn't have naturally wavy hair. His hair is straight; it's his head that's wavy.

5 She had her hair tinted red but now it clashes with her nose.

6 She's got lovely, shiny, long black hair running down her back. Pity it isn't on her head.

7 She's thinking of having her hair dyed back to its original colour – but she can't remember what it is!

8 The best way to get your friends to appreciate your old hair-style is to get a new one.

9 What I want to know is, when one barber cuts another barber's hair, who does the talking?

10 CUSTOMER: What have you got for grey hair?
HAIRDRESSER: The greatest respect, sir.

11 How do you like my hair? I spent a long time over it.
Really? I spend a long time under it!

12 I've decided to let my hair grow.
How would you stop it?

13 What do you think of my toupee?
It's fantastic. I couldn't tell it from a wig.

14 What have you done to your hair? It looks like a wig.
It *is* a wig.
You know, you could never tell.

15 Who was that blonde I saw you with on Friday?
That was the brunette you saw me with on Thursday.

16 Men! Are you worried because you have thinning hair? Relax – nobody has fat hair.

Try Harry's Happy Hair Restorer. For twenty years, the public has been taking Harry's – and for twenty years Harry has been taking the public.

Harry's Happy Hair Restorer will put hair on a billiard ball. Mind you, it slows the game up a little.

Harry's Happy Hair Restorer doesn't come with a guarantee. It comes with a comb.

See Police 3, Weather – Cold 7; *see also* Appearance, Baldness, Barbers, Beards and Moustaches, Faces

Happiness

1 Money can't buy happiness, but it helps you look for it in a lot more places.

2 Real happiness is when you marry a girl for love and find out later she has money.

3 A lifetime of happiness: no man alive could bear it; it would be Hell on Earth.
George Bernard Shaw

4 Grief can take care of itself, but to get the full value from joy you must have somebody to divide it with.
Mark Twain

5 Happiness is like coke – something you get as a by-product in the process of making something else.
Aldous Huxley

6 Happiness is having a large, loving, caring, close-knit family in another city.
George Burns

7 Happiness isn't something you experience. It's something you remember.
Oscar Levant

8 Happiness: an agreeable sensation arising from contemplating the misery of another.
Ambrose Bierce

9 I can sympathize with people's pains, but not with their pleasures. There is something curiously boring about somebody else's happiness.
Aldous Huxley

10 The search for happiness is one of the chief sources of unhappiness.
Eric Hoffer

11 The secret of happiness is to face the fact that the world is horrible, horrible, *horrible*.
Bertrand Russell

See Infidelity 5, Introductions 26, Prudery 9, Sailing 2, The Sexes 4; *see also* Optimism, Optimism and Pessimism

Hard times

1 Business is so bad these days that even those people who don't intend to pay aren't buying.

2 I don't go to restaurants any more. You know what they say: 'Never eat on an empty pocket!'

3 I need a pay increase now. My problem is there's too much month left at the end of the money.

4 I'm broke. The trouble is last week I blew all my money on the rent.

5 I'm fascinated by the way the Chancellor tries to talk up the economy. As I understand it, we've just reached the lowest peak in history.

6 I'm haunted by two worries: first, will we ever get back to the good old days? And secondly, these may be them!

7 Cheer up! The less you have, the more there is to get!

8 If this isn't a Depression, it's the worst boom in history.

9 It used to be news when a man bit a dog. Now it's news if a man bites a sandwich.

10 Just when you're about to make both ends meet, someone comes along and moves the ends.

11 Last year it was my doctor who put me on a diet. This year it was my accountant.

12 Let's look on the bright side. Twenty years from now, they'll be calling these the good old days.

13 An income is what you can't live without – or within.

14 Nothing's happening. I think life has put me on hold!

15 The economy hasn't reached rock-bottom yet – but if we keep climbing, it soon will.

16 The husband worked out their budget and told his wife, 'One of us will have to go!'

17 They say the economy is bouncing back. So are my cheques.

18 Things are so bad, the mice in our house bring their own food.

19 Things are tough. Even the Joneses

are having trouble keeping up with themselves!

20 Things are really bleak. The only business that can claim to be looking up is periscope manufacture.

21 This recession is affecting everyone. I just heard that Snow White has laid off three dwarfs.

22 We're now at the bridge we were going to cross when we came to it.

23 We're spending most of our money on food. My family won't eat anything else!

24 We've discovered a new use for stale old food – we eat it.

25 Years ago I used to dream about the salary I'm starving on now.

26 A recession is when your neighbor loses his job. A depression is when you lose yours. A recovery is when Jimmy Carter loses his.
Ronald Reagan

27 There were times my pants were so thin, I could sit on a dime and tell if it was heads or tails.
Spencer Tracy

See Accountants 6, Business 2, 12, 14, Christmas 18, Clothes 9, Cross Jokes 1, Drink 6, Food 18; *see also* Begging, City Life, Debt, Economics, Inflation, Pessimism, Poverty, Saving Stock Market, Thrift

Hats

1 He wore a big flat hat.
Why?
He had a big flat head.

2 Your hat's on the wrong way!
How do you know which way I'm going?

3 Her hat looked as if it had made a forced landing on her head.

See Age 2, Neighbours 4, Women –

The Male View 3; *see also* Clothes, Fashion, Hair

Health

1 A little honey is good for you – until your wife finds out.

2 An osteopath works his fingers to your bone.

3 Doctor, I'm sick and tired of being sick and tired.

4 Hay fever is much achoo about nothing.

5 I knew I was in trouble when the doctor put on his best graveside manner.

6 I sent her out to get something for my liver. She came back with a pound of onions.

7 I take a cold shower every morning – after the rest of my family has taken hot ones.

8 My health is so bad, my doctor has advised me not to start reading any serials.

9 My housemaid's knee has been giving me trouble. My wife caught me sitting on it.

10 Nobody is sicker than a man who is sick on his day off.

11 OSTEOPATH TO WOMAN PATIENT: What's a joint like this doing in a girl like you?

12 The human body, with proper care, will last a lifetime.

13 Whenever I get the flu, I go to bed and take a bottle of whisky with me – and within three or four hours it's gone. Mind you, I've still got the flu.

14 I've been in bed all day with a hot water bottle and a thermometer in my mouth.
Well, there's certainly room for both.

15 The doctor said I could get rid of my cold by drinking a glass of freezing orange juice after a hot bath.
Really? And did it work?
I don't know. I haven't finished drinking the hot bath yet.

16 Attention to health is the greatest hindrance to life.
Plato

17 The only way to keep your health is to eat what you don't want, drink what you don't like and do what you'd rather not.
Mark Twain

18 I personally stay away from health foods. At my age, I need all the preservatives I can get!
George Burns

See Drink 22, Intelligence 2; *see also* Dentists, Diets, Doctors, Exercise, Hearing, Hypochondria, Illness, Hospitals, Medicine, Plastic Surgery, Psychiatry

Hearing

1 I've got a terrific new hearing aid.
Marvellous! Does it work?
Half past three!

See Art and Artists 14, Hospitals 15

Heaven

1 A black man arrived at the Pearly Gates and was stopped by Saint Peter. Saint Peter was very apologetic. He said to the black man, 'I'm terribly sorry but we're a little overcrowded at the moment, so we're only taking heroes.'
And the black man said, 'But I *am* a hero!'
'So what did you do that was heroic?'
And the black man said, 'Well, I got married to a beautiful blonde white girl at an outdoor ceremony in Little Rock, Arkansas.'
'And when was this?'
'About thirty seconds ago!'

2 Heaven is the place where the donkey at last catches up with the carrot.
Anon.

3 In heaven all the interesting people are missing.
F. W. Nietzsche

4 It is a curious thing that every creed promises a paradise which will be absolutely uninhabitable for anyone of civilized taste.
Evelyn Waugh

5 My idea of heaven is eating foie gras to the sound of trumpets.
Sydney Smith

See Driving 8, Golf 25, Texas and Texans 3; *see also* Death, God, Hell, Religion

Hecklers

Responses to . . .

1 Do you come from a happy family? Or do you go home at night?

2 Do you have a chip on your shoulder? Or is that your head?

3 Don't move. I want to forget you exactly the way you are!

4 Would you like to step outside and say that? Good – I'll stay inside and finish my speech.

5 I look forward to running into you again – some day when you're walking and I'm driving.

6 I'd like to help you out. Which way did you come in?

7 I'm fascinated by what you have to say. I could sit and talk to you for minutes.

8 If I've said anything to insult you, please believe me!

9 If they ever put a price on your head, take it!

10 If you had a half a brain, you'd be dangerous!

11 If you were alive, you'd be a very sick man.

12 Is that your real face or are you still celebrating Halloween?

13 Let's play horse. I'll be the front and you can be yourself!

14 Listen, when I want your opinion, I'll give it to you!

15 Sir, there are some things in life that go without saying. Would you mind being one of them?

16 Look, it's all right to donate your brain to science, but shouldn't you have waited until you died?

17 I've listened to your humble opinion – and it has every right to be.

18 I can see you have a ready wit. Let me know when it's ready.

19 There he is, America's Most Un-wanted.

20 You have all the makings of a perfect stranger.

21 Thank you, I used to know a funny version of that joke.

22 The next time you want to time anything, just let the sand run out of your head.

23 The next time you throw your old clothes away, why don't you stay in them?

24 What's on your mind – if you'll pardon the exaggeration?

25 With luck you might get elected an honorary human being.

26 You know something? You ought to be on TV – so we could turn you off.

27 You know, you remind me of my uncle – except *he* was human.

28 Do you know the meaning of '*rigor mortis*'? Well, you will in a minute!

See also Appearance, Bores, Clothes, Ethnic Jokes, Failure, Insults, Introductions, Laziness, Losers, Stupidity, Ugliness

Height – short

1 He's so short, when he pulls his socks up, he can't see where he's going.

2 He's so short, he's the only man I know who has turn-ups on his boxer shorts.

3 I'm not saying he's small or superstitious – but he *does* think it's unlucky to walk under a black cat.

4 Is she tiny? Let's put it this way: she'd make a great fridge magnet.

5 She stood five feet in her socks. Mind you, I prefer it when there's only two feet in them.

6 She was so short, her miniskirt dragged along the floor.

7 She's so small, she buys second-hand miniskirts to use as ballgowns.

See Dancing 5, Drink 32, Psychiatry 5, Sex 27, Song Titles 5, Texas and Texans 2; *see also* Appearance, Clothes, Figures – Fat, Figures – Thin, Height – Tall

Height – tall

1 He was worried about being too tall, so he joined Height Watchers. And already he's down to 5 feet 3 on his way to a target height of 4 feet 7.

2 He's so tall he can stand on his head.

3 He's so tall, he has to stand on a chair to brush his teeth.

4 He's so tall, he gets the bends when he sits down.

5 He's so tall, for six months of the

year he goes around with snow on his head.

See also Appearance, Clothes, Figures – Fat, Figures – Thin, Height – Short

Hell

1 Hell is other people.
Jean-Paul Sartre

2 Maybe this world is another planet's Hell.
Aldous Huxley

See Nostalgia 3, Texas and Texans 4; *see also* God, Heaven, Religion, Weather – Hot

Heredity

1 Heredity is what makes a father wonder more than ever about his wife's parents.

2 They didn't believe in heredity until they produced this brilliant, good-looking child.

3 Breeding isn't everything.
Maybe, but it's certainly lots of fun!

See Insanity 1, Politics and Politicians 36, Sex 13; *see also* Ancestors, Aristocracy, Birth, Families, Snobbery

History

1 It's amazing how much we can learn from history – and how little we have.

2 It's no wonder the Red Indians got fed up with the early settlers – always paying their bills before six o'clock in the morning.

3 One of my American ancestors was killed because he wouldn't pay a buccaneer.
And we think corn is expensive today!

4 When you hear two eyewitness accounts of the same traffic accident, you begin to worry about history.

5 STUDENT: What were the main effects of the French Revolution?
PROFESSOR: I think it's a little too early to say.

6 A group of American tourists were visiting Runnymede and the tour guide was explaining its significance. 'This is where the Magna Carta was signed,' he told them.
'When was that?' came a voice from the crowd.
The guide replied, '1215.'
'Goddammit,' said the voice. 'We missed it by twenty minutes.'

7 Though God cannot alter the past, historians can.
Samuel Butler

See also America and the Americans, Ancestors, School

Hobbies

1 The best thing about a hobby is that it gives you something to do while you're worrying.

See Arguments 15; *see also* Do It Yourself, Exercise, Games, Sport

Holiday camps

1 Every night in this holiday camp the AA man used to come round.
The AA man? In a holiday camp? What was he doing?
He was going round saying, ''Ay, 'ay, you can't do that!' and ''Ay, 'ay, cut that out!'

2 It was a terrible holiday camp. I went to the office and I said, 'It's about the roof of our chalet.'
The man said, 'What about it?'
And I said, 'We'd like one.'

3 We went to this holiday camp last

year for a couple of weeks. Actually we were only there for seven days. They gave us a week off for good behaviour!

4 We were doing self-catering. But the walls were so thin, that when I opened the oven door to look at the Sunday joint, the man from next door was dipping his bread in our gravy.

See also Beach, Holidays, The Sea

Holidays

1 A holiday is something that turns someone who's tired into someone who's exhausted.

2 A man I know won a free trip to China. He's out there now trying to win a trip back.

3 America is just wonderful. If you ever go there, don't miss it.

4 Every year the kids tell me we can go on holiday to anywhere I like. Then they give me a list of the places I'd like.

5 Honolulu – it's got everything: sand for the children, sun for the wife, sharks for the wife's parents.

6 I drove across America from coast to coast. For every day driving I spent two days folding the road maps.

7 I get two vacations a year: one when the kids go to camp and the other when the wife goes to California.

8 I met my husband at a travel agent's. I was looking for a holiday and he was the last resort.

9 I pack just about everything when I go on holiday. The only thing I leave behind is a note for the milkman.

10 I went on holiday to forget everything. And when I opened my suitcase, I found I had.

11 I'm going to somewhere quieter next year. Yesterday the beach was so crowded I had to dive in five times before I hit the water!

12 I've got one of those bargain holiday deals: ten days and four nights.

13 I've no problem deciding about holidays – the boss tells me when, the kids tell me where!

14 Labor Day is a day when nobody does any.

15 My next-door neighbour had a great holiday this year. He bought a big new Volvo estate, put all the kids in the back – and then took himself off on a cruise.

16 This resort was so dull, one day the tide went out and never came back.

17 We were in Spain for our holidays and saw this sign that said: TOPLESS BAR. Turned out to be a café without a roof.

18 We're going on a short trip to Lapland. Three glorious nights and three glorious nights.

19 If you go to the Caribbean for your holidays, it shows you have money. Wrong! It shows you had money!

20 That's a great tan. Did you get it in the Caribbean?
You bet. It cost me £23.50 per square inch.

21 The heat was intense by the side of the pool. Eventually I fainted. But fortunately my wife brought me to. Then I fainted again and my wife brought me two more.

22 Why don't you ever take any time off work?
I just can't get away.
Can't the firm do without you?
On the contrary – and I don't want them to find out!

See Sex 24, Stinginess 5, 20, Teaching 3, Weather 4, 6; *see also* Beach,

Flying, Flying – Economy, Flying –
Fear of, Summer, The Sun, Travel,
Weather – Hot

Hollywood

1 Did you hear about the Hollywood
producer who liked his wife so
much that he decided to hold her
over for a second week?

2 Hollywood is a place where all the
girls are looking for husbands and
all the husbands are looking for
girls.

3 Hollywood is where no one gives
their right age, except in time of
war.

4 Hollywood – where people accept
you for what you're not.

5 In Hollywood they only know one
word of more than one syllable.
And that's 'fillum'.

6 In Hollywood, if you don't have a
psychiatrist, people think you're
crazy.

7 They had a quiet Hollywood wedding. Only the press agents of the
immediate family were present.

8 An associate producer is the only
guy in Hollywood who will associate with a producer.
Fred Allen

9 Hollywood brides keep the bouquets and throw away the grooms.
Groucho Marx

10 I knew Doris Day before she was a
virgin.
Oscar Levant

11 Once in Hollywood they almost
made a great picture, but they
caught it just in time.
Wilson Mizner

12 Working for Warner Brothers is
like fucking a porcupine; it's 100
pricks against one.
Wilson Mizner

13 You can take all the sincerity in
Hollywood, place it in the navel of
a fruit fly and still have room
enough for three caraway seeds and
a producer's heart.
Fred Allen

See Bosses 17, Divorce 1, Losers 4,
Marriage 49, Plastic Surgery 4,
Ronald Reagan 5; *see also* Actors
and Actresses, America and the
Americans, California, Fame, Films,
Los Angeles, Show Business, Tele-
vision

Home

1 Home is a place to stay while the car
is being serviced.

2 Home is that place where, no matter
where you're sitting, you're looking
at something that needs doing.

3 Home is the place where teenagers
go to refuel.

4 My wife said, 'I'm homesick.'
I said, 'But this *is* your home.'
And she said, 'Yes, and I'm sick of
it.'

5 There's no place like home – once in
a while.

6 There's no place like home – which
is why I go out most nights.

7 Home is where you hang your head.
Groucho Marx

See also Antiques, Decoration, Furniture, Homes, Homes – Squalid,
Houses, Landlords, Poverty

Homes

1 I live in a third-floor room overlooking the rent.

2 I love living in a penthouse. It's
great to have a roof under my feet!

3 I've got a room in Chelsea and she's
got a flat behind.

4 In my apartment building you're not allowed to have children. The woman next door loves the place so much, she's in her fifteenth month.

5 My room's so small, I can only boil one egg at a time.

6 The walls are so thin you can hear the people next door changing their minds.

7 The walls of our flat are so thin that one day I asked my wife a question and got four different answers.

8 They had a house so big that when it was seven o'clock in the dining room, it was ten o'clock in the kitchen.

9 LANDLADY: I've come to tell you that I'm going to raise the rent.
LODGER: Oh good, because I was just about to tell you that I can't.

10 TENANT: There's no ceiling in my bedroom!
LANDLORD: That's OK, the man upstairs doesn't walk around much!

11 I had to complain to the landlord about the walls being so thin. I said, 'You've got to do something about the next-door neighbour's television.'

He said, 'You mean you can hear it?'

I said, 'No, I can *see* it!'

See Inflation 27; *see also* Decoration, Home, Homes – Squalid, Hotels – Cheap, Hotels – Small Rooms, Houses, Housework, Landlords

Homes – squalid

1 I'm not saying the place was scruffy but last year some vandals broke in and decorated it.

2 Our house was such a mess when I was a kid that I used to wipe my feet before going *out*.

3 The dust was so thick on the floor that the cockroaches were going round on stilts.

4 We've got so much grease in the sink, the cockroaches slide to their death.

See Poverty 8; *see also* Cleanliness, Home, Homes, Hotels – Cheap, Hotels – Small Rooms, Houses, Housework, Pests, Poverty, Tidiness

Homosexuality

1 Lesbian: a mannish depressive with delusions of gender.

2 I must tell you I'm a lesbian.
No problem. How are things back in Beirut?

3 What do you call a man who marries another man?
A vicar.

4 MY MOTHER MADE ME A HOMOSEXUAL!
If I gave her the wool, would she make me one too?
Graffiti

See Parties 10; *see also* Sex

Honesty

1 I trade in antiques
Honestly?
Mind your own business!

2 Honesty is a good thing, but it is not profitable to its possessor unless it is kept under control.
Don Marquis

3 Honesty is the best policy – when there is money in it.
Mark Twain

4 Some people are likeable in spite of their unswerving integrity.
Don Marquis

5 There is only one way to find out if a man is honest: ask him. If he says 'Yes', you know he's crooked.
Groucho Marx

See Business 15, Games 1

Honeymoons

1 After the honeymoon I felt like a new man. The trouble was, so did she.

2 I knew the honeymoon was over when I realized that everything she said or cooked disagreed with me.

3 We were so happy on honeymoon. Every night we'd sit together in the moonlight while she ran her fingers through my money.

4 The current trend is towards shorter honeymoons – but more of them.

5 BOSS: So how long do you want to be away on your honeymoon?
MAN: I don't know. How long would you say?
BOSS: How would I know. I haven't seen the bride!

6 So their honeymoon wasn't a success?
Well, suffice to say that when they came down to breakfast on the first morning, they asked for separate bills.

7 When we went on holiday last year there were lots of honeymooners at our hotel.
How could you tell?
They all started yawning at six o'clock in the evening.

See Nudity 4; *see also* Holidays, Newlyweds, Sex, Weddings

Horse-racing

1 I once backed a horse which finished in front of the winner in the 1989 Grand National. Unfortunately, the horse started running in the 1988 Grand National.

2 Many horses are given peculiar names – especially if they don't finish in the first three.

3 My horse was so slow, he won the next race.

4 The horse was so slow, the jockey died of starvation.

5 The way my horses run can be summed up in one word: last.

See Optimism and Pessimism 1, Superstition 1; *see also* Defeat, Gambling, Horses, Losers, Sport, Victory

Horses

1 I rode through town on my fine white steed. People said that I cut a fine figure on that horse. They were right. I'd sat on my sword.

2 Of course I can shoe a horse. I just look it in the eye and go, 'Shoo, shoo!'

3 There's nothing like your first horse-back ride to make you feel better off.

4 It takes a good deal of physical courage to ride a horse. This, however, I have. I get it at about forty cents a flask, and take it as required.
Stephen Leacock

See Psychiatry 28; *see also* Animals, Farming, Horse-racing

Hospitality

1 The young bachelor, just returned from a weekend in a stately home, was telling a friend how it had been.
'If the soup had been as warm as the wine and the wine as old as the chicken, and the chicken as tender as the upstairs maid and the upstairs maid as willing as the duchess, it would have been perfect.'

See also Drink, Entertaining, Food, Holidays

Hospitals

1 Before they admitted me to this private hospital, the doctor interviewed me to find out what illness I could afford to have.

2 Definition of a minor operation: one performed on somebody else.

3 I haven't recovered from my operation yet. I've still got two more payments to go.

4 If all men are born free, why hasn't anyone told the maternity hospital about it?

5 Nurse! Will you never listen? I said, 'Prick his boil . . .'

6 She's a lousy nurse. She couldn't even put a dressing on a salad!

7 The operation was in the nick of time. In another two hours, the patient would have recovered.

8 The things those doctors and nurses get up to at night. Once I heard a nurse tell a doctor to cut it out – and she wasn't talking about an appendix.

9 The X-ray specialist married one of his patients. Everybody wondered what he saw in her!

10 They called her Nurse Tonsils – all the doctors wanted to take her out!

11 They don't allow you to leave this private hospital until you're strong enough to face the accounts department.

12 This patient was so rich he wouldn't accept a local anaesthetic – he insisted on having a foreign one.

13 To save money our local hospital now gets its patients to make their own beds. When you check in, they give you a toolbox and some wood.

14 DOCTOR: This operation is quite routine and not at all complicated.
PATIENT: Well, just remember that when you send me the bill!

15 CONSULTANT: Well, you'll be pleased to know that the operation to cure your deafness has been a complete success.
PATIENT: Pardon?

16 I had an operation and the surgeon left a sponge in me.
Do you feel any pain?
No, but I don't half get thirsty!

17 I reckon old Harry will be in hospital for some time yet.
Why, have you seen his doctor?
No, I've seen his nurse.

18 My brother's a naval surgeon.
Wow, they do specialize these days, don't they?

19 NURSE: Look at that operating table – it's ruined!
DOCTOR: I'm sorry, I must try and learn not to cut so deeply!

20 NURSE: Take your clothes off.
MAN: Where shall I put them?
NURSE: On top of mine.

21 PATIENT: After the operation, will I be able to play tennis?
SURGEON: Of course you will!
PATIENT: That's great, because I never could before!

22 What did they do before they invented X-ray machines?
They used to hold the patient up to the light.

23 Why do the doctors wear those masks during the operations?
So if anything goes wrong, they can't be identified.

24 You're coughing a lot more easily this morning.
I should think so. I've been up all night practising!

25 I don't understand that nurse. She keeps saying to me, 'How are we today?' and 'Have we eaten this morning?' But when I put my hand on her knee, she slapped our face!

26 MATRON: Why are you making that patient jump up and down?

NURSE: Because I've just given him some medicine and I forgot to shake the bottle!

27 The doctor sat down beside the bed, looked the patient square in the eye and said, 'I'm afraid I've bad news for you. You have only four minutes to live.'

'Four minutes! Is there really nothing you can do for me?'

'Well, I could just about boil you an egg.'

28 The patient, drowsily coming to after his operation, recognized the figure of the surgeon at the end of his bed. 'So how was it?' said the patient.

'Well,' replied the doctor, 'I've got some bad news and some good news. The bad news is that I'm afraid we amputated the wrong leg.'

'Amputated the wrong leg! What sort of good news can there be after you tell me that?'

'Well,' said the surgeon, 'the good news is that your bad leg is getting better.'

29 The phone rang in the ward and the matron picked it up. The caller said, 'I wonder if you can tell me how your patient Mr Grossmann is.'

And the matron said, 'He's getting better all the time. In fact, he'll be ready to leave hospital in a couple of days. Who is this calling?'

And the voice said, 'This is Mr Grossmann. The doctor won't tell me anything!'

30 When I was in hospital I said to the nurse, 'Last night I dreamed I was eating an enormous marshmallow. It was terrible.'

And she said, 'Well, you're all right now – but where's your pillow?'

See Insults 47, Restaurants – Waiters 36, Sex 29; *see also* Doctors, Health, Hypochondria, Illness, Medicine, Plastic Surgery, Psychiatry

Hotels

1 Business is so bad on the Costa Brava, some hotels are stealing towels from the guests.

2 I'm not saying the staff were greedy, but when we arrived, they welcomed us with open palms.

3 I've got some marvellous digs – they've only been dug a month.

4 I'd never stayed in a hotel where the room service was so slow. If you ordered anything from them, you had to leave a forwarding address.

5 In this grand hotel in Morocco we were surrounded by tropical plants – mostly outstretched palms.

6 They advertised running water in every room, but I didn't expect to find it running down the walls.

7 The guys in room service would do anything to earn a tip. I ordered a pack of cards and they made fifty-two separate trips!

8 The hotel was supposed to be air-conditioned. I've never seen air in that condition. On a clear day you could see the bathroom!

9 The landlady said she wanted me to treat the place like my home. So I did – I didn't pay the rent.

10 We got a double room with bath – too bad they were in separate buildings.

11 What a hotel! They change the sheets twice a day – from one room to the other!

12 DESK CLERK: Do you have a reservation?

GUEST: What do you think I am, a Red Indian?

13 LANDLADY: Rooms overlooking the sea are five pounds extra.
LODGER: How much if I promise not to look?

14 Room service? Can you send up a towel?
As soon as we can, sir. Someone's using it at the moment!

15 This is the house detective! Have you got a lady in there?
Hold on a minute, I'll ask her!

16 RECEPTIONIST: Would you like the thirty-five-pound room or the fifty-pound room?
TRAVELLER: What's the difference?
RECEPTIONIST: In the fifty-pound room, you get free TV.

17 The family had waited in line for more than an hour to check into the hotel. When they finally reached the desk, the receptionist said snootily, 'Do you have any reservations?'

'Plenty, but now we're here we might as well stay.'

See Las Vegas 13, Sex 34; see also Holiday Camps, Holidays, Hotels – Cheap, Hotels – Large, Hotels – Luxury, Hotels – Small Rooms, Landlords, Restaurants, Travel

Hotels – cheap

1 I remember lying in bed in this cheap hotel with the moonlight streaming in through the holes in the ceiling.

2 It called itself a three-star hotel – and two of them were shining through my ceiling.

3 It may have been a cheap hotel but they still changed the sheets every day – Room 237 changed with 238, Room 239 with 240, and so on.

4 The hotel walls were so thin, we couldn't just hear the radio in the next room, we could see the television.

5 The landlady said the rooms cost only five pounds a night if you made your own bed. I said, 'OK'. So she gave me a hammer and nails.

6 There were always two choices for dinner every night – take it or leave it.

7 We stayed at this over-priced, second-rate hotel in Florida, where we paid good dollars for poor quarters.

8 LODGER: I'd like to complain about the facilities in this hotel – they're practically non-existent.
LANDLADY: Well, well. Who got up on the wrong side of the floor this morning?

See also Holiday Camps, Homes – Squalid, Hotels, Hotels – Large, Hotels – Luxury, Hotels – Small Rooms, Landlords, Poverty, Restaurants, Thrift, Travel

Hotels – large

1 My room was so far from the front desk that by the time I got to my room, I owed two days' rent.

2 The hotel was enormous – to call the front desk you had to dial long-distance.

3 This hotel was so enormous that when I asked for my breakfast, it came by Federal Express.

See also Holidays, Hotels, Hotels – Cheap, Hotels – Luxury, Hotels – Small Rooms, Restaurants, Wealth

Hotels – luxury

1 I stayed in a hotel that was so posh, room service was ex-directory.

2 I stayed in a hotel so posh that even

the guests had to use the service entrance.

3 It was the poshest hotel I've ever stayed in. When you rang for the bellboy, he sent his valet up.

4 What a classy hotel! The towels were so thick and fluffy I could hardly close my suitcase.

See also Holidays, Hotels, Hotels – Cheap, Hotels – Large, Hotels – Small Rooms, Restaurants, Travel, Wealth

Hotels – small rooms

1 My room was so small, I couldn't brush my teeth sideways.

2 My room was so small, the furniture was painted on the walls.

3 My room was so small, the mice went around hunchback.

4 My room was so small, I had to open the window to throw my chest out.

5 The room was so small, when you put the key in the door, you broke the window!

6 GUEST: My room is tiny!
MANAGER: It's an optical illusion. It looks like that because the mice are so big!

See also Holiday Camps, Hotels, Hotels – Cheap, Hotels – Large, Hotels – Luxury, Landlords, Restaurants, Thrift, Travel

Houses

1 By the time we'd paid for our house in the suburbs, it wasn't.

2 People who live in glass houses might as well answer the doorbell.

3 The house is so old, the only thing that keeps it standing is the woodworm holding hands.

4 It cost me 2,000 pounds to have my house painted.
Wouldn't it have been cheaper to have it photographed?

5 So how do you like my room as a whole?
As a hole, it's all right. But as a room, no.

6 When we were finishing our house, we found we had a little cash left over, on account of the plumber not knowing it.
Mark Twain

See Alimony 9, Inflation 12, Wealth 19; *see also* Decoration, Home, Homes, Homes – Squalid, Housework, Landlords

Houses of Parliament

1 Parliament is a place where a man gets up to speak, says nothing and nobody listens and then everyone disagrees.

2 Five hundred men, ordinary men, chosen accidentally from among the unemployed.
David Lloyd George

3 The House of Lords must be the only institution in the world which is kept efficient by the persistent absenteeism of most of its members.
Herbert Samuel

4 The other night I dreamed that I was addressing the House of Lords. Then I woke up and by God I was.
Duke of Devonshire

See also Congress, Conservatives, Democracy, Government, Politics and Politicians, Speakers and Speeches, Margaret Thatcher.

Housework

1 My wife didn't know much about housekeeping. She kept clogging up the dishwasher with paper plates.

2 WIFE: When are you thinking about mowing the lawn?
HUSBAND: When I've finished thinking about mending the gate.

3 Housework is something you do that nobody notices until you don't.
Alfred McFote

4 I hate housework. You make the beds, you do the dishes. And six months later you have to start all over again.
Joan Rivers

See also Cleanliness, Do It Yourself, Home, Homes, Homes – Squalid, Houses, Servants, Tidiness

Humour

1 My wife knows all my jokes backwards – at least, that's how she tells them.

2 On his first night in prison, a convict is glumly eating his dinner when another convict leaps to his feet, shouts 'Thirty-seven', and all the other inmates laugh hysterically.

Later, another shouts, 'Four hundred and twenty', with exactly the same result.

'What's going on?' says the convict to his cell-mate, sitting next to him.

'It's like this: we only have one joke book in the prison and everyone knows all the jokes off by heart. So instead of telling the whole joke, we just stand up and shout a number.'

A few days later, the new convict decides that it's time to try it out for himself. So he stands up and shouts, 'Fourteen.'

Silence.

Turning to his cell-mate, he asks, 'What went wrong?'

'Must be your delivery.'

3 A difference of taste in jokes is a great strain on the affections.
George Eliot

See Appearance 17; *see also* Comedians, Laughter

Hunting

1 A man out hunting in the Highlands today climbed over a fence with his rifle cocked. He is survived by his wife, three children and one rabbit.

2 I came face to face with an angry lion but I knew exactly what steps to take – long ones.

3 My uncle is a great tracker. He once followed these tracks into a cave – and shot a train.

4 The hunter came across a sign that read: BEAR LEFT. So he gave up and went home.

5 Any luck?
Yes, I managed to shoot ten ducks.
Were they wild?
No, but the farmer who bred them was!

6 I have a stuffed tiger at home that reminds me of my uncle.
What's it stuffed with?
My uncle.

7 I was hunting in the jungle. Suddenly I turned round and there was a lion just 6 feet away!
What did you do?
I jumped to try and catch a branch 10 feet above my head.
And did you?
No, I missed, but fortunately I caught it on my way down!

8 The drunken hunter aimed his gun at a bird and fired. But he missed and hit a frog instead.
When he picked up the poor frog's lifeless body, the hunter said, 'Well, at least I knocked its feathers off.'

9 We hunted all day in the jungle but ended up with only a snake and a pygmy. So that's what we had for dinner: snake and pygmy pie.

10 A sportsman is a man who, every now and then, simply has to go out and kill something.
Stephen Leacock

11 Support the Right to Arm Bears!
Anti-hunting slogan

See Aristocracy 7; *see also* Animals, Birds, Guns, Sport

Husbands

1 A husband is a man with lots of small mouths to feed and one big one to listen to.

2 He was so henpecked, he had to wash and iron his own apron.

3 He wears the trousers in his house – right under his apron!

4 He's a model husband – but not a working model!

5 I can say anything I like in my own home – because nobody listens anyway.

6 I may not be the best-informed husband, but I'm certainly the most informed.

7 I'm sure my husband would leave home if only he knew how to pack his bag.

8 A husband like yours is hard to find.
I know. He still is!

9 Can you think of anything worse? My wife never stops talking about her last husband.
I can. *My* wife never stops talking about her *next* husband!

10 Husbands never become good. They merely become proficient.
H. L. Mencken

11 I started as a passion and ended as a habit, like all husbands.
George Bernard Shaw

12 The husband who wants a happy marriage should learn to keep his mouth shut and his check book open.
Groucho Marx

See Holidays 8, Retirement 8; *see also* Fathers, Husbands and Wives, Marriage, Wives

Husbands and wives

1 As far as our marriage goes, there's nothing I wouldn't do for her and there's nothing she wouldn't do for me. And that's the way it goes – nothing doing.

2 Every man needs a wife, because of all the things that go wrong that can't be blamed on the government.

3 Grandma and Grandpa have been married for fifty years and they still hold hands. If they didn't, they'd kill each other.

4 I couldn't ask for a better husband – much as I'd like to.

5 I don't know if my wife and I will ever get on. She can't stand me when I'm drunk and I can't stand her when I'm sober.

6 I finally figured out why my wife closes her eyes when we're making love. She hates to see me having a good time!

7 I haven't spoken to my wife for three years. I don't like to interrupt her.

8 I just wish I had as much fun as my wife thinks I do.

9 I made a big mistake putting my wife on a pedestal. Now she can't reach the floor to clean it.

10 I married my wife for her looks –

but not the ones she's been giving me lately.

11 I met my wife under unfortunate circumstances. I was single!

12 I put my wife on a pedestal. It makes it easier for her to paint the ceiling.

13 I take my wife out every night – but she keeps coming back!

14 I take my husband everywhere I go. It's better than kissing him good-bye.

15 I was cleaning out the attic last night with my husband – filthy, dusty, covered in cobwebs. Still, he's good to the kids!

16 I'll never forget the day I first met my husband – and don't think I haven't tried.

17 I've just got back from a pleasure trip. I took my husband to the airport.

18 I've just about had enough of my wife saying she does everything for me. I'd leave home tomorrow if I knew how to pack my suitcase.

19 It was time to tell my wife who was the boss. I said, 'You're the boss.'

20 My husband's as strong as a horse. I just wish he had the IQ of one.

21 My only regret is that I have but one wife to send to the country.

22 My wife always lets me have the last word. It's usually, 'Yes.'

23 My wife and I have an understanding. One night a week I go out with the boys. And one night a week she does the same thing.

24 My wife and I have an agreement: I do what I want and I do what she wants.

25 My wife and I have an agreement that we never go to sleep angry with each other. We've been awake now for nearly six months.

26 My wife is so difficult to please. I offered to take her on a trip around the world but she wanted to go somewhere else.

27 My wife isn't talking to me today and I'm in no mood to interrupt her.

28 Of course, every now and then I'll do something that hurts my wife – like breathe.

29 She was his secretary before they got married. Now she's his treasurer.

30 She's got her husband eating right out of her hand. It saves having to do the washing-up.

31 The only thing my wife doesn't know is why she married me.

32 The way my wife finds fault with me, you'd think there was a reward.

33 There's nothing he wouldn't do for me. And that's what he does – nothing.

34 My brother got a girl into trouble. He married her.

35 We have an understanding. I bring home the bacon and she burns it!

36 What a couple! They remind me of psychotherapy. She's therapy.

37 Why is it that the man your wife gave up to marry you always turns out to be more successful?

38 Women, did you get up this morning with a pain in the neck? Or did your husband get up before you?

39 Has your wife learned to drive yet? Only in an advisory capacity.

40 HUSBAND: One more word from you and I'm leaving home.
WIFE: Taxi!

41 I heard your husband was dangerously ill.
That was last week. This week he's dangerously well again.

42 Is your husband hard to please?
I don't know. I've never tried.

43 My wife thinks I'm perfect.
I know. I heard her say it.
When?
When she called you an idiot.

44 POLICEMAN: Did you get the number of the woman who knocked you over?
DRIVER: No, but I'd recognize that laugh anywhere.

45 Sorry, I'm late darling. Is my dinner hot?
It should be. It's been on the back of the fire since half past seven!

46 What do you and your wife fight about all the time?
I don't know. She won't tell me!

47 Why do you keep reading our marriage licence?
I'm looking for a loophole!

48 WIFE: Before we were married, you told me you were well off.
HUSBAND: Yes, but I didn't know just how well off.

49 WIFE: If you ever spent a Sunday with me instead of on that damned golf course, I think I'd drop down dead!
HUSBAND: There's no point in trying to bribe me!

50 WOMAN: Can I have more sleeping tablets for my husband?
DOCTOR: Why?
WOMAN: He's woken up!

51 A loving wife will do anything for her husband except stop criticizing and trying to improve him.
J. B. Priestley

52 Wives are people who feel they don't dance enough.
Groucho Marx

53 You mustn't think that, because a woman abuses her husband, she will allow you to do so.
Anon.

See Arguments 15, Defeat 1, Golf 23, Hobbies 1, Shopping 3; *see also* Arguments, Husbands, Marriage, Men and Women, The Sexes

Hypochondria

1 He has an infinite capacity for faking pains.

2 Hypochondria is about the only disease she doesn't think she has.

3 My uncle was such a hypochondriac that he insisted on being buried next to a doctor.

4 No doubt about it, she certainly enjoys bad health.

5 The hypochondriac was complaining to his doctor that he was suffering from a fatal liver disease.
'Impossible,' said the doctor. 'You wouldn't be able to tell. With that disease, there's no pain, there's no discomfort.'
And the patient said, 'But those are exactly my symptoms!'

6 The best cure for hypochondria is to forget about your own body and get interested in somebody else's.
Goodman Ace

See also Doctors, Health, Hospitals, Illness, Psychiatry

Hypocrisy

1 A hypocrite is someone who writes a book in praise of atheism – and then prays for it to be a bestseller.

Ice hockey

1 Ice hockey? Isn't that the game where you take a stick and hit the puck, or anyone who has recently hit the puck?

2 Hockey's the only place where a guy can go nowadays and watch two white guys fight.
Frank Deford

See also Sport

Ideas

1 I've got a hunch.
I thought you were just round-shouldered.

2 An idea isn't responsible for the people who believe in it.
Don Marquis

Illness

1 He's never had a day's illness in his life. He always makes it last a week!

2 I'm afraid I've got Parkinson's disease – and he's got mine.

3 I've got this terrible headache. I was putting some toilet water on my hair and the lid fell down.

4 Virus: a Latin word used by doctors and meaning, 'Your guess is as good as mine.'

See Alcoholism 1, The Army 22, Cannibals 4, Husbands and Wives 41, Insurance 5, School 30; *see also* Doctors, Health, Hospitals, Hypochondria, Medicine, Psychiatry

Incentives

1 Every morning I take out my bankbook, stare at it, shudder – and turn quickly to my typewriter.
Sydney J. Harris

2 My sole inspiration is a telephone call from a producer.
Cole Porter

See Wealth 22; *see also* Ambition, Success

Indecision

1 He's so indecisive, he's got a seven-year-old son he hasn't named yet.

2 The only way she can make up her mind is to powder her forehead.

3 They call him 'Jigsaw'. Every time he's faced with a problem, he goes to pieces.

4 I don't know what to do. My heart says yes but my brain says no.
Have you heard from your liver yet?

5 I've changed my mind.
Thank goodness. Does it work any better now?

See also Decisions, Fear, Timidity

Infidelity

1 All the world loves a lover – except the husband.

2 As the wife said when she ran into her husband's mistress, 'Harold has told me so little about you!'

3 Guns don't kill people. Husbands who come home early kill people.

4 I thought my marriage was secure but a month after moving from London to Edinburgh I discovered that I still had the same postman.

5 I'm only interested in my wife's happiness. In fact, I'm so interested that I've hired a private detective to find out who's responsible for it.

6 I've got the most beautiful wife in the world. Unfortunately, her husband wants her back.

7 My neighbour must think I'm in the coastguard. Every few days he phones my wife to ask if the coast is clear.

8 My wife's very clever. She's even discovered a way of protecting her clothes from theft. Every now and then I come home from work and there's a man in the wardrobe watching them.

9 She accused me of infidelity – but I've been faithful to her lots of times!

10 The only time I find my wife entertaining is when I come home unexpectedly.

11 Today is my wedding anniversary and let me tell you, for the last six years I've been in love with the most beautiful girl in the whole world. And if my wife ever finds out, she'll kill me.

12 Did you sleep with my wife last night?
Not a wink!

13 GIRL: Before we get serious about each other, I've got to tell you about the affairs I've had in the past.
BOY: That's OK, you told me about those two weeks ago.
GIRL: But it's what happened since two weeks ago that I'm worried about!

14 I'm furious. My wife's been seeing a psychiatrist.
Why does that make you furious?
Because she's also been seeing a bartender, a pilot, a salesman and the milkman.

15 Where did you get that nice blazer?
It was a present from my wife. I came home early the other night and there it was, hanging on the back of a kitchen chair.

16 A husband staggers home in the small hours of the morning and, as he undresses, his wife wakes up and sees that he's not wearing his underwear.
She says, 'Where are your jockey shorts?'
The husband looks down and then, quick as a flash, yells, 'My God, I've been robbed!'

17 I didn't realize how much my wife loved me until I was off work for a few days with flu. She was so thrilled to have me in the house that every time the postman or the milkman called, she'd run out into the street, shouting, 'My husband's at home! My husband's at home!'

18 The woman was telling her lawyer how she feared that her husband had been cheating on her and she wanted a divorce. 'Just last night,' she explained, 'I was walking through town and I saw my husband going into a cinema with another woman.'
And the lawyer said, 'So why didn't you follow him into the cinema and confront him. There may have been a completely innocent explanation.'
'I couldn't do that,' said the woman. 'The man I was with had already seen the film.'

See Beauty 4, Mothers-in-Law 10; *see also* Alimony, Divorce, Marriage

Inflation

1 A bargain these days is something that's only a little overpriced.

2 A bargain is something that costs no more this month than it did last month.

3 Apples are so expensive these days, you may as well have the doctor.

4 At today's prices you can hardly make *one* end meet.

5 Complaints about the high cost of living are just propaganda put out by people who eat.

6 I'll try to keep my remarks brief because I'd like to finish speaking before prices go up again.

7 I'm just popping along to the butcher's. I'll be back in twenty-five minutes or twenty-five pounds, whichever comes first.

8 One thing is true, people are certainly getting stronger. Ten years ago it took two people to carry ten pounds worth of groceries. Today, a child can do it.

9 Our parents used to tell us that money isn't everything. Now we tell our kids that money isn't *anything*.

10 The cost of living is getting ridiculous! Soon, newlyweds will have to start having to do without some of the things their parents could never afford.

11 The cost of living is always the same – all you have.

12 The great thing about inflation is that it makes it possible for people from all walks of life to live in more expensive neighbourhoods without even moving.

13 The latest statistics indicate that the best time to buy anything is a year ago.

14 The pound today will go further than you think. In fact, you can carry it round with you for days without finding anything you can buy with it.

15 Things are so bad, my take-home pay can hardly survive the trip.

16 To work out the cost of living, take your income and add 10 per cent.

17 You know you've got inflation when something that cost five pounds to buy now costs twenty-five pounds to fix.

18 I'm seriously worried about the pound these days. I looked at one this morning and the Queen had her fingers crossed.

19 I've got enough money to last me the rest of my life – unless I want to buy something.

20 I've never had it so good – or parted with it so fast.

21 Inflation is when your pockets are full and your stomach isn't.

22 Inflation is when you want to pay cash for something and they ask for two pieces of identification.

23 Inflation wouldn't be so bad if prices didn't keep on rising.

24 Inflation is when you earn more and more of less and less.

25 Inflation is a fate worse than debt.

26 Inflation is when nobody has enough money because everybody has too much money.

27 Of course, everyone has the right to a roof over his head. But if you want floors and walls as well, you may be getting out of your price range.

28 You know you've got inflation when one can live as cheaply as two.

29 Are you against inflation?
Three hundred per cent!

30 The husband rushed in and em-

braced his wife. He said, 'Darling, I've got some wonderful news. We don't have to move to a more expensive apartment. The landlord just raised the rent!'

31 One good thing about inflation is that the fellow who forgets his change nowadays doesn't lose half as much as he used to.
Kin Hubbard

32 There was a time when a fool and his money were soon parted, but now it happens to everybody.
Adlai Stevenson

See also Debt, Economics, Hard Times, Money

Insanity

1 Insanity is hereditary. You get it from your children.

2 Does he suffer from insanity?
No, he enjoys every minute of it!

3 Everyone is more or less mad on one point.
Rudyard Kipling

4 Insanity is often the logic of an accurate mind overtaxed.
Oliver Wendell Holmes

5 Show me a sane man and I will cure him for you.
Carl Gustav Jung

6 When we remember that we are all mad, the mysteries disappear and life stands explained.
Mark Twain

See Courtroom 12, Families 11; *see also* Hypochondria, Illness, Psychiatry, Psychology

Insomnia

1 But first a word for people who can't get to sleep at night: insomniacs.

2 I've got insomnia so bad, I can't even sleep when it's time to get up.

3 Doctor, I've got insomnia.
Well, go home and sleep it off.

See also Sleep

Insults

1 Scientists are trying to build the ultimate idiot and they're using him as a blueprint.

2 Disliked? You could count his enemies on the fingers of the Royal Philharmonic Orchestra.

3 Every year he finishes last in the company popularity poll. And he only finishes that high because he votes for himself.

4 He and I have a personality clash. I've got one and he hasn't.

5 He came here determined to speak his mind. Unfortunately, we've no time for Marcel Marceau impersonations.

6 He claims he's got an open mind. In fact, it's just vacant.

7 He doesn't know his own mind – and he hasn't missed much.

8 He has a nice personality – but not for a human being.

9 He has a soft heart – and a head to match.

10 He speaks his mind – which tends to limit the conversation a bit.

11 He's the sort of man who wins hearts wherever he goes – and doesn't stay.

12 He was put on earth to teach us that not everything in nature has a purpose.

13 He was the life of the party. Which gives you an idea of how dull it was.

14 He's a man who has no equals – only superiors.

15 He's a self-made man who obviously gave the job to the lowest bidder.

16 He's always been nasty. When he dies, he wants to be cremated and thrown in somebody's face!

17 He's always been unbearable. In fact, when he was seven, his parents ran away from home.

18 He's been compared to many great men – for the most part, unfavourably.

19 He's got a split personality. If you could call either one a personality.

20 He's got a wonderful personality – but not for a human being.

21 He's got just one fault. He's insufferable!

22 He's got no class. Last night he decided to spit out of my car window. What made it worse was that the window wasn't even open.

23 He's smarter than he looks – but then, he'd have to be.

24 He's someone who can bring an atmosphere of happiness, laughter and merriment into the office – simply by being absent.

25 He's the most underrated president the country's ever had. And deservedly so.

26 He's the sort of person Doctor Spooner would have referred to as a shining wit.

27 He's the sort of guy to whom you'd like to bid a welcome adieu.

28 His boss stopped him having his five-minute tea-breaks. It was taking too long to retrain him.

29 His main problem? He has delusions of adequacy.

30 I never forget a face – but in your case, I'll make an exception.

31 I only know him superficially, but I've a feeling that may be enough.

32 I've nothing but admiration for him – and I've very little of that.

33 I'd love to know what makes you tick. And not only that, but what makes you go cuckoo every half-hour.

34 If brains were dynamite, he wouldn't have enough to blow his nose.

35 If he ever killed himself, he'd get the right man.

36 If ignorance is bliss, he must be Mr Happy!

37 If intelligence was sunshine, he'd be a snowstorm.

38 If you ever have your life to live all over again, please do it somewhere else.

39 Men like him don't grow on trees – they swing from them.

40 My brother's got a split personality – and I hate both of them!

41 Next time you pass my house, I'd appreciate it.

42 Don't go away, I want to forget you exactly as you are.

43 I'm not going to ask you to act like a human being. I know you don't do imitations!

44 Let's play horse. I'll be the front end and you can just be yourself.

45 No one has a higher opinion of you than I have – and I think you're third-rate.

46 She's not such a bad person – until you get to know her.

47 The last time he was in hospital he got Get Well Soon cards from all the nurses.

48 There are some things in life that go without saying. He, unfortunately, is not one of them.

49 They call him a wit. They're half right.

50 They gave him a dope test – and he passed.

51 This is a man who had greatness thrust upon him – and ducked.

52 We need him like we need a banjo player for Beethoven's Fifth.

53 What he lacks in intelligence, he more than makes up for in stupidity.

54 Years ago he agreed to donate his brain to medical science. Most people would have waited to do it until after they'd died.

55 Yesterday his library burned down and both books were destroyed – *including* one he hadn't finished colouring yet.

56 You are the excess baggage in the airport of my life.

57 You'll have to excuse him. He's going through a nonentity crisis!

58 You'll have to excuse him. He's feeling a bit depressed. This is the year his age caught up with his IQ.

59 You've all heard the expression, 'The worst is yet to come.' Well, he's just arrived!

60 You've got to feel sorry for him at the moment. He's not allowed to have anything sharp – like a mind.

61 At least he's kind to his inferiors. Where on earth does he find them?

62 I go to Liverpool once a year to see my auntie Vera.
But I thought she lived in Manchester.
She does. She just looks better from Liverpool.

63 I'm not feeling myself tonight.
Yes, I noticed the improvement!

64 To me, he's a complete pain in the neck!
Funny, I've got a much lower opinion of him.

65 What do you mean, telling the boss I'm a fool?
I'm sorry. I didn't realize it was a secret.

66 Why does everybody take such an instant dislike to me?
Because it saves time!

67 You're a low-down, ignorant, worthless piece of pond-scum!
Well, nobody's perfect!

68 He looked at me as if I was a side-dish he hadn't ordered.
Ring Lardner Jr of President William Taft

69 I may not know much, but I know chicken shit from chicken salad.
Lyndon Johnson of a speech by Vice-President Richard Nixon

70 No wonder you're going home alone!
Sign above mirror in men's room, Ed Debevic's Diner, Beverly Hills

71 Ordinarily he is insane, but he has lucid moments when he is only stupid.
Heinrich Heine

72 The guy's no good. He never was any good. His mother should have thrown him away and kept the stork.
Mae West

73 Waldo is one of those people who would be enormously improved by death.
Saki of Ralph Waldo Emerson

74 When they circumcised Herbert Samuel, they threw away the wrong bit.
David Lloyd George

See also Appearance, Bores, Clothes, Ethnic Jokes, Failure, Hecklers, Introductions, Laziness, Losers, Stupidity, Ugliness

Insurance

1 Accidents will happen. Unless you have an accident policy.

2 An insurance salesman just signed me up for a marvellous retirement policy. If I keep up the payments for ten years, he can retire.

3 BUPA? That's the company that docks my pay to pay my doc.

4 I'm with an extremely reliable insurance company. In all the thirty years I've been with them, they've never missed sending me the bill.

5 I've got an extremely comprehensive health-insurance policy. For instance, if I should ever come down with yellow fever, they'll repaint my bedroom so I don't clash with the walls.

6 I've got no-fault car insurance. If I have an accident, I just call the insurance company and they tell me it isn't their fault.

7 I've got this new fire-and-theft insurance. Trouble is, they only pay up if your house is burgled while it's burning.

8 I've got this new life-insurance policy, but I don't understand the small print. The only thing I know is that after I die, I can stop paying.

9 I've got wonderful health insurance. If I ever get knocked on the head, they pay me a lump sum.

10 In every insurance policy, the big print giveth and the small print taketh away.

11 Insurance is what keeps you poor so you can die rich.

12 People who live in glass houses should take out insurance.

13 If I take out life insurance on my husband and he dies tomorrow, what will I get?
At least ten years.

14 A friend of mine had two wooden legs. One day his house burned down and unfortunately his legs got caught in the blaze. But the insurance company refused to pay up. They said he didn't have a leg to stand on.

15 So when will your husband's leg be better so he can return to work?
Not for a long time yet, I'm afraid.
But I thought it was almost healed.
It was, but then compensation set in.

16 The broker received a phone call from an excited woman. She said, 'I want to insure my house. Can I do it over the phone?'
And the broker said, 'I'm sorry, but I have to see it first.'
And the woman cried, 'Well, you better get over here fast, the place is on fire!'

17 The factory owner took out fire insurance on Friday. Later that day his premises were burned to the ground.
Not surprisingly, the insurance agent was suspicious. He looked the factory owner straight in the eye and said, 'You took out fire insurance at ten in the morning. The fire started at noon. Can you explain the delay?'

18 Insurance: an ingenious modern game of chance in which the player is permitted to enjoy the comfortable conviction that he is beating the man who keeps the table.
Ambrose Bierce

See Losers 15; *see also* Accidents, Cars

Intellectuals

1 An intellectual is a man who doesn't know how to park a bike.
Spiro Agnew

2 The dullard's envy of brilliant men is always assuaged by the suspicion that they will come to a bad end.
Max Beerbohm

3 The intellectuals' chief cause of anguish are one another's works.
Jacques Barzun

4 There is nothing so stupid as the educated man if you get off the thing he was educated in.
Will Rogers

5 An 'egghead' is someone who stands firmly on both feet in midair on both sides of an issue.
Senator Homer Ferguson

See also Education, Intelligence

Intelligence

1 My brother is incredibly intelligent. If he doesn't know the answer to a question, there isn't one.

2 I have come to the conclusion that a good, reliable set of bowels is worth more to a man than any quantity of brains.
Josh Sillings

3 There is nobody so irritating as somebody with less intelligence and more sense than we have.
Don Herold

See California 3, Marriage 50, Tributes 7; *see also* Education, Intellectuals, Stupidity

Introductions

1 A man like him is certainly hard to find. Tonight, for instance, we had to look in three pubs and a wine bar.

2 And now a husband and wife who need no introduction. They've already met.

3 As soon as this man is introduced, things start to pick up speed. Which is what happens when a show starts going downhill!

4 But this man is not just a buffoon in baggy trousers. He's a *red-nosed*, cross-eyed buffoon in baggy trousers.

5 He's a man who's going places – and, frankly, the sooner the better.

6 He's here under embarrassing circumstances. He wasn't asked!

7 I have not known our next guest long, but I've known him as long as I intend to.

8 I'd like you to meet one of the cleverest, wittiest, most charming, most handsome actors of his generation. And that's not just my opinion. It's his too.

9 I'll never forget the first time I laid eyes on him – and don't think I haven't tried.

10 I'm not going to stand around telling you a lot of old jokes. I'm going to introduce you to a man who can do that much better than I can.

11 If you were listening last week, you'll have heard our deliberate mistake. And here he is again . . .

12 In my book, he's one of the nicest men around. But then, my book *is* a work of fiction.

13 It isn't often that I have the pleasure of introducing a truly great comedian – and tonight is no exception. Please welcome . . .

14 It's been said of our next guest that he's one of the funniest men in the country. And here's the man who said it . . .

15 Much has been written and said about him, and he is here with us tonight to deny it.

16 Next I'd like to introduce a man to whom success did not come easy.
They all laughed at Franklin when

he invented the lightning conductor.

They all laughed at Newton when he discovered gravity.

They all laughed at Columbus when he said the world was round.

But nobody laughs at this man – especially when he tells a joke. Ladies and gentlemen, please welcome . . .

17 Of all the speakers I have ever heard, our next guest is certainly one of them.

18 Once in every lifetime a really beautiful song comes along . . . until it does, I'd like to sing this one.

19 Our next guest needs no introduction. He already knows who he is!

20 Our next performer is working under a handicap tonight. He's sober!

21 Our next performer has everything a girl singer should have – *and* a terrific voice!

22 Our next speaker will certainly add something to the evening. I estimate about three-quarters of an hour.

23 Usually at this point in the evening we introduce a man of unusual intelligence, integrity, achievement and wisdom. Tonight we depart from that tradition.

24 Our next speaker tonight needs no introduction – he hasn't turned up!

25 Right, now we've finished our chicken, it's time for some baloney.

26 Some people bring happiness wherever they go. Our next guest brings happiness *whenever* he goes.

27 The last time she spoke she had the audience glued to their seats – which was a very good idea.

28 This is a man who's been admired for years – but none of them recently.

29 Good evening, ladies and gentlemen. I assume that takes care of most of you!

30 This man has got more talent in his little finger than he has in his big finger.

31 Tonight I'm not going to bore you with a long, rambling speech, but I am going to introduce you to a man who will!

32 We have, I'm afraid, two disappointments tonight. The Prime Minister couldn't make it and our next guest could.

See Name 4, Singing 4; *see also* Introductions – Responses, Speakers and Speeches, Tributes

Introductions – responses

1 Thank you for that generous introduction – wonderfully restrained, I thought.

2 Well, after an introduction like that, I can hardly wait to hear what I'm going to say.

3 Well, of all the introductions I've ever received, that was certainly the most recent.

4 What a coincidence! As you were saying all those terrific things about me, I was thinking exactly the same thing!

5 At least we have one thing in common – none of us knows what I'm going to say.

See also Insults, Introductions, Tributes

Ireland and the Irish

1 TEACHER: Are you Irish?
FIRST PUPIL: Yes.
TEACHER: What's your name?
FIRST PUPIL: Pat.
TEACHER: You can't be Irish. If you

were Irish, you'd say 'Patrick'. Anyway, what's *your* name?
SECOND PUPIL: Mickrick.

2 I'm engaged to marry an Irishman. Oh, really?
No, O'Reilly.

3 FIRST IRA MAN: Did you see there's been more bombs going off in Belfast?
SECOND IRA MAN: I did. Oh, 'tis a terrible war!
FIRST IRA MAN: You're right, but it's better than no war at all.

4 God is good to the Irish, but no one else is; not even the Irish.
Austin O'Malley

5 I showed my appreciation of my native land in the usual Irish way by getting out of it as soon as I possibly could.
George Bernard Shaw

6 The Irish are a fair people – they never speak well of one another.
Samuel Johnson

See also Britain and the British

J

Jealousy

1 I didn't realize how jealous my wife was until the wedding – and I saw the male bridesmaids.

2 Nothing is more humiliating than to see idiots succeed in enterprises we have failed in.
Gustave Flaubert

See Luck 3; *see also* Love

Jewellery

1 My diamonds once belonged to a millionaire – Mr Woolworth.

See Separation 1; *see also* Clothes, Fashion

Jews

1 There's a new cruise ship goes to Israel. It goes across the Mediterranean at full speed – but to you, half-speed.

2 There's a new Jewish disco in Golders Green. It's called the Let My People A Go-Go.

3 I've just graduated from law school.
NYU?
And vy not?

4 My son is training to be a rabbi.
A rabbi? What kind of job is that for a Jewish boy?

5 SON: Dad, what is a vacuum?
FATHER: A vacuum is a void.
SON: I know it's a void, but vot does dat void mean?

6 What do you call a Jewish baby who isn't circumcised?
A girl.

7 Why do Jews always answer a question with another question?
Well, why not?

8 A Jew walking along the street in Berlin accidentally bumped into a Nazi stormtrooper. The stormtrooper turned round and shouted, '*Schweinhund!*'
   The Jew turned round and shouted, 'Mandelstein!'

9 Jesus was a Jew, yes, but only on his mother's side.
Archie Bunker

See Charity 3, Light-bulb Jokes 4, Religion 10, 12; *see also* Religion

Jokes

1 Do you get people sending in funny jokes to your show?
All the time.
Then why don't you use them?

2 I heard a new joke the other day. I wonder if I told it to you?
Is it funny?
Yes.
Then you haven't.

3 A young travelling salesman was driving in an isolated country area when his car broke down. He got out and walked and eventually he came to a farmhouse.
   He knocked on the door and when the farmer came he said, 'I'm a travelling salesman and my car has broken down. Can I spend the night here?'

And the farmer said, 'Of course you can, but I'm afraid you'll have to sleep with my son.'

And the salesman said, 'I'm sorry, I can't stay, I'm in the wrong joke.'

See Ethnic Jokes 12, Hecklers 21, Retirement 10; *see also* Comedians, Humour, Laughter

Journalism

1 Doctors bury their mistakes. Lawyers hang theirs. And journalists put theirs on the front page.

2 It was long ago in my life as a simple reporter that I decided that facts must never get in the way of truth.
James Cameron

3 Journalism consists in buying white paper at two cents a pound and selling it at ten cents a pound.
Charles A. Dana

4 Journalism is still an underdeveloped profession and, accordingly, newspapermen are quite often regarded as were surgeons and musicians a century ago, as having the rank, roughly speaking, of barbers and riding masters.
Walter Lippman

5 The secret of successful journalism is to make your readers so angry they will write half your paper for you. C. E. M. Joad

6 There is but one way for a newspaperman to look at a politician, and that is down.
Frank H. Simonds

See Government 6; *see also* News, Newspapers, Writers and Writing

Kindness

1 You never forget a kind deed – especially if it was one of yours.

2 He was so benevolent, so merciful a man that, in his mistaken passion, he would have held an umbrella over a duck in a shower of rain.
Douglas Jerrold

See also Philanthropy

Kissing

1 I've kissed so many girls now, I can do it with my eyes closed.

2 It takes a lot of experience for a girl to kiss like a beginner.

3 Am I the first girl you ever kissed? You might be. Your face looks familiar.

4 BOY: Wow! Where did you learn to kiss like that?
GIRL: I used to be a tester in a bubblegum factory.

5 GIRL: Am I the first girl you ever kissed?
BOY: Could be. Were you anywhere near Weston-super-Mare in 1983?

6 She looks on me as her brother.
How do you mean?
Well, every time I kiss her, she says, 'Oh, brother!'

7 That girl over there is a fantastic kisser.
How do you know?
I had it from her own lips.

8 When I kiss a girl, she certainly knows she's been kissed.
Why, who tells her?

9 Where did you get that black eye?
From kissing the bride.
But that's the convention, isn't it?
Yes, but not two years after the wedding!

10 Who said you could kiss me?
Everybody!

See The Bible 2, Dating – Chat-up Lines 8, Driving 16, Song Titles 2; *see also* Dating, Love, Romance, Sex, Sexual Attraction

Knock-knock jokes

1 Knock, knock.
Who's there?
Hawaii.
Hawaii who?
Fine until you turned up!

2 Knock, knock.
Who's there?
Yah.
Yah who?
Ride 'em, cowboy!

3 Knock, knock.
Who's there?
Tank.
Tank who?
My pleasure!

4 Knock, knock.
Who's there?
Astronaut.
Astronaut who?
Astronaut what your country can do for you but what you can do for your country.

5 Knock, knock.
Who's there?
Boo.
Boo, who?
No need to cry!

6 Knock, knock.
Who's there?
Xavier.
Xavier, who?
Xavier breath, I'm not leaving!

7 Knock, knock.
Who's there?
Who.
Who who?
Sorry, I don't speak to owls.

8 Knock, knock.
Who's there?
Major.
Major who?
Major answer a knock-knock joke!

9 Hey, listen. I've got this great knock-knock joke for you! OK? Knock-knock!
Who's there?
Sorry! Sorry! I've completely forgotten the rest of the joke.
Sorry! Sorry! I've completely forgotten the rest of the joke *who*?

See also Cross Jokes, Light-bulb Jokes, Tom Swifties

Landlords

1 So how much are they asking for your rent now?
About three times a week.

2 TENANT: Where can I buy 10,000 cockroaches?
LANDLORD: Why do you want to know?
TENANT: Because the lease says I have to leave the premises exactly the way I found them.

3 LANDLORD: I know you're an actor and I know times are hard, but you're months behind with your rent.
ACTOR: But just think – ten years from now you'll be able to point at this place and tell people that a great actor used to live here.
LANDLORD: Look, I can start saying it tomorrow!

See also Home, Homes, Homes – Squalid, Hotels

Languages

1 I speak Spanish like a native – of Czechoslovakia.

2 She's a brilliant linguist. She speaks Esperanto like a native.

3 Did you have any difficulty with your French in Paris?
No, but the French people did!

See Los Angeles 2; *see also* The English Language, Holidays, Speakers and Speeches, Travel

Las Vegas

1 A friend of mine has got property in Las Vegas. Caesar's Palace has got his luggage.

2 A terrible thing happened to me on my way to Las Vegas. I got there safely.

3 I took a nine to five job in Las Vegas. I didn't like the job but the odds were great.

4 In Las Vegas now they've got some 100-dollar slot machines. They're for the man who has everything – but not for long.

5 Las Vegas, or as it's better known, 'Weight Watchers for Your Wallet'.

6 My uncle once gambled away his car in Las Vegas. The people at Hertz were furious.

7 My uncle tells me he did very well in Las Vegas. He drove there in a 10,000-dollar car. And drove home in a 100,000-dollar bus.

8 One piece of advice: if you want to leave Las Vegas with a small fortune, go there with a large one.

9 The first time I went to Las Vegas I parked my car on a meter, put a couple of quarters in – then three little wheels spun round and I lost the car.

10 There's a sign above the dice tables. It says: SHAKE WELL BEFORE LOSING.

11 They don't take marriage very seriously in Las Vegas. The shops keep their wedding gowns in the sporting-goods department.

12 They're so friendly in Las Vegas, they welcome you with open palms.

13 When I went to Las Vegas, there was a sign on the back of my hotel door. No, not HAVE YOU LEFT ANYTHING? This one said, HAVE YOU ANYTHING LEFT?

See also America and the Americans, Gambling, Weddings

Lateness

1 Ever since I told my secretary that I'm a stickler for punctuation, she hasn't been late for work once.

2 He's always running late. In fact, if anyone gets to the airport after him, they've missed the plane.

3 He's always been late for everything. That's why his twin brother is six months older than he is.

4 I'm not normally late. It just takes me longer than most people to start to begin to commence to get ready.

5 I'm not really late. I just took my coffee-break before I came in!

6 My brother is the world's greatest procrastinator. At his wedding, when the vicar said, 'You may now kiss the bride,' he said, 'Later.'

7 The boss came up with a great way of getting people to work on time: ninety-five parking spaces for every hundred employees.

8 BOSS: You should have been here at nine o'clock.
JUNIOR: Why, what happened?

9 BOSS: You're twenty minutes late again! Don't you know what time we start work at this office?
JUNIOR: No, sir. You're always hard at it when I arrive.

10 HUSBAND: If you'd run a bit faster, we would have caught that train!

WIFE: If you hadn't run so fast, we wouldn't have to wait so long for the next one!

11 Why do you call the boss 'Musketeer'?
Because he says I musketeer by 9.30!

See Railways 5, Unemployment 5; *see also* Bosses, The Office, Procrastination

Laughter

1 He who laughs last . . . doesn't get the joke.

2 My wife laughs like a cackling hen. I'd get rid of her if I didn't need the eggs.

3 Show me a man who laughs when everything goes wrong and I'll show you an idiot.

4 There's nothing so hollow as the laugh of the man who intended to tell the story himself.

5 You might as well laugh at yourself once in a while – everyone else does.

6 In my mind, there is nothing so illiberal and ill-bred as audible laughter.
Earl of Chesterfield

See Bosses 14; *see also* Comedians, Humour, Jokes

Law, The

1 A judge is a man who ends a sentence with a sentence.

2 A jury is one thing that never works properly after it's been fixed.

3 A jury is twelve people whose job it is to decide which side has the better lawyer.

4 A jury is a group of citizens who will try anyone once.

5 He became a High Court judge – an honour few people receive while they're still alive.

6 I began to get suspicious of the contract when I saw that the first paragraph forbade you from reading any of the others.

7 I don't understand. How come they lock the jury up overnight and let the prisoner go home?

8 I thought I was intelligent until I was tried by a jury of my peers.

9 If you can't get a lawyer who knows the law, get one who knows the judge.

10 In the old days there was one law for the rich and one law for the poor. Today there are thousands of laws for everyone.

11 It takes a thief to catch a thief – and a jury to let him go.

12 These days we'll try anything once – except criminals.

13 JUDGE: There's far too much of this sexual intercourse going on. And I'm not having it!

14 The Old Bailey, where justice is dispensed with.

15 What causes all this trouble is that we have 10,000 laws to enforce the Ten Commandments.

16 What's the difference between unlawful and illegal?
Unlawful is against the law. Illegal is a sick bird.

17 You've been found guilty of not stopping at a red light. Do you have anything to say in mitigation?
Well, I've often stopped at green lights when I haven't had to.

18 For certain people, after fifty, litigation takes the place of sex.
Gore Vidal

19 I know of no method to secure the repeal of bad or obnoxious laws so effective as their stringent execution.
Ulysses S. Grant

20 I learned law so well, the day I graduated I sued the college, won the case and got my tuition back.
Fred Allen

See also Courtroom, Crime, Lawyers, Prison, Wills

Lawyers

1 A lawyer is a man who helps you get what's coming to him.

2 A lawyer is someone who prevents somebody else from getting your money.

3 Did you hear about the lawyer who was so clever he didn't bother to graduate? He just settled out of class.

4 God bless lawyers. If we didn't have them, how would we ever get out of the trouble they got us into?

5 Hell hath no fury like the lawyer of a woman scorned.

6 I've got a brilliant lawyer. He can look at a contract and in less than a minute tell you whether it's oral or written.

7 Old lawyers never die, they just lose their appeal.

8 Remember, if there had never been any lawyers, there would never have been any need for them.

9 Talk is cheap, until you call a lawyer.

10 CLIENT: Can you tell me what your fees are?
LAWYER: Well, I charge 100 pounds to answer three questions.
CLIENT: That's rather steep, isn't it?
LAWYER: Yes, now what's your final question?

11 I'm a criminal lawyer.
Thank you for being so frank.

12 Q: What's the difference between a proud rooster and a lawyer.
A: The rooster clucks defiance . . .

13 What's the difference between a lawyer and a catfish?
One is a scum-sucking bottom dweller and the other is a fish.

14 Why does California have the most lawyers and New Jersey the most toxic waste dumps?
Because New Jersey had first choice.

15 A builder, an electrician and a lawyer were arguing over whose profession was the oldest.
'The first thing God did,' said the builder, 'was to build the Earth.'
'Ah, yes,' countered the electrician, 'but before that he said, "Let there be light."'
'True,' said the lawyer, 'but before the light, there was chaos – and who do you think created that?'

16 A lawyer called a plumber to fix a leaking pipe and got charged fifty pounds an hour.
The lawyer said, 'Fifty pounds! I don't make that as a lawyer!'
And the plumber said, 'Neither did I when I was a lawyer!'

17 A man telephones a law firm and a voice answers, 'Hello. Wilson, Wilson, Wilson and Wilson.'
The man says, 'Hello, may I speak to Mr Wilson.'
'I'm afraid he's not in.'
'Well may I speak to Mr Wilson?'
'He's at lunch.'
'OK, then is Mr Wilson there?'
'I'm afraid he's away.'
'How about Mr Wilson?'
'Speaking.'

18 Two scientists are discussing their latest research methods. One says, 'We've started something new. For some of our experiments now, we're using lawyers instead of rats.'
'Lawyers instead of rats? What's the advantage of that?' said the other.
'Well you know how it is,' replied the first scientist, 'you get so attached to rats.'

19 A town that cannot support one lawyer, can always support two.
Lyndon B. Johnson

20 I do not care to speak ill of any man behind his back, but I believe the gentleman is an attorney.
Samuel Johnson

21 My definition of utter waste is a coachload of lawyers going over a cliff with three empty seats.
Lamar Hunt

22 You've heard about the man who got the bill from his lawyer which said, 'For crossing the street to speak to you and discovering it was not you . . . twelve dollars.'
George S. Kaufman

See The Office 7; *see also* Courtroom, Crime, Divorce, The Law, Wills

Laziness

1 Ever since he's been old enough to hold down a steady job, he hasn't.

2 He has the strangest hobby. All day long he sits in the corner and collects dust.

3 He was born with a silver spoon in his mouth – and he hasn't stirred since.

4 He's devised this great labour-saving device. It's called 'tomorrow'.

5 He's got two desks in his office – one for each foot.

6 He's so lazy, he won't even exercise discretion.

7 He's so lazy, he even married a widow with five children.

8 I don't think my uncle can be serious about getting a job. He says the only one he'll take is marriage-guidance counsellor to the Pope.

9 I hate mornings. I get up at the crack of noon.

10 I keep telling my brother to learn a trade, so at least he'll know what sort of work he's out of!

11 I missed my nap today. I slept right through it.

12 I'll tell you how lazy he is – he's dating a pregnant woman!

13 I've got a great way of starting the day: I go back to bed.

14 I've stopped drinking coffee in the morning, because it keeps me awake for the rest of the day.

15 My brother works almost every day – almost on Monday, almost on Tuesday, almost on Wednesday . . .

16 My brother was very religious. He wouldn't work if there was a Sunday in the week.

17 My secretary is extremely efficient. She hasn't missed a coffee-break in ten years.

18 My uncle does absolutely nothing around the house. Recently his wife had him searched for a socket. She wondered if maybe she had to plug him in!

19 My uncle is very superstitious. He won't work in any week that has a Friday in it.

20 My uncle once thought about getting a job. Then he decided that would be the coward's way out.

21 My uncle was rejected by the army because he had a problem with his back. He couldn't get off it.

22 No wonder my brother doesn't work very often. He describes himself as a Coronation programme-seller.

23 The greatest pleasure in life is having lots to do – and not doing it.

24 They offered me a raise if I worked hard. I knew there was a catch there somewhere.

25 They recently gave him a little job to tackle – his.

26 You can tell a British workman by his hands – they're always in his pockets.

27 DOCTOR: I'm afraid, Mrs Waver-tree, that your husband will never work again.
MRS WAVERTREE: Well, that'll certainly cheer him up!

28 What do you do for a living?
As little as possible.

29 You labourers are so lazy. You've been sitting there all day, doing absolutely nothing.
How do you know?
I've been sitting here watching you.

30 The boss found an employee asleep on the job so he woke him up. Coming to his senses, the employee said, 'Good heavens, can't a man even close his eyes for a few moments of prayer?'

31 Laziness is nothing more than the habit of resting before you get tired.
Jules Renard

See Advertising 8, Congress 4, Economics 7, Gifts 7, Gold-diggers 6, Marriage 12, Ronald Reagan 7; *see also* Procrastination, Work

Legs

1 She was so bow-legged, she could walk down a bowling alley during the game.

2 He was so bow-legged, he looked like one bite out of a doughnut.

3 He was so bow-legged, he could get out of both sides of a cab at the same time.

4 He's so bow-legged, his wife has to iron his underpants on a boomerang.

5 His wife's bow-legged and he's knock-kneed. When they stand together, they spell the word 'ox'.

6 She was so knock-kneed, her legs walked in single file.

7 She's got two of the best legs in Chelsea. And I should know – I've counted them.

8 The last time I saw legs like those, there was a message tied to them.

9 Was I embarrassed? I told this girl her stockings were wrinkled – and she wasn't wearing any.

10 Well, at least no one could say that he's bow-legged – he's knock-kneed!

See also Appearance, Figures – Thin

Libraries

1 My sister is a librarian. She carries a card that reads: IN CASE OF EMERGENCY, SSHHHH!

2 READER: Can you tell me where the 'Self-help' section is?
LIBRARIAN: But doesn't that defeat the whole purpose?

3 Who told you you're a good bookkeeper?
The librarian.

4 The local library was moving to the other side of town. To save costs, residents were asked to help out by borrowing ten books each and returning them three weeks later.

See Entertaining 1, Insults 55; *see also* Books, Literature

Lies

1 Don't talk to me about lie-detectors – I married one.

2 I can tell when he's lying. His lips are moving!

3 Half the lies they tell about me aren't true!

4 I'm afraid I just don't trust my partner. Even if he promised me he was lying, I still wouldn't be sure he wasn't telling the truth.

5 I'm not saying he's a liar. Let's just say he lives on the wrong side of the facts.

6 My father was a very honest man. All the years that he lived, a lie never passed his lips. He talked through his nose.

7 THE WORLD'S BIGGEST LIES
The cheque is in the post.
I'm from the government and I'm here to help you.
Of course I'll respect you in the morning.
You don't look a day over forty.
It doesn't look like a wig.
Of course I won't tell anyone else.
Hello – no, I wasn't asleep.
But, officer, I've only had a couple of beers.

8 What you're saying is as false as the teeth you're saying it through!

9 I support my party right down the line.
Neither do I.

10 I think my wife's deceiving me. Last night she came home and said that she'd spent the evening with her friend, Annie. But she can't have.
Why not?
Because I did.

11 My wife couldn't tell a lie to save her life.
You're lucky! My wife can tell a lie the moment it leaves my mouth.

12 It is hard to believe that a man is telling the truth when you know that you would lie if you were in his place.
H. L. Mencken

13 The aim of the liar is simply to charm, to delight, to give pleasure. He is the very basis of civilized society.
Oscar Wilde

14 The liar's punishment is not in the least that he is not believed, but that he cannot believe anyone else.
George Bernard Shaw

See Birthdays 6, Church 6, Doctors 25, Fishing 3, Government 6, Old Age 10; *see also* Truth

Life

1 I am confused, therefore I am.

2 Just when I thought I knew all the answers, life started asking me all the wrong questions.

3 Life can be marvellous. Try not to miss it!

4 Life is a sexually transmitted disease.

5 Life is what happens to us while we're making other plans.

6 Life is what you make it – until somebody makes it worse.

7 Life isn't all beer and skittles. In fact, it's ages since I last touched a skittle.

8 Life may not be all you want, but it's all you have.

9 Life may not always be worth living, but what else can you do with it?

10 There's one good thing about life – it's only temporary.

11 I heard a bit of good news today. We shall pass this way but once.
George Price

12 Life . . . is much too short to be taken seriously.
Nicolas Bentley

13 Life is an incurable disease.
Abraham Cowley

14 Life is just one damned thing after another.
Elbert Hubbard

15 Life is one crisis after another.
Richard Nixon

16 The basic fact about human existence is not that it is a tragedy, but that it is a bore.
H. L. Mencken

17 The golden rule is that there are no golden rules.
George Bernard Shaw

See Gifts 2, Insanity 6; *see also* Modern Times

Light-bulb jokes

1 How many Californians does it take to screw in a light bulb?
Four. One to screw in the bulb and three to share the experience.

2 How many psychiatrists does it take to screw in a light bulb?
One. But the bulb has really got to want to change.

3 How many yuppies does it take to screw in a light bulb?
None. Yuppies only screw in a Jacuzzi.

4 How many Jewish mothers does it take to screw in a light bulb?
None. It's OK, I'll just sit here in the dark.

See Sociology 1; *see also* Cross Jokes, Knock-knock Jokes, Tom Swifties

Limericks

1 The limerick packs laughs anatomical
Into space that is quite economical,

But the good ones we've seen
So seldom are clean
And the clean ones so seldom are comical.

2 There was a young man of Calcutta,
Who had the most terrible stutta,
He said, 'Pass the h-ham
And the j-j-j-jam,
And the b-b-b-b-b-b-butta.'

3 There was an old man from Darjeeling
Who boarded a bus bound for Ealing,
He saw on the door,
'Please don't spit on the floor',
So he stood up and spat on the ceiling.

4 There was a young lady from France
Who decided to just take a chance.
For an hour or so,
She just let herself go.
And now all her sisters are aunts.

5 There was a young lady of Tottenham,
Who'd no manners, or else she'd forgotten 'em.
At tea at the vicar's
She tore off her knickers,
Because, she explained, she felt 'ot in 'em.

6 There was a young girl of Madras
Who had the most beautiful ass,
But not as you'd think
Firm, round and pink,
But grey, with long ears, and eats grass.

7 There was a young lady from Exeter
So pretty that men craned their nexeter.
One was even so brave
As to take out and wave
The distinguishing mark of his sexeter.

See Drink 56, Farming 12, News-papers 6, Sex 33; *see also* Poets and Poetry

Literature

1 Whenever I'm reading really bad prose, I always remember it could be verse.

2 You should take a look at my bookshelves. I've got the complete works of Shakespeare, Whitman, Proust, Longfellow and Jane Austen. And I've also got some books for reading.

3 Have you read any of Shakespeare's plays?
Only two of them.
Which ones?
Romeo and Juliet.

4 Literature is the orchestration of platitudes.
Thornton Wilder

5 Literature is always a good card to play for honours. It makes people think that Cabinet ministers are educated.
Arnold Bennett

See also Books, Books – The Critics, Libraries, Literature – The Critics, Poets and Poetry, Writers and Writing

Literature – the critics

1 I was very excited by his last book, mainly because I hoped it was.

2 A bad review is even less important than whether it is raining in Patagonia.
Iris Murdoch

3 I was so long writing my review that I never got around to reading the book.
Groucho Marx

4 Nature, when she invented, manufactured and patented her authors, contrived to make critics of the

chips that were left.
Oliver Wendell Holmes

5 To literary critics, a book is assumed to be guilty until it proves itself innocent.
Nelson Algren

See also Books, Books – The Critics, Libraries, Poets and Poetry

Loneliness

1 Solitude is much more enjoyable if you have someone to share it with.

2 Doctor, I'm so alone. Nobody seems to notice me.
Next patient, please!

See Losers 2

Los Angeles

1 What happens when the smog lifts over Los Angeles?
UCLA.

2 Two Korean businessmen bumped into each other in a Los Angeles street. One started talking in Korean but the other interrupted him. He said, 'You're in America now, remember. Speak Spanish!'

3 Disneyland can be found in Los Angeles. Wherever you look.
David Frost and Michael Shea

4 Isn't it nice that people who prefer Los Angeles to San Francisco live there?
Herb Caen

See Psychiatry 18; see also America and the Americans, California, Hollywood, Pollution – Air

Losers

1 My brother-in-law is practically a genius. He can do almost anything – except make a living.

2 He applied to join a Lonely Hearts Club – but they wrote back and told him that they weren't that lonely.

3 He came in like a lion and went out like a lamp.

4 He wanted to be a big movie star or nothing. He got his wish. He's a big nothing!

5 He was an only child, and he still wasn't his father's favourite.

6 He works a lot for charity. He has to – no one's ever likely to pay him.

7 He'd love to be a Don Juan. But the girls Don Juan to have anything to do with him.

8 He's willed his body to science – and science is contesting the will.

9 He's only dull and dreary until you get to know him. After that, he's just plain boring.

10 He's so dull, he couldn't even entertain a doubt.

11 He's the only man I know who had a paternity suit filed against him by his own children.

12 He's very keen on self-improvement at the moment. Every day he reads until his lips get tired.

13 His life is so dull, the only thing he looks forward to is going to the dentist's.

14 His problem is, he's the son his father never had.

15 When I was born, my father tried to collect on his accident insurance.

16 I must be really unpopular. My phone doesn't even ring when I'm in the bath!

17 She was never popular. One day a man took her out – and left her there.

18 Unpopular? He couldn't even get a date on his gravestone!

19 When he was a child he was kidnapped. His parents got a ransom note which read, 'Give us 10,000 pounds or you'll see your kid again.'

20 You won't find him in *Who's Who*. You *will* find him in *What's That?*

See also Defeat, Failure, Insults, Victory

Love

1 I believe in love at first sight. It saves such a lot of time.

2 Love is the feeling that you feel when you feel you're going to feel a feeling that you never felt before.

3 My philosophy is that it's better to have loved a short girl than never to have loved at all.

4 Adam invented love at first sight, one of the greatest labor-saving devices the world ever saw.
Josh Billings

5 Because women can do nothing except love, they've given it a ridiculous importance.
W. Somerset Maugham

6 Love is a gross exaggeration of the difference between one person and everybody else.
George Bernard Shaw

7 Love is just another four-letter word.
Tennessee Williams

8 Love is the delusion that one woman differs from an other.
H. L. Mencken

9 Love is the delightful interval between meeting a beautiful girl and discovering that she looks like a haddock.
John Barrymore

10 Love is the triumph of imagination over intelligence.
H. L. Mencken

11 Love is what happens to a man and a woman who don't know each other.
W. Somerset Maugham

12 Love: a temporary insanity, curable by marriage . . .
Ambrose Bierce

13 Many a man has fallen in love with a girl in a light so dim he would not have chosen a suit by it.
Maurice Chevalier

14 Many a man in love with a dimple makes the mistake of marrying the whole girl.
Stephen Leacock

See Advice 4; *see also* Dating, Kissing, Romance, Sex

Luck

1 A rabbit's foot may be lucky – but not for the original owner.

2 For years he waited for Dame Fortune to come knocking on his door. Finally, someone did knock, but when he opened the door it was Dame Fortune's daughter, Miss Fortune.

3 I don't actually believe in luck, but how else do you explain other people doing well?

4 If I didn't have bad luck, I wouldn't have any luck at all.

5 Just my luck! When my ship came in, I was stuck at the airport!

6 When opportunity finally knocked on his front door, he was out in the back yard looking for four-leafed clovers.

7 If you put the milk in your tea first, it's extremely unlucky. My great-aunt Clarice one day put the milk

in first and over the course of the next fifty years, she lost all her teeth.

8 I am a great believer in luck, and I find the harder I work the more I have of it.
Stephen Leacock

M

Mafia

1 The two hoodlums paid a return visit to the shopkeeper who was refusing to pay them protection money. 'So are you going to pay up or not?' they asked him.

'No way!' said the shopkeeper stubbornly.

So the two thugs pushed him into the back room, pinned him against the wall and took turns to pummel him. When he collapsed on the floor, they kicked him in the side, pulled him back to his feet and started to punch him again.

'OK, OK, I'll pay!' cried the shopkeeper.

The thugs pushed him on to a chair and one of them said, 'So why didn't you agree earlier?'

'Because,' said the shopkeeper, 'you hadn't explained it before.'

See Scotland and the Scots 7, Sociology 2; *see also* Corruption, Crime

Magic and magicians

1 AGENT: So what can you do?
MAGICIAN: I've got this unique act. I saw a lady in half.
AGENT: Unique? Every magician I know can saw a lady in half!
MAGICIAN: Lengthways?

See Arguments 10, Psychology 2; *see also* Show Business

Mankind

1 I finally know what distinguishes man from the other beasts: financial worries.
Jules Renard

2 I love mankind – it's people I can't stand.
Charles M. Schultz

3 Man is a dog's ideal of what God should be.
Holbrook Jackson

4 Man is Nature's sole mistake.
W. S. Gilbert

5 The noblest work of God? Man.
Who found it out? Man.
Mark Twain

See Sleep 4

Manners

1 A bird in the hand is bad table manners.

2 I haven't forgotten *all* my manners. I still say 'Excuse me!' to anyone over 6 feet 6.

3 I still think politeness is important. I always offer my seat to a lady as I get off the bus.

4 I'm always a gentleman on the train. If I see an empty seat, I point it out to a lady – and then I race her for it.

5 I'm normally very polite. I always take my shoes off before I put my feet on the table.

6 She's very refined. She wears a T-shirt to serve tea.

7 Soup should be seen and not heard.

8 He has the manners of a gentleman. I knew they couldn't belong to him!

9 OUTRAGED HUSBAND: How dare you belch in front of my wife!
FELLOW DINNER GUEST: I'm terribly sorry. I didn't realize it was her turn!

10 When are you justified in spitting in a man's face?
Only when his moustache is on fire.

11 Don't tell your friends about your indigestion:
'How are you!' is a greeting, not a question.
Arthur Guiterman

12 Good breeding consists in concealing how much we think of ourselves and how little we think of other persons.
Mark Twain

13 I think she must have been very strictly brought up, she's so desperately anxious to do the wrong thing correctly.
Saki

14 Manners are especially the need of the plain. The pretty can get away with anything.
Evelyn Waugh

15 Nothing is less important than which fork you use.
Emily Post

16 Politeness: the most acceptable hypocrisy.
Ambrose Bierce

See Limericks 3, 5; see also Embarrassment

Marriage

1 A good marriage lasts for ever. A bad one just seems to.

2 Every morning I take my wife her tea in my pyjamas. She loves it but my pyjamas are getting a bit soggy.

3 Finally I took her for my wife. Trouble was, my wife didn't want her.

4 Five years ago I asked for her hand – and it's been in my pocket ever since.

5 For twenty-five years my husband and I were deliriously happy. Then we met.

6 Her husband is not exactly homeless – but he's home less than most husbands.

7 I can remember *when* I got married. And *where* I got married. What I just can't remember is *why*?

8 I got married twenty-five years ago and I haven't regretted a single day since. The day I'm thinking of was 5 October 1987, when my wife went to visit her sister in Birmingham.

9 Every man waits for the right girl to came along, but in the meantime he gets married.

10 I never knew what happiness was until I got married – and then it was too late.

11 I think my wife's grown tired of me. She keeps wrapping my sandwiches in a road map.

12 I told my wife that I don't believe in combining marriage and a career – which is why I haven't worked since our wedding day.

13 I'm so looking forward to being married – coming home from work, opening a beer, sitting on the sofa and spending the evening watching my wife's favourite television shows.

14 I've been happily married for ten years. Ten out of thirty isn't bad.

15 I've decided to end it all. I'm getting married!

16 I've found marriage to be a continuous process of getting used to things I hadn't expected.

17 In many Eastern countries a woman never sees her husband before marriage. In many Western countries, she doesn't see him very much afterwards.

18 It seems like only yesterday I got married. If it was tomorrow, I'd call the whole thing off!

19 Marriage isn't a word, it's a sentence.

20 Marriage is a fine institution. But who wants to live in an institution?

21 Marriage is the price men pay for sex; sex is the price women pay for marriage.

22 Marriage is a good way for a woman to keep active until the right man comes along!

23 My grannie told me that all girls should learn how to cook and clean the house. She said it would come in handy in case I couldn't find a husband.

24 My husband added some magic to our marriage. He disappeared.

25 My parents were absolutely inseparable. In fact, it used to take six people to pull them apart.

26 My wife and I have been married for twenty-three years and we're still blissfully in love – she with the doctor and me with the woman next door.

27 My wife should get a job in earthquake prediction. She can find a fault quicker than anyone!

28 No, I'm not married. I've always been round-shouldered.

29 Of course, I'm the master in my own house. I run everything: the parties, the holidays, the gardening, the errands.

30 Our marriage was a love match pure and simple – she was pure and I was simple.

31 She says she doesn't believe in marriage because, after all, it's just a piece of paper. Well, so is a fifty-pound note and she certainly believes in those!

32 She wanted to marry a big movie star or nothing. She got her wish – she married a big nothing.

33 Marriage is just another union that defies management.

34 Something terrible has happened. My best friend has run away without my wife!

35 The first part of our marriage was blissfully happy. Then, on the way back from the ceremony . . .

36 The time had come to take a wife. The question was: whose wife to take?

37 There's only one thing that keeps me from being happily married – my wife.

38 We don't communicate any more. My wife gave up sex for Lent – and I didn't find out till Easter.

39 We had a perfectly happy marriage until my wife found out that the Book of the Month Club doesn't hold meetings.

40 You know the honeymoon's over when the groom stops helping his wife with the dishes – and starts doing them himself!

41 'Tis better to have loved and lost than to have loved and married.

42 Did your wife have anything to say when you got home late last night?
No, but it didn't stop her talking for hours.

43 Do you think the fun and excitement have gone out of our marriage?
I'll discuss it with you during the next commercial break.

44 Every night my wife takes my shoes off.
When you get in?
No, when I want to go out!

45 If you marry two men it's bigamy.
What is it if you marry just one man?
Monotony.

46 The truth is, I regret the day I was married.
You're lucky. I was married for a whole month!

47 What did you do before you married?
Anything I wanted to!

48 What do you normally have for breakfast?
Arguments about dinner.

49 You know that beautiful film star you were talking about?
Is she married?
Occasionally.

50 I think I want to get married.
Don't. You're not intelligent enough.
And when will I be intelligent enough?
When you stop thinking you want to get married.

51 A man took his wife along to a marriage counsellor. The counsellor asked him to explain their problem. The man said, 'What's 'er name here claims I don't pay her enough attention.'

52 Do you know what it's like to go home every night to a slap-up three-course supper?
It means you've gone home to the wrong house, that's what it means.

53 A young couple rush into a register office and the young woman says, 'Could you marry us, please? Now!'
And the registrar says, 'I'm sorry, but you have to wait forty-eight hours to get married.'
And the young man says, 'In that case, could you just say a few words to tide us over for the weekend?'

54 An old gentleman was reminiscing to a fellow pensioner about his late wife. 'Yes, she was a remarkable woman – extremely religious. When she woke up in the morning, she would sing a hymn, then she would ask me to join her in prayer. Then, over breakfast, she would recite a psalm, and that's how it went on all day – praying, singing and reciting until she finally climbed into bed, said her prayers, sang a hymn and said her prayers again. And then one morning, she was dead.'
'What happened?'
'I strangled her.'

55 Harry took his friend Frank home for dinner one evening and was greeted at the door by his wife, who flung her arms round him and kissed him passionately.
'That's fantastic,' said Frank. 'You've been married all these years and yet your wife still welcomes you home like that. It's amazing!'
'Don't be fooled,' said Harry. 'She only does it to make the dog jealous.'

56 When people ask me the secret of our long marriage, I tell them. Twice a week we take time off to go to this romantic little restaurant we know. There's dinner by candle-light, soft music and dancing under the stars.
She goes on Mondays, I go on Thursdays.

57 A man may be a fool and not know it, but not if he is married.
H. L. Mencken

58 Before marriage a man will lie awake all night thinking about some-

thing you said; after marriage, he'll fall asleep before you've finished saying it.
Helen Rowland

59 He marries best who puts it off until it is too late.
H. L. Mencken

60 It destroys one's nerves to be amiable every day to the same human being.
Benjamin Disraeli

61 It isn't tying himself to one woman that a man dreads when he thinks of marrying; it's separating himself from all the others.
Helen Rowland

62 Marriage is a very good thing, but I think it's a mistake to make a habit of it.
W. Somerset Maugham

63 One should always be in love – that is one reason why one should never marry.
Oscar Wilde

64 The days just prior to marriage are like a snappy introduction to a tedious book.
Wilson Mizner

See Happiness 2, Humour 3, Old Age 31; see also Arguments, Bigamy, Children, Divorce, Families, Gold-diggers, Honeymoons, Husbands, Husbands and Wives, Men and Women, Newlyweds, The Single Life, Weddings

Maths

1 How much is 5q plus 5q?
10q
My pleasure!

2 Mathematics may be defined as the subject in which we never know what we are talking about, nor whether what we are saying is true.
Bertrand Russell

3 Mathematics is a tentative agreement that two and two make four.
Elbert Hubbard

See Banks and Banking 7, Golf 17; see also School, Statistics

Medicine

1 I called my acupuncturist and told him I was in terrible pain. He told me to take two safety pins and call him in the morning.

2 My brother is a brilliant medical researcher. He's just invented a cure for which there is no known illness.

3 There are two ways of dealing with the common cold: if you *don't* treat it, it lasts six or seven days, and if you *do* treat it, it lasts about a week.

4 This latest wonder drug is so powerful, you have to be in perfect health to take it.

5 We live in a world of increasing medical specialization. Today four out of five doctors recommend another doctor.

6 CUSTOMER: Do you have some talcum powder?
PHARMACIST: Certainly, sir, walk this way.
CUSTOMER: If I could walk that way, I wouldn't need the talcum powder.

7 A man rushed into the chemist's and said to the assistant, 'Do you have anything that'll stop hiccups?'
The assistant leaned over the counter and slapped the man's face.
The man said, 'What did you do that for?'
The assistant replied, 'Well, you don't have any hiccups now, do you?'
And the man said, 'I never did have. I wanted something for my wife. She's out in the car.'

8 The consultant was showing the young medical student a set of X-rays.

'As you will observe,' said the consultant, 'one hip seems to be higher than the other. What do you expect to find wrong with the patient?'

'I would expect him to walk with a limp.'

'Good, and so what would *you* do in the circumstances.'

'I suppose I'd walk with a limp too.'

9 The patient stood nervously in the consulting room of an eminent Harley Street specialist.

'So who did you consult before you came to me?' asked the specialist.

'My local GP.'

'Your GP? They're hopeless. Complete waste of time. Tell me, what sort of useless advice did he give you?'

'He told me to come and see you.'

10 The art of medicine consists of amusing the patient while Nature cures the disease.
Voltaire

See Space 1; *see also* Doctors, Health, Hospitals, Illness

Memory

1 Do I have a good memory? I even remind elephants!

2 I have a photographic memory, but just occasionally I forget to take off the lens cap.

3 I'm getting so forgetful. Yesterday I put my shoes on the wrong feet – then I just couldn't remember whose feet I put them on.

4 I've got a superb memory. I can recite ten pages of the London tele- phone directory by heart! Ready? 'Smith, Smith, Smith, Smith . . .'

5 My wife has a terrible memory. She never forgets a thing.

6 PATIENT: Doctor, I can't remember anything.
DOCTOR: Tell me all about it.
PATIENT: All about what?

See Birthdays 7, Drugs 4; *see also* Amnesia

Men – the female view

1 Ninety per cent of men give the other 10 per cent a bad name.

2 She's attracted to the simple things in life – like men.

3 You can talk to my husband about any subject. He doesn't understand, but you can talk to him.

4 Can you imagine a world without men? No crime and lots of happy, fat women.
Nicole Hollander

5 I like men to behave like men – strong and childish.
Françoise Sagan

See also Men and Women, Women – The Male View

Men and women

1 I worship the ground she walks on. I don't think much of her – but the ground is sensational.

2 Is he reliable? Let's just say that whenever he wants me, there he is.

3 My trouble is, I put women under a pedestal.

4 There are two periods in his life when a man doesn't understand women – before marriage and after marriage.

5 They're a very trying couple. Maybe one day she'll let him.

6 She struggled for years to get a mink coat. And then, when she was about to give up, she finally got one.
How?
She stopped struggling.

7 WIFE: Derek Jones next door blows his wife a kiss every morning as he leaves the house. I wish you'd do that.
HUSBAND: But I hardly know the woman!

8 Last night my girlfriend was complaining that we have nothing in common. She said we didn't agree on anything.
I said, 'I wouldn't say that. For instance, if you had to spend the night in a room with two big beds and there was a man in one and a woman in the other, whose bed would you choose?'
And she said, 'The woman's, of course.'
And I said, 'Well, so would I.'

9 A man is in general better pleased when he has a good dinner upon his table, than when his wife talks Greek.
Samuel Johnson

10 Brigands demand your money or your life; women require both.
Samuel Butler

11 Men have a much better time of it than women: for one thing, they marry later; for another thing, they die earlier.
H. L. Mencken

12 No matter how much a woman loves a man, it would still give her a glow to see him commit suicide for her.
H. L. Mencken

13 Only men who are not interested in women are interested in women's clothes; men who like women never notice what they wear.
Anatole France

See The Bible 3; see also Husbands and Wives, Marriage, Men – The Female View, Women – The Male View

Middle age

1 An adult is someone who's stopped growing at both ends and started growing in the middle.

2 Middle age is when, if you have a choice between two temptations, you choose the one that'll get you home earlier.

3 Middle age is when work is a lot less fun and fun is a lot more work.

4 Middle age is when women stop worrying about becoming pregnant and men start worrying about looking like they are.

5 Middle age is when your age starts to show around your middle.

6 Remember, you're only middle-aged once.

7 She admitted she was forty but she didn't say when.

8 She recently had bad luck – she ran into someone she knew when they were the same age.

9 When I went to my class reunion, all the guys were so fat and bald they hardly recognized me.

10 She says she's approaching middle age.
Yes, for the third time!

11 Boys will be boys – and so will a lot of middle-aged men.
Kin Hubbard

12 Middle age is the time when a man is always thinking that in a week or two he will feel as good as ever.
Don Marquis

13 Pushing forty? She's clinging on to it for dear life!
Ivy Compton-Burnett

See also Age, Birthdays, Old Age

Mistakes

1 A man who can smile when things go wrong has probably just thought of someone he can blame it on.

2 I'm generous to a fault – especially if it's my own.

3 If you don't learn from your mistakes, what's the point in making them?

4 The greatest mistake in life is to be in constant fear that you'll make one.

5 If I wasn't making mistakes, I wasn't making decisions.
Robert W. Johnson

See also Accidents, Failure

Moderation

1 Doing things in moderation is fine – as long as you do it in moderation.

See also Excess

Modern times

1 Have you noticed how these modern developers operate? They bulldoze the trees and then name the streets after them!

2 I've just bought one of these new talking washing-machines. The first time it spoke was to tell me what it did with the other sock.

3 Take it from me: if you're not confused, you don't know what's going on.

4 The problem with trying to get away from it all is that wherever you go, there you are.

5 This is getting ridiculous. My plumber is now refusing to do house calls.

6 It's hard for me to get used to these changing times. I can remember when the air was clean and sex was dirty.
George Burns

7 The world is moving so fast these days that the man who says it can't be done is generally interrupted by someone doing it.
Elbert Hubbard

See also City Life, Gadgets, Life, Progress

Money

1 It's my wife who makes our budget work – the secret is that we go without a lot of things I don't need.

2 Ladies and gentlemen, a fifty-pound note has been found in the theatre. Will the person who lost it please form a queue at the stage door.

3 Money can't buy you love, but it certainly puts you in a better bargaining position.

4 Money doesn't go as far as it used to, but at least it goes faster.

5 Money isn't everything. Sometimes it's not even enough.

6 Money isn't everything. There's also credit cards and traveller's cheques.

7 Money isn't everything. I've had money and I've had everything – and believe me, they're not the same.

8 Money isn't everything, but it's a long way ahead of whatever comes next.

9 Money isn't everything, but it's cer-

tainly handy if you don't have a credit card.

10 They say money brings only misery. With money, though, you can afford it.

11 A money-grabber is anybody who grabs more money than you do.

12 Does your husband confide in you about his business problems?
Yes, every time I come home with a new outfit.

13 Money isn't everything.
Who told you that?
My boss.

See Happiness 1, Religion 6; *see also* Accountants, Bankruptcy, Banks and Banking, Borrowing and Lending, Credit, Credit Cards, Debt, Gold-diggers, Hard Times, Inflation, Saving, Spending, Thrift, Wealth

Morality

1 I said to the vicar, 'Do you believe in sex before the wedding?' And he said, 'Not if it delays the ceremony.'

2 Morality is that instinctive sense of what's right and what's wrong that tells some people how everyone else should behave.

3 I didn't sleep with my wife before I got married. How about you?
I don't know. What was her maiden name?

4 Moralizing and morals are two entirely different things and are always found in entirely different people.
Don Herold

5 Morality is simply the attitude we adopt towards people whom we personally dislike.
Oscar Wilde

See also Prudery, Sex

Mothers

1 I did something really special for my mum on Mother's Day. I opened the door for her when she put my laundry in the washing-machine!

2 It isn't easy being a mother. If it were, fathers would do it.

3 Never forget: a mother's place is in the wrong.

4 You should be ashamed of yourself, Laura. All your girlfriends are divorced already and you're not even married!

5 On her son's birthday, his mother gave him two splendid silk ties – a green one and a red one. That night at dinner the son arrived at the table proudly wearing the green one.
His mother, struggling to conceal her disappointment, cried, 'And what was wrong with the red one?'

6 If a mother's place is in the home, how come I spend so much time in the car?
Bumper sticker

7 My mother had a great deal of trouble with me, but I think she enjoyed it.
Mark Twain

See also Children, Families, Fathers, Parents

Mothers-in-law

1 Behind every successful man stands an amazed mother-in-law!

2 I keep telling my wife that I like her mother-in-law a lot better than I like mine!

3 I said to my mother-in-law, 'Our house is your house.' Last week she sold it.

4 I'm leaving my wife because of another woman – her mother.

5 It's strange. One day I wasn't good enough to marry her daughter. The next, I've fathered the brightest grandchild on earth.

6 My mother-in-law may live with us for ever. I can't really complain – it *is* her house!

7 And what's more, Mummy says she thinks you're effeminate!
Well, compared to her, I am!

8 I'm going home to mother! I should have listened to her twenty years ago!
Go ahead. She's still talking!

9 You know, there was one time when I would have cut my throat if it wasn't for my mother-in-law.
How was that?
She was using my razor.

10 My mother-in-law broke up my marriage. My wife came home and found us in bed together.
Lenny Bruce

See Christmas 18, Weddings 31; *see also* Husbands and Wives, Marriage

Motorcycling

1 Motorcyclists who don't wear helmets should have their heads examined. And usually do!

See also Cars, Driving, Driving – Police

Mouths

1 Her mouth is so big, she can sing duets all by herself.

See also Appearance, Conversation, Faces, Talkers, Teeth

Murder

1 He killed his parents then asked for leniency on the grounds that he was an orphan.

2 You throttled your wife? I must go! My mother told me never to speak to stranglers.

3 It was obvious a murder had been committed. I lined up all the suspects except the butler.
Why didn't you line up the butler?
He was the one who'd been murdered.

4 Sergeant, this could be the murder weapon!
I doubt it. There's rust in the barrel, the trigger's missing, it's the wrong calibre and, most important of all, the victim was strangled.

5 Suddenly there was a gunshot. He fell to the ground. I ran up to him and examined him. There were no bullet holes.
No bullet holes?
Obviously this was an inside job.

6 The gunman fired two bullets at him, one of which came within 12 inches of his shoulder.
Phew!
Unfortunately, the other went straight between his eyes.

See also Courtroom, Crime, Death, Law, Police

Music

1 I was a musical prodigy. At three I composed an opera. At four I wrote a minuet. At five I wrote a complete symphony. And at five thirty, as usual, I went downstairs and had a cup of tea.

2 A true gentleman is someone who knows how to play the bagpipes – but doesn't.

3 Classical music is music written by famous dead foreigners.

4 Each of these musicians is a soloist in his own right. If you don't believe me, listen to what happens when they try and play together.

5 He loves music so much that one day he heard Dolly Parton singing in the bath and he put his ear to the keyhole.

6 He took up the trombone because he likes to let things slide.

7 I started my musical career in a three-piece band. We only knew three pieces!

8 My brother's a trumpet player. He recently had to move house. It was either him or the neighbours.

9 I play the piano just like Rachmaninov – with both hands!

10 I'd never buy a Stradivarius. I've heard that he's stopped making spare parts for them.

11 I'm trying to write this drinking song but I can't get past the first few bars.

12 Modern music isn't always as bad as it sounds.

13 There are three types of harmony: polyphonous, contrapuntal and lousy.

14 They laughed when I sat down at the piano. I'd forgotten to bring a stool.

15 What a violinist! He's been asked to join the Bournemouth Symphony Orchestra. By the Glasgow Symphony Orchestra!

16 When I was five years old my father gave me a drum and told me to beat it.

17 Can you play the violin?
I don't know. I've never tried.

18 Doctor, doctor, come quickly. My wife's just broken a leg.
But I'm a Doctor of Music!
That's all right. It's the piano leg.

19 Excuse me, how do I get to the Albert Hall?
Practise, my boy, practise.

20 Good morning, I'm the piano tuner.
But I didn't send for you.
No, but the neighbours did.

21 I play by ear.
What a coincidence. I listen the same way!

22 I play in a small quartet.
A small quartet?
Yes, there are only three of us.

23 Music has certainly given me the opportunity to travel. I've played in front of the King of Spain, the Queen of Denmark and the Prince of Wales.
The crowned heads of Europe?
No, the pubs of south London.

24 POLICEMAN: Excuse me, sir, but have you got permission to play that violin in the street?
BUSKER: Well, actually, no.
POLICEMAN: In that case I must ask you to accompany me.
BUSKER: Certainly, officer. What would you like to sing?

25 What would you have been if you hadn't been a musician?
A drummer.

26 When I was three years old I could play the trumpet.
Only by ear, of course.
Naturally, it was an ear trumpet.

27 Will the band play requests?
Certainly.
Then ask them to play dominoes!

28 Musical people always want one to be perfectly dumb at the very moment when one is longing to be absolutely deaf.
Oscar Wilde

29 Of all noises, I think music is the least disagreeable.
Samuel Johnson

30 Piano: a parlor utensil for subduing the impenitent visitor. It is operated by depressing the keys of the machine and the spirits of the audience.
Ambrose Bierce

31 Play us a medley of your hit.
Oscar Levant to George Gershwin

32 Nothing soothes me more after a long and maddening course of pianoforte recitals than to sit and have my teeth drilled.
George Bernard Shaw

See Bosses 16, Doctors 47, Drinks 11, 48, Golf 4, Heaven 5, Incentives 2, Insults 52, Neighbours 2, Records 1, 2, Robbery 4, Weather 5; *see also* Dancing, Music – The Critics, Opera, Singing, Singing – Insults

Music – the critics

1 He is nothing if not a brilliant pianist. In other words, he is nothing.

2 I am sitting in the smallest room in my house. I have your review in front of me. Soon it will be behind me.
Max Reger

3 The chief trouble with jazz is that there is not enough of it; some of it we have to listen to twice.
Don Herold

4 Wagner's music is better than it sounds.
Mark Twain

5 You have Van Gogh's ear for music.
Billy Wilder

See also Music, Singing, Singing – Insults

N

Names

1 His parents called him Bill, because he was born on the first day of the month.

2 I had a brother who was named after my father. We called him Dad.

3 I'm glad my parents called me Horatio.
Why's that, Horatio?
Because that's what everybody else calls me.

4 VICAR: Do you know my daughter, May?
YOUNG BACHELOR: No, I didn't, but thanks for the tip.

See The Army 15, Babies 3, 12, 20, 26, Bosses 8, Boxing 2, 15, Cars 7, Cats 2, Church 8, Dogs 4, 19, Families 13, Indecision 1, 3, Ireland and the Irish 1, Lawyers 17, School 31; *see also* Babies, Birth

Navy, The

1 I joined the navy to see the world – and spent two years in a submarine.

2 Two young sailors went to sea for the first time and, as they left port and saw the wide expanse of ocean before them, one said to the other, 'Did you ever see so much water in your whole life?'
And the other said, 'No, and we're only looking at the top of it!'

See Congress 1, Ethnic Jokes 17, Hospitals 18, Vanity 8; *see also* The Army, Boats and Ships, Sailing, The Sea

Neighbours

1 My wife never knows what she wants until the people next door get it.

2 There should be music in every home – except the one next door.

3 We've made a deal with our next-door neighbours. We'll stop trying to keep up with them if they'll stop trying to keep up with us!

4 I can't believe it! The woman next door has just bought a hat exactly like mine. I'm going to have to buy another one.
Well, it would certainly be cheaper than moving!

5 I'm looking for the people who live here.
Well, you came to the right place.

See Men and Women 7, Music 8, 20, Religion 4, Sales and Selling 11, Singing – Insults 15, Television 17, Wealth 21; *see also* Home

Nepotism

1 I made my money the old-fashioned way. I inherited it!

2 My boss had to do it the hard way. He had to be nice to his father.

3 Our company is one big happy family. Mainly because I only give jobs to my relatives.

4 This is my son, who's just joined the company. He's going to start at the bottom for a few days.

5 When I say he's a born executive, I mean his father owns the business.

6 When it comes to having qualifications, it's hard to beat having a father who owns the company.

7 Can you find a job for my son?
Sure, what can he do?
If he could do anything, *I'd* hire him!

8 I heard an amazing overnight success story the other day. This teenager joined the firm as a messenger boy as soon as he left school – about a year ago.

Just last week the president of the company called the kid into his office. He told him that he'd been watching his progress through the firm with great interest and that a place on the board had just fallen vacant and he was going to take a gamble and make this eighteen-year-old managing director.

You can imagine the teenager's reaction – from messenger boy to managing director in just one year!

When he tried to speak, he just couldn't. Finally he managed to utter just a few words. He said, 'Why, thanks, Dad!'

See also Families, Fathers, The Office, Relatives, Work

New Year

1 I've decided on my New Year's resolution: from the beginning of February, I'm resolving not to procrastinate.

2 My wife was furious with me because I came home late from a New Year's Eve party – in August.

3 New Year is resolution time – when we practise giving up things for Lent.

4 The best way to keep a New Year's resolution is to yourself.

5 Most New Year's resolutions go in one year and out the other.

6 My New Year's resolution is to start giving up giving up.

7 There's only one thing more depressing than staying in on New Year's Eve and that's going out.

See also Anniversaries, Christmas, Parties

New York

1 They don't give you the key to the city in New York any more. They just send someone over who tells you how to pick the lock.

2 Do people fall off the Empire State Building often?
No, just the once.

3 I met a Texan here in New York the other day. He was telling me that Texas is so vast, you can get on a train and after twenty-four hours' travelling you're still in Texas.

I wasn't too impressed. We have got the same experience here on the subway.

4 When I had looked at the lights of Broadway by night, I said to my American friends: what a glorious garden of wonders this would be to anyone who was lucky enough to be unable to read.
G. K. Chesterton

See also America and the Americans, California, City Life, Los Angeles

Newlyweds

1 We've just had the first row of our marriage. It's over whether we should have a 'his 'n' hers' honeymoon.

2 Darling, when are you going to learn to make the bread my mother makes?
Just as soon as you learn to make the dough my father makes!

3 GROOM: Darling, was I the first?
BRIDE: Why does everyone have to ask me that question?

4 The newlyweds had both led very sheltered lives and had no idea of what to do on their wedding night. So they went to see their doctor and asked him for a demonstration of the sexual act.

The doctor asked the woman to undress and lie down on his couch and then he began to make love to her.

When he'd finished, he turned to the man and said, 'So that's the sexual act. Any questions?'

And the man said, 'Yes, so how often do I have to bring her in?'

See also Honeymoons, Marriage, Weddings

News

1 Don't you sometimes wish that newscasters would cast their news somewhere else?

2 The trouble with today's news is that, most of the time, it's too true to be good.

3 We all want to get the news objectively, impartially and from our own point of view.
Bill Vaughan

See also Modern Times, Newspapers, Television

Newspapers

1 HEADLINES
Girl disappears in swimsuit.
Three men held in cigarette case.
Egg-laying contest won by local man.
Man refuses to give up biting dog.

2 My very first day working on the newspaper I got two scoops – one strawberry and one vanilla.

3 The best way of getting your name in the newspaper is to walk across the street reading one.

4 I'm calling about the announcement of my death in your paper this morning.
I see. Can you tell me where you're calling from?

5 The *Daily Chronicle* is proud of its record in breaking the big stories. Last week we were the first paper in the land to report that the Prime Minister was about to resign. Two days later, we were again the first paper to inform its readers that this report was entirely without foundation.

6 There was a young girl from St Paul
Who attended a newspaper ball
Where her dress caught on fire
And burnt the entire
Front page, sporting section and all.

7 Freedom of the press is limited to those who own one.
A. J. Liebling

8 I read about eight newspapers a day; when I'm in a town with only one newspaper, I read it eight times.
Will Rogers

9 The morning paper is just as necessary for an American as dew is to the grass.
Josh Billings

10 Lickspittle: a useful functionary, not infrequently found editing a newspaper.
Ambrose Bierce

11 Never trust a smiling reporter.
Ed Koch

See Government 7, Optimism 6, Small Towns 8, 10, Smoking 2; *see also* Journalism, News, Writers and Writing

Nonsense

1 Why does a chicken go to sleep on one leg?
I don't know.
Because if he took the other leg away he'd fall over.

2 Why is a tin of condensed milk like a mad dog?
I don't know.
Neither can ride a bike.

Noses

1 Does he have a big nose? Let's put it this way: he only has to breathe in once and it lasts all day.

2 His nose is so big, it's got it's own post code!

3 His nose is so big he can smoke a cigar in the shower!

4 Is that your nose or are you eating a banana?

5 JIMMY DURANTE: Where are my glasses?
FRIEND: They're on your nose!
JIMMY DURANTE: Be more specific!

See Plastic Surgery 4, Wealth 17; *see also* Appearance, Faces, Smells

Nostalgia

1 Nostalgia sure ain't what it used to be.

2 Nostalgia is a longing for a place you'd never think of moving back to.

3 Things were so much nicer in the old days. I used to belong to a gang called 'Heck's Angels'.

See Drugs 4; *see also* Memory, Old Age

Nudity

1 A nudist camp is a place where the peeling is mutual.

2 A nudist camp is a place where men and women air their differences.

3 A nudist camp is a place where nothing goes on.

4 On my wedding night I stood in front of my bride in my birthday suit. She told me it needed ironing!

5 SIGN AT AIRBASE: Absolutely no flying over nudist camp 9.7 miles SSW on a true course of 177 degrees.

6 There was lots of nudity in the film. In one scene you could actually hear more pants than you could see.

7 What I don't understand about nudist weddings is, where do they keep the ring?

O

Office, The

1 A secretary is someone you pay to learn to type while she looks for a husband.

2 He found his secretary sitting in front of two typewriters, working one with her left hand and one with her right. She said, 'I couldn't find the carbon paper.'

3 The boss has two secretaries – one for each knee.

4 The typing pool had a collection for a young man at the office – but they still couldn't afford one.

5 SECRETARY: I can do thirty words a minute.
BOSS: Typing or shorthand?
SECRETARY: Reading.

6 BOSS: You know something, Nugent, it hasn't escaped my notice that every time there's a mid-week game on, for some reason you have to take your granny to the doctor's.
NUGENT: Good heavens, you're right, sir. You don't think she's faking it by any chance?

7 The boss called in his secretary and said, 'OK, I make the occasional pass at you, but who told you you could do as you like around the office?'
And the secretary said, 'My lawyer.'

8 A memorandum is written, not to inform the reader, but to protect the writer.
Dean Acheson

See Christmas 16, Pregnancy 1, Prudery 8; *see also* Business, Work

Old age

1 At seventy-five, I feel like a twenty-year-old – but unfortunately there's never one around.

2 Just when you've learned to make the most of your life, most of your life is gone.

3 He's definitely getting more cautious in his old age. Nowadays he slows down when the traffic lights are red.

4 He's so old he can remember when Heinz had only one variety.

5 He's so old, his passport number is 7.

6 His face is so wrinkled, it can hold five days of rain!

7 I come from a family of long livers. My father had a liver 2 feet long.

8 I don't think I'll lust much longer.

9 I must be getting old. I can't take yes for an answer.

10 I never lie about my age. I just tell people I'm as old as my wife – and then I lie about *her* age!

11 I was always told to respect my elders. It's just getting harder and harder to find one.

12 I'll say he's old! At his last birthday, the candles cost more than the cake.

13 I'm at the age when, if a girl says no, I'm grateful.

14 I'm at the age now when, if I put five pounds in the collection plate,

14 it's not so much a contribution but more of an investment.

15 I'm not saying he's old, but his birthday cake has just been declared a fire hazard.

16 If I'd known how old I was going to get, I'd have taken much better care of myself.

17 Mr Horace Hattersley of Norwich, England, was told by seven doctors that he had just a year to live – yet he died at the age of 102.
The doctors told him when he was 101.

18 My parents are having an age problem. He won't act his and she won't tell hers.

19 People who knew him forty years ago say he still looks like he looked then – old!

20 She's eighty-five years old and she still doesn't need glasses. She drinks it straight from the bottle!

21 She's discovered the secret of eternal youth. She lies about her age!

22 The secret of longevity is deep breathing – as long as you can keep it up for eighty or ninety years.

23 The worst thing is growing old by yourself. My wife hasn't had a birthday for five years.

24 They've just opened a new disco for pensioners – it's called the Whisky a Ga-Ga.

25 You know you're getting old when you bend down to tie your shoelaces and you try to think of other things you ought to do while you're down there.

26 FIRST PENSIONER: You know the stuff they used to put in our tea during the war?
SECOND PENSIONER: Yes, why?
FIRST PENSIONER: Well, I think it's beginning to work.

27 How does an eighty-year-old man like you persuade a twenty-two-year-old to be your bride?
Easy. I lied about my age. I told her I was ninety!

28 Tell me, have you lived here all your life?
Not yet.

29 To what do you attribute your old age?
To the fact that I was born a long time ago.

30 Will you still love me when I'm old and feeble?
Of course I do!

31 A 109-year-old man was getting married and a reporter asked him, 'Why would you want to get married at your age?'
And the man said, 'I don't *want* to get married – I *have* to get married!'

32 Ellsworth ran into his fellow old age pensioner Mortimer and he said, 'You look tired. What have you been up to?'
Mortimer replied, 'I've just come back from Paris.'
'How was it?'
'It was fine, but I just wish that I'd been there fifty years ago.'
'You mean when Paris really was Paris?'
'No, when Mortimer really was Mortimer.'

33 I don't date women my own age – there *are* no women my own age.
George Burns

34 I prefer old age to the alternative.
Maurice Chevalier

35 I will never be an old man. To me, old age is always fifteen years older than I am.
Bernard Baruch

36 Old age is the out-patients' department of purgatory.
Lord Cecil

37 The greatest problem about old age is the fear that it may go on too long.
A. J. P. Taylor

38 When I get up in the morning, the first thing I do is read the obituaries. If my name's not in there, I shave.
George Burns

See Advice 5, Children 3, Divorce 26, Hair 10, Health 18, Parents 11, Parties 7; *see also* Age, Birthdays, Grandparents, Middle Age, Nostalgia, Retirement

Opera

1 Grand opera is so called because that's what you'd give not to go.

2 I go to the opera whether I need to sleep or not.

3 I've been going to the opera since I was a tiny child. I can remember *Madame Butterfly* when she was a caterpillar.

4 If you get to the opera before the end, you're on time.

5 The diva was furious as she took her bows at the end of the opera, because she received only nine bouquets. The problem was, she'd paid for ten.

6 What did you hear at the opera yesterday?
Lots of things – the Hughes are going to Boston this summer, the Mortimers are selling up, Lucy's pregnant . . .

7 How wonderful opera would be if there were no singers.
Gioachino Rossini

8 I sometimes wonder which would be nicer – an opera without an interval or an interval without an opera.
Ernest Newman

9 I would rather sing grand opera than listen to it.
Don Herold

10 Opera is when a guy gets stabbed in the back and, instead of bleeding, he sings.
Ed Gardener

See also Music, Singing, Theatre

Opinions

1 Thank you for giving us the benefit of your inexperience.

2 I've changed my mind.
Good. Does it work any better now?

3 When I say, 'Everybody says so', I mean *I* say so.
Ed Howe

See Teenagers 3, 4, Women – The Male View; *see also* Prejudice

Optimism

1 An optimist is a man who gets married at eighty-five and then buys a house near a school.

2 An optimist is someone who starts filling in his crossword puzzle with ink.

3 He's the eternal optimist. If he fell out of a window on the fortieth floor, as he passed the twentieth he'd still be saying, 'So far, so good.'

4 Never borrow money from an optimist. He always expects to get it back!

5 You've got a flat tyre.
Yes, but only at the bottom.

6 An optimist is someone who hasn't gotten around to reading the morning papers.
Earl Wilson

See also Happiness, Optimism and Pessimism, Pessimism

Optimism and pessimism

1 A pessimist is an optimist on his way home from the racetrack.

2 A pessimist is a man who thinks all women are bad. An optimist is a man who hopes they are.

3 An optimist is someone who sees the opportunity in every catastrophe; a pessimist is someone who sees the catastrophe in every opportunity.

4 What's the difference between an optimist and a pessimist?
An optimist invented the aeroplane; a pessimist invented the seat belts.

5 There is no sadder sight than a young pessimist, except an old optimist.
Mark Twain

See also Optimism, Pessimism

P

Parents

1 He's very good to his mother. He never goes home!

2 I was a war baby. As soon as they saw me, my parents started fighting.

3 I've got lots of distant relatives – including my mother and father.

4 It's terribly hard to keep young these days – especially if you have four or five of them.

5 My father and mother are first cousins. That's why I look so much alike.

6 My parents were totally unsuited to having kids. One day my father took me aside and left me there.

7 School days are the happiest days of your life – but only if the kids are old enough to attend!

8 There is nothing like the joy of motherhood – especially when the children are in bed.

9 When I was a kid I wanted to grow up to be an orphan.

10 What's the matter, son?
I've just had a fight with your wife!

11 Would you like to make a contribution to the old folks' home?
Certainly. You can have my parents.

12 Parenthood remains the greatest single preserve of the amateur.
Alvin Toffler

13 The real menace in dealing with a five-year-old is that in no time at all you begin to sound like a five-year-old.
Jean Kerr

14 There may be some doubt as to who are the best people to have charge of children, but there can be no doubt that parents are the worst.
George Bernard Shaw

See Insults 17, Weddings 9; see also Children, Families, Fathers, Grandparents, Mothers

Parking

1 After he's parked the car, it's normally just a short walk to the pavement.

2 Don't leave caravans parked on the side of hills. They can leave if so inclined.

3 I solved my parking problem – I bought a parked car.

4 I was in a parking lot last night full of compact cars. Of course, they weren't like that when they arrived!

5 Remember the good old days, when it cost more to run a car than to park it?

6 POLICEMAN: What are you doing lying in the gutter? Were you knocked over?
MAN: No, I'm OK. But I just found this parking space so I've sent my wife out to buy a car!

7 I had a terrible experience with one of those really tight parking spaces yesterday. This man walking past insisted on helping me. He was going, 'Left, left, right, another few

inches, forward, forward, right, left
... that's it!'

There I was, nestled snugly between these two cars, and the man
said, 'OK?'

And I said, 'No, I was trying to
get out!'

See America and the Americans 3,
Dating 19, Las Vegas 9, Lateness 7,
Retirement 1; *see also* Cars, City
Life, Driving

Parties

1 She believes in the two-party
system: one in the evening and one
a bit later.

2 Then we played Cowboy's Knock
– same thing as Postman's Knock
but there's more horsin' around.

3 We went to a fancy-dress party.
First prize went to a woman with
varicose veins who went as a
roadmap.

4 We're having a coming-out party
for my sister. She's just done six
months in Holloway.

5 What a great party! We played
Chef's Knock. It's like Postman's
Knock but you make more of a
meal of it.

6 Great party, isn't it?
Yes. I wonder who's giving it!

7 I went to a smashing rave-up last
week. It was my grandad's one hundred and third birthday party.
Well, he must have had a great
time.
No, he wasn't there. He died when
he was eighty-seven.

8 OUTRAGED NEIGHBOUR: But didn't
you hear me pounding on the ceiling?
PARTYGOER: Oh, that's OK. We
were making lots of noise ourselves.

9 Did you have a good time at the
party?
So they tell me.

10 So how was last night's party?
Terrible. It was a Gay Nineties
Party. All the men were gay and all
the women were ninety!

See Insults 13, Weddings 7; *see also*
Anniversaries, Birthday Parties,
Christmas, Drink, Games, New
Year, Weddings

Patriotism

1 I am ready to die for my country –
even if it costs me my life.

2 Patriotism, for some, is the willing-
ness to make any sacrifice – as long
as it doesn't hurt business.

3 Every man loves and admires his
own country because it produced
him.
Lord Lytton

4 Patriotism is your conviction that
this country is superior to all others
because you were born in it.
George Bernard Shaw

5 Patriotism is the last refuge of a
scoundrel.
Samuel Johnson

6 Patriotism is the *first* refuge of a
scoundrel.
Ambrose Bierce

See The Army 7; *see also* Politics
and Politicians

Peace

1 Did you hear about the politician
who was a well-known dove – until
one flew over him?

2 He's decided to bury the hatchet –
between his enemy's shoulder
blades.

3 Peace is a period of confusion and
unrest between two wars.

See also Arguments, Fighting, Politics and Politicians, War

Pessimism

1 A pessimist is a man who burns all his bridges in front of him.

2 A pessimist is someone who looks both ways before crossing a one-way street.

3 A pessimist is someone who feels bad when he feels good for fear he'll feel worse when he feels better.

4 A pessimist is a man who gets a clean bill of health from the doctor, then demands a second opinion.

5 A pessimist is someone who sees a cloud in every silver lining.

6 I have to tell you that things are going to get a lot worse before they get worse.

7 My brother is the complete pessimist. He carries a card in his wallet that reads, 'In the event of an accident – I'm not surprised.'

8 A pessimist is a person who has had to listen to too many optimists.
Don Marquis

See also Optimism, Optimism and Pessimism

Pests

1 One flea said to the other, 'Shall we walk home or shall we catch a dog?'

2 These mothballs are hard to use. I've thrown them all now and I still haven't hit a single moth.

3 When Noah built the ark, why didn't he swat those two flies when he had the chance?

4 CUSTOMER: I'd like some rat poison, please.
ASSISTANT: I'm afraid we're out of it. Have you tried Boots?
CUSTOMER: I want to poison them, not kick them to death!

5 Is this aerosol spray good for mosquitoes?
Certainly not. It kills them stone dead.

6 LANDLADY: You won't find a single flea in any of my beds.
LODGER: I know. They're all married with families.

7 Were the mosquitoes big?
Well, I'll tell you something, they showed up on radar!

See Hard Times 18, Lawyers 19; see also Cleanliness, Homes – Squalid, Modern Life

Pets

1 I came home one night and the wife said that the cat had upset her. I told her it was her own fault for eating it.

2 Are you taking that lobster home for tea?
No, he's had his tea. Now I'm taking him to the cinema.

3 Don't be ridiculous! We can't keep a pig in the house. Think of the smell.
Don't worry. He'll soon get used to it.

4 Have you given your goldfish some fresh water?
No, he hasn't finished what I gave him yesterday.

5 I used to have a parrot once that laid square eggs.
Did it ever speak?
Well, it occasionally said, 'Ouch!'

See Earthquakes 3, The English Language 5; see also Animals, Birds, Cats, Dogs, Fish

Philanthropy

1 A philanthropist is a man who gives away publicly the fortune he stole privately.

2 A philanthropist is someone who gives away what he should really be giving back.

3 To enjoy a good reputation, give publicly and steal privately.
Josh Billings
See also Animals, Birds, Cats, Dogs, Fish

4 She's the sort of woman who lives for others. You can always tell the others by their hunted expression!
C. S. Lewis

See also Begging, Gifts, Money, Wealth

Philosophy

1 A route of many roads leading from nowhere to nothing.
Ambrose Bierce

2 I think I think; therefore, I think I am.
Ambrose Bierce

3 Philosophy consists largely of one philosopher arguing that all others are jackasses.
H. L. Mencken

4 Philosophy: unintelligible answers to insoluble problems.
Henry Brooks Adams

5 Philosophy: a blind man in a dark room looking for a black hat which isn't there.
Anon.

6 Any philosophy that can be put 'in a nutshell' belongs there.
Sydney J. Harris

See also Ideas, Intellectuals, Life

Photography

1 A bad photographer is someone who always takes a dim view of things.

2 A good photographer is someone whose photographs always do him justice.

3 If you really look like your passport photograph, the chances are you're not well enough to travel.

4 Smile, please! If only for one hundredth of a second.

5 My photographs don't do me justice.
You don't want justice, you want mercy!

See Figures – Fat 19, Houses 4, Post Office 10; *see also* Art and Artists, Films, Holidays

Plastic surgery

1 She's had her face lifted so many times, it's out of focus.

2 She had her face lifted – but it turned out there was one just like it underneath.

3 She's had so many face-lifts that when she raises her eyebrows, she pulls up her stockings.

4 Q: How does a Hollywood wife pick her nose?
A: From a catalogue.

5 She got her good looks from her father. He's a plastic surgeon.
Groucho Marx

See also Appearance, Beauty, Cosmetics, Doctors, Faces, Hollywood, Hospital, Uglinesss

Poets and poetry

1 Generally speaking, nobody knows a poet is alive until he's dead.

2 A poet more than thirty years old is simply an overgrown child.
H. L. Mencken

3 Poetry is to prose as dancing is to walking.
John Wain

4 Poets are born, not paid.
Wilson Mizner

5 Roses are red,
Violets are blue,
If a poem doesn't rhyme,
Some people think it's somehow
superior to one that does.
Frederick Oliver

6 There are two ways of disliking
poetry: one way is to dislike it, the
other is to read Pope.
Oscar Wilde

See also Books, Limericks, Literature, Writers and Writing

Police

1 He's a lousy detective. He'd have
trouble tracking down an elephant
having a nosebleed in the snow.

2 The police are doing a marvellous
job. I mean, look at the prisons –
they're all full.

3 Three tons of human hair were
stolen last night from a wig factory
in Yeovil. Local police are reported
to be combing the area.

4 We've just got a new Chief Constable. His first job was to arrest the
old Chief Constable.

5 Have you ever been picked up by
the fuzz?
No, but I bet it really hurts!

6 Open up! It's the CID!
Could you spell that for me please?

7 POLICEMAN: I'm going to have to
lock you up for the night.
SUSPECT: What's the charge?
POLICEMAN: There's no charge. It's
all part of the service.

8 The next morning I got up early
and grilled them individually for ten
minutes.
That's the way to treat your
suspects.

Who said anything about suspects?
I'm talking about my sausages!

9 The police are looking for a man
with one eye.
Typical police efficiency!

10 The police are looking for a man
with one eye called Roger.
What's the other eye called?

11 Wait a minute! If you're a police
officer, why are you wearing that
black-and-white patterned suit?
Just a routine check, sir.

See Art and Artists 11, Eyes 1, Figures – Fat 28, Music 24, Stinginess
33, Work 13; see also Courtroom,
Crime, Driving – Police, The Law,
Lawyers, Murder

Politics and politicians

1 A liberal is a man who has enemies
right and left.

2 Do you want a strong, honest,
straight-talking Prime Minister? Or
do you want me?

3 He says he's the man to get the
country moving. He's right! If he
gets in, I'm moving!

4 He tells us that he's standing on his
record – that's one way of making
sure we can't see it.

5 His popularity has hit rock bottom.
Even if he ran unopposed, he'd lose.

6 I admire the straightforward way in
which my opponent dodges the
issues.

7 I bear no ill-will to my opponent.
He did what any despicable little rat
would do in the circumstances.

8 I don't support any organized party.
I vote Labour!

9 I vow to keep the promises I made
during the election campaign – in a
small filing cabinet in the basement
of Number Ten.

10 I wouldn't call him a cheap politician. He's costing this country a fortune!

11 I've got lots of friends in politics. They're the best that money can buy.

12 If you have half a mind to read their manifesto, that's all you'll need.

13 In crime, they say take the money and run. In politics, they say run, *then* take the money.

14 In making your choice, vote for the man who'll do least harm.

15 In the Cabinet you can say what you like about the Prime Minister. But God help you if you say what you *don't* like.

16 Looking at the two candidates, it makes you grateful only one of them can get elected.

17 Many people today vote Conservative because their fathers voted Conservative. On the other hand, many people today vote Labour because their fathers voted Conservative.

18 Not a very responsible politician? I was responsible for losing the last election, wasn't I?

19 Of course our party is looking up. It has to. It's flat on its back!

20 Please support me in my ambition to get the country back on its knees.

21 Politicians are people who put in their place people who put them in their place.

22 Politics is the art of looking for trouble, finding it everywhere, diagnosing it incorrectly, applying the wrong solutions and finding somebody else to blame.

23 Politics is the art of the passable.

24 Socialism is when the state owns everything; capitalism is when your bank does.

25 The French elections: the Socialists stand accused of staying in Toulon and deserving Toulouse.

26 The hotel is expecting a political convention. They're putting their Gideon Bibles on chains.

27 The only president who didn't blame the previous administration for all his troubles was George Washington.

28 There are two sides to every question – and a good politician takes both.

29 There are two lunatics living in Westminster who think they're the Prime Minister. And one of them's right!

30 Things are really tough for the Prime Minister at the moment. I popped into a pub near Downing Street the other night and there he was, propped up against the bar, telling the bartender, 'My country doesn't understand me.'

31 To err is human; to blame it on someone else is politics.

32 What an unstable country! They have so many *coups* and revolutions, the Cabinet meets in a revolving door.

33 What we need is more people giving up politics – but staying in office.

34 When I was a kid I was told anyone could become Prime Minister. I'm beginning to believe it.

35 When I was a kid, fairy-tales used to begin, 'Once upon a time ...' Now they begin, 'If I'm elected ...'

36 Why spend good money having your family tree traced? Go into politics and your opponents will do it for you.

37 You always know when the middle classes have joined the revolutionar-

ies: the Molotov cocktails have olives in them.

38 Which is the most neutral country in the world?
Tibet. It doesn't even interfere in its own internal affairs.

39 Capitalism is the exploitation of one man by another.
And Communism?
Communism is the opposite.

40 I'd join your party if it wasn't so full of self-serving hypocrites.
Oh, there's always room for one more.

41 I'm thinking of standing for the town council.
Yes, but d'you think they'll stand for you?

42 It's said that every new president of the United States should carry with him three envelopes. At the end of his first year in office, when the going is usually rough, he should open the first envelope. Inside he will find a note that reads, 'Blame the previous administration!'
At the end of the second year, if things don't get any better, he should open the second envelope. Inside he will find a note that reads, 'Blame Congress!'
And at the end of the third year, if things still haven't got any better, he should open the third envelope. Inside he will find a note that reads, 'Prepare three envelopes!'

43 My father was a Socialist, my grandfather was a Socialist and that's why I'm a Socialist.
But that's no argument. What if your father was a swindler and your grandfather was a swindler? Would that make *you* a swindler?
No, that would make me a Conservative.

44 A candidate was addressing an election meeting.

'When my party comes to power, workers' wages will be doubled.'
A woman shouted out, 'And what about the tarts and prostitutes who defile our streets?'
The candidate replied, 'When my party comes to power, they will be driven underground.'
And a voice from the back shouted, 'There you go again, favouring the bloody miners.'

45 Within hours of the death of the sitting MP, an ambitious young hopeful rang the local party agent.
'I hope you don't mind me ringing at this time,' he said, 'but I was wondering whether I might take the place of the deceased . . .'
'I hadn't really thought about it,' replied the agent, 'but if the undertaker doesn't mind, then neither will I.'

46 A fanatic is one who can't change his mind and won't change the subject.
Winston Churchill

47 Any party which takes credit for the rain must not be surprised if its opponents blame it for the drought.
Dwight W. Morrow

48 Being in politics is like being a football coach. You have to be smart enough to understand the game . . . and dumb enough to think it's important.
Eugene McCarthy

49 Conservative: a statesman who is enamoured of existing evils, as distinguished from the Liberal, who wishes to replace them with others.
Ambrose Bierce

50 Do not criticize your government when out of the country. Never cease to do so when at home.
Winston Churchill

51 Generosity is a part of my character, and I therefore hasten to assure this government that I will never make an allegation of dishonesty against it wherever a simple explanation of stupidity would suffice.
Leslie Lever

52 I have learned that one of the most important rules of politics is poise – which means looking like an owl after you've behaved like a jackass.
Ronald Reagan

53 I never dared be radical when young, for fear it would make me conservative when old.
Robert Frost

54 I never vote for anyone. I always vote against.
W. C. Fields

55 I once said cynically of a politician, 'He'll double-cross that bridge when he comes to it.'
Oscar Levant

56 I seldom think of politics more than eighteen hours a day.
Lyndon B. Johnson

57 I sometimes marvel at the extraordinary docility with which Americans submit to speeches.
Adlai Stevenson

58 In order to become the master, the politician poses as the servant.
Charles de Gaulle

59 My opponent has a problem. He won't get elected unless things get worse – and things won't get worse unless he's elected.
George Bush

60 No party is as bad as its leaders.
Will Rogers

61 Politics is supposed to be the second oldest profession. I have come to realize that it bears a very close resemblance to the first.
Ronald Reagan

62 Politics: a strife of interests masquerading as a conflict of principles. The conduct of public affairs for private advantage.
Ambrose Bierce

63 The middle of the road is all of the usable surface. The extremes, right and left, are in the gutters.
Dwight D. Eisenhower

64 The politician is an acrobat. He keeps his balance by saying the opposite of what he does.
Maurice Barrès

65 Too bad 90 percent of politicians give the other 10 percent a bad reputation.
Henry Kissinger

See Apathy 1, Birthdays 8, Gambling 5, Intellectuals 5, Journalism 6, Lies 9, Parties 1; see also Capitalism, Communism, Congress, Conservatives, Democracy, Economics, Government, Houses of Parliament, The Presidency, Ronald Reagan, Speakers and Speeches, Margaret Thatcher

Pollution

1 The car-makers have devised a 100 per cent effective anti-pollution device – an ignition key that doesn't fit!

2 It's difficult to escape from pollution these days. Did you hear the story of the ninety-seven-pound weakling who was lying on the sand with his girlfriend and a bully came along and kicked oil in his face?

See Lawyers 14; see also Environment, Pollution – Air, Pollution – Water

Pollution – air

1 Air pollution is getting really bad in London. Yesterday, the West End After Dark tour started at lunchtime.

2 How wonderful it is to wake up in the middle of London every morning to the sounds of the birds coughing.

3 The air pollution was so bad that when a majorette threw her baton into the air, it stuck there.

4 The smog is so bad in Los Angeles, they've started making the freeway signs in Braille.

5 The smog was so bad yesterday, I opened my mouth to speak and chipped a tooth.

6 We have beautiful weather here. When the fog lifts, you can see the smog.

See Modern Times 6; *see also* Environment, Los Angeles, Pollution, Pollution – Water

Pollution – water

1 Bad news from scientists this morning. The chemical formula for water is now H2Ugghhh!

2 I saw a depressing sign at the beach today. It said: PLEASE DON'T THROW STONES IN THE SEA. IT DENTS THE WATER.

3 The fish coming on to the market now are from the area of that oil spill. You've got a choice of two types: regular or unleaded.

4 The fish in the bay are so riddled with mercury, they can take their own temperature.

5 The pollution in our river is unbelievable. I was walking by it the other day and I heard the fish coughing!

6 You want to know how polluted some of our reservoirs are? Last week a dam gave way and the water didn't.

7 Water pollution is getting so bad, there's been a 200 per cent increase

in the sales of scuba-diving equipment.
What's so bad about that?
Most of the customers are fish.

8 Why did your company spill half a million gallons of oil into the Bay of Biscay?
It was a public service. Who wants a squeaky ocean?

See also Environment, Pollution, Pollution – Air

Popularity

1 I was so popular at school that everyone hated me!

2 His fan mail keeps ten secretaries busy.
Answering it?
No, writing it.

3 Why is Alice so unpopular?
She won a popularity contest.

See Telephones 3; *see also* Fame, Friends

Pornography

1 If the purpose of pornography is to excite sexual desire, it is unnecessary for the young, inconvenient for the middle-aged and unseemly for the old.
Malcolm Muggeridge

See also Books, Literature, Sex, Sexual Attraction

Post Office

1 I got my new driving licence in the post this morning. It expired last week!

2 The Post Office is asking staff to be more careful. In future, if the package is marked 'Fragile', they have to throw it underarm.

3 They've increased the cost of postage again.
Why don't they just make the stamps smaller?

4 We've got problems with our postman. He's stopped making house calls.

5 I wrote her a letter every day for three years.
Then what happened?
She married the postman.

6 POSTMAN: I've had to walk five miles to deliver this letter to your farm.
FARMER: You should have posted it!

7 What's the difference between a postbox and an elephant?
I don't know.
Well, I'm not giving you any letters to post.

8 This letter's too heavy. You're going to have to put more stamps on it.
And that's going to make it lighter?

9 You've put too many stamps on this letter.
Oh dear, does that mean it'll go too far now?

10 I got a package in the post today. On the outside was printed: PHOTO-GRAPHS – DO NOT BEND.
Across the bottom was scrawled, 'Oh yes, they do!'

See Drought 6

Poverty

1 He's money-mad. He doesn't have any money and it makes him mad!

2 I started out with nothing. I still have most of it.

3 I've been on the dole so long, they even sent me a ticket for their staff dance.

4 If you saw a cat with a tail on round our way, you knew it was a tourist.

5 In an ideal world, what I'd like to see is drive-in soup kitchens.

6 My dad couldn't afford to buy me a yo-yo for Christmas. All he could afford was a yo.

7 My parents were so poor, they got married just for the rice.

8 Our house was in such a terrible state, it had to be done up before the council would condemn it.

9 Our old age pensioners don't know when they're well off – because they never are.

10 Poor? We were so poor, burglars used to break in and leave things.

11 The only bar in town was like a pigsty with a jukebox. Only there wasn't a jukebox.

12 There's one thing that money can't buy – and that's poverty.

13 They've recently improved my old neighbourhood. They tore it down and put up a slum.

14 Things were so bad that on Sunday lunchtime the family would fight over who got the middle cut of the sardine.

15 We had a fire in our bathroom one night. Fortunately, it didn't spread to the house.

16 We were so poor, the tooth fairy used to leave IOUs.

17 We were so poor I bought one shoe at a time.

18 When I was a kid my family was so poor I had to wear my brother's hand-me-downs – at the same time that he was wearing them.

19 When I was a kid the wolf was at the door so often we called him Rover.

20 When I was a kid, my mother couldn't afford talcum powder so

she used to use self-raising flour. When I got hot, I used to break out in pancakes!

21 When the wolf was at our door, it used to bring its own sandwiches.

22 Without my wife I'd never be what I am today – broke.

23 I can't afford it. I'm a pauper.
You're a pauper? Congratulations! Boy or girl?

24 I wish I had the money to buy Buckingham Palace.
Why on earth do you want to buy Buckingham Palace?
I don't. I just wish I had the money.

25 You'll never believe what happened to me this morning. I found this unopened wage packet!
You lucky devil!
Lucky? You must be kidding! Look at the tax I've paid!

26 I hate the poor and look forward eagerly to their extermination.
George Bernard Shaw

27 Look at me; I worked my way up from nothing to a state of extreme poverty.
Groucho Marx

28 Poverty is an anomaly to rich people. It is very difficult to make out why people who want dinner do not ring the bell.
Walter Bagehot

29 Poverty is no disgrace to a man, but it is confoundedly inconvenient.
Sydney Smith

30 When you meet someone who tells you that poverty is good for the character, you know you're talking to someone who's not suffering from it.
Frederick Oliver

See Ronald Reagan 6, Writers and Writing 23; see also Begging, Debt, Hard Times, Homes – Squalid, Money, Stinginess, Thrift

Pregnancy

1 The young secretary sent her boss a memo which read: 'The reason for my resignation will soon become apparent – and so will I.'

2 DOCTOR: Well, Mrs Harris, I've got some good news for you.
PATIENT: It's not Mrs Harris, it's Miss Harris.
DOCTOR: In that case I've got some *bad* news for you.

3 Mother, there's something I have to tell you. I'm pregnant.
My God! This is terrible! Who's the father?
How should I know? You never let me go steady.

See Figures – Thin 6, Homes 4, Middle Age 4, Old Age 31, Proposals 7, Sex 31, see also Babies, Birth, Birth Control, Sex

Prejudice

1 He's so narrow-minded, he won't even listen to both sides of a cassette.

2 I am free of all prejudice. I hate everyone equally.
W. C. Fields

See also Opinions, Race

Presidency, The

1 Every kid brought up in America has the chance to become President of the United States. It's one of the risks he has to take.

2 I know how Nixon felt about Vietnam. I tried to get out of a book club once.

3 Mothers all want their sons to grow up to be president, but they don't want them to become politicians in the process.
John F. Kennedy

4 Mr Coolidge is the best Democrat we ever had in the White House. He didn't do nothin' but that's what we wanted done.
Will Rogers

5 The pay is good, and I can walk to work.
John F. Kennedy

6 Within the first few months I discovered that being a president is like riding a tiger. A man has to keep riding or be swallowed.
Harry S. Truman

See Hard Times 26; *see also* America and the Americans, Congress, Democracy, Politics and Politicians, Republicans, Ronald Reagan

Prison

1 I'll never forget what my mother said when I first went to prison. She said, 'Hello, son!'

2 I'm in prison for my beliefs. I believed that the bank had sacked its security guards.

3 My uncle went to jail for something he didn't do. He didn't pay his taxes!

4 The judge gave him a total of 300 years in prison. He was lucky not to get life.

5 GOVERNOR: Do you think you can handle this job as a prison guard? We've got some pretty tough customers in here.
NEW GUARD: No problem. I'll tell them what to do and if they don't do it, out they go!

6 I'm in prison because I made big money.
How much?
About a quarter of an inch too big.

7 I've got a brother but he won't be home for three months.
Why, what's he doing?

Three months.

8 My father went to prison for something he didn't do.
What didn't he do?
He didn't run fast enough.

9 Remember, 'Stone walls do not a prison make nor iron bars a cage.'
Well, just don't tell my uncle. He'll be furious that he's been sitting where he has for the last three years.

10 My uncle Ronnie is in prison. Since he's been there he's had his tonsils out, his appendix out and his wisdom teeth out. The governor thinks he's escaping bit by bit.

11 Two prisoners were being shown into a new cell.
One said to the other, 'How long are you in for?'
'Seventy years,' came the reply.
'I'm in for ninety. Take the bed nearest the door since you're getting out first.'

See Drought 4, Gardening 11, Humour 2, Parties 4, Speakers and Speeches 28, Sport 6; *see also* Courtroom, Crime, The Law, Murder, Police

Problems

1 I put my problems down to three things: women, money – and both those two.

2 The problems of the world today are so complex that even teenagers don't have the answer.

3 Q: Can you tell me the best way to remove a patch of white paint from the seat of a pair of blue trousers?
A: It's quite simple. All you need is a bottle of turpentine, a stiff brush and an ordinary pair of scissors.

4 Q: I am a Boy Scout. Is it true that the best way to start a fire is to have two pieces of wood?

A: You're right. The best way to start a fire *is* to have two pieces of wood, but just make sure that at least one of them is a match.

Procrastination

1 A procrastinator is someone who puts off until tomorrow the things he's already put off until today.

2 I'm really going to do something about my procrastination – just as soon as I can get round to it.

3 Never put off until tomorrow what you can put off for good.

4 Never put off until tomorrow what you can do the day after tomorrow.
Mark Twain

See also Lateness

Professions

1 A profession is something you study for years to get into, then work for the rest of your life trying to earn enough money to get out of.

2 I'm trying to sell my house at the minute and I've come to the conclusion that estate agents are people who couldn't make the grade as second-hand car salesmen.

3 Professionals built the *Titanic*; amateurs built the Ark.

4 Incomprehensible jargon is the hallmark of a profession.
Kingman Brewster

See Actors and Acting 17, Teaching 7; *see also* Accountants, Banks and Banking, Business, The Office, Work

Progress

1 Keeping things pretty much the same as they've always been is enough progress for me.

2 Progress is the continuing effort to make the things we eat, drink and wear as good as they used to be.

3 Progress is going around in the same circles – but faster.

4 What we call progress is the exchange of one nuisance for another nuisance.
Havelock Ellis

See also Gadgets, Modern Times

Proposals

1 When I asked her father for her hand, he said, 'You can take the whole girl or nothing!'

2 BOY: Can I change your name to mine?
GIRL: Do you think 'Christopher' would suit me?

3 Can I have your daughter for my wife?
Well, bring your wife round and we'll see.

4 Darling, will you marry me?
Have you seen my father?
Lots of times, but I still want to marry you.

5 FATHER: So you want to marry my daughter. Don't you think you ought to see my wife first?
YOUNG MAN: I *have*, sir, and I *still* want to marry your daughter.

6 GIRL'S FATHER: So you want to become my son-in-law?
BOYFRIEND: No, I don't. But since I want to marry your daughter, I can't see any way out of it.

7 How do most young men propose?
'You're going to have a what?'

8 I've been asked to get married lots of times.
Who asked you?
My mother and father.

9 Let's get married!
But who'd have us?

Prudery

10 Marry my daughter? But she's only a girl!
I know. That's why I want to marry her!

11 Sir, I have been going out with your daughter for five years now . . .
So what do you want – a pension?

12 Sir, I wish to marry your daughter.
Are you sure you can support a family?
I'm certain.
But you do realize there are eight of us?

13 Sir, I've come to ask you for your daughter's hand.
Good. You can take the one that's always in my pocket!

14 What would you say if I asked you to marry me?
Nothing. I can't talk and laugh at the same time!

15 HE: May I have your hand in marriage?
SHE: What?
HE: May I change your name to mine?
SHE: Pardon?
HE: You don't seem to understand. I want you to be the mother of my children.
SHE: Goodness. How many have you got?

16 A young man wrote, 'Dear Alice, Please forgive me but I'm becoming forgetful. I proposed to you last night but I've forgotten whether you said "Yes" or "No".'
And Alice replied, 'Dear Laurence, So glad to hear from you. I remember saying "No" to somebody last night but I'd forgotten who it was.'

17 I said to her father, 'Sir, the bright sunshine of your daughter's smile dispels the dark clouds of my life.'
And he said, 'Are you proposing or is this the weather forecast?'

18 Marry me and I'll never look at another horse!
Groucho Marx

See also Dating, Engagements, Marriage, Romance, Weddings

Prudery

1 A prude is someone who wants her conscience to be your guide.

2 Blessed are the pure, for they shall inhibit the earth.

3 I led a very sheltered life – I was twenty before I was allowed to have a full-length mirror.

4 If God had wanted us to go naked, we would have been born that way.

5 Sex, unlike justice, should not be seen to be done.

6 She's so modest, she wears a blindfold when she takes a bath.

7 There's nothing wrong with sex. It's a perfectly natural, disgusting act.

8 SECRETARY: I always warn people new to the office about Mr Rogers. He's got an absolutely filthy mind – judging by all the dirty songs that he knows.
NEW GIRL: But surely he doesn't sing them around the office!
SECRETARY: Well, maybe not – but he certainly whistles them!

9 There is only one honest impulse at the bottom of Puritanism, and that is the impulse to punish the man with a superior capacity for happiness.
H. L. Mencken

See Accountants 13, Thanksgiving 2; *see also* Censorship, Morality, Nudity, Sex

Psychiatry

1 A psychiatrist is called a shrink because that's what he does to your wallet.

2 A psychiatrist is someone who will listen to you as long as you don't make sense.

3 A psychiatrist is a mental detective.

4 Anyone who goes to a psychiatrist ought to have his head examined.

5 He won't go to a shrink. He thinks he's small enough already.

6 I couldn't afford to go to a psychiatrist so I went into group therapy. Instead of couches, we had bunk-beds.

7 I don't really trust my psychiatrist. First of all, he tells me he doesn't believe in shock therapy. Then he gives me the bill.

8 I had a very friendly psychiatrist. In fact, he was so friendly he used to lie down on the couch with me.

9 I started going to a psychiatrist when I was slightly cracked – and kept going until I was completely broke.

10 Kleptomaniacs are people who help themselves because they can't help themselves.

11 My psychiatrist has helped me a lot. I used to be too afraid to answer the phone. Now I answer it whether it rings or not.

12 My psychiatrist and I are making real progress. He's taken all my little fears and turned them into one big phobia.

13 The funny thing about going to a psychiatrist is that you have to lie down to learn how to stand on your own two feet.

14 Psychiatry is the only business where the customer is always wrong.

15 Roses are red,
Violets are blue,
I'm a schizophrenic
And so am I.

16 She's so pathologically tidy that her doctor sent her to a psychiatrist. But it was a complete waste of time. She spent the first forty minutes rearranging the couch.

17 The good thing about being a kleptomaniac is that you can always take something for it.

18 There's a new instant psychiatrist in Los Angeles. He's got a sign outside that says: TWO COUCHES. NO WAITING.

19 Are you troubled by improper thoughts?
Certainly not. I enjoy them!

20 Everybody hates me.
Of course they don't. Everybody hasn't met you yet.

21 For years I used to think I was a dog. Then I went to a psychiatrist and he soon put things right.
So how are you now?
Fine. Feel my nose.

22 How much did the psychiatrist charge the elephant?
Twenty pounds for the session and 200 pounds for the couch.

23 My son has never been to a psychiatrist.
Why? What's wrong with him?

24 My wife thinks she's the Queen of England.
Have you ever told her she isn't?
What, and blow my chances of a knighthood!

25 PATIENT: Doctor, I think I'm suffering from schizophrenia.
DOCTOR:
a) That makes four of us.
b) Oh, go chase yourself.

c) Well, sit down and tell me all about yourselves.

26 PATIENT: Every evening, about seven o'clock, my husband imagines he's a light bulb.
PSYCHIATRIST: Well, why don't you tell him he isn't?
PATIENT: What, and eat in the dark!

27 PATIENT: I suppose what makes me different is that I always get my own way. I'm completely selfish. Whatever I want – women, possessions, money, power – I just go out and get, regardless of others.
PSYCHIATRIST: I see. So how long have you had this complaint?
PATIENT: Who's complaining?

28 PATIENT: I'm worried. I keep thinking I'm a horse.
PSYCHIATRIST: Well, I think I can cure you. But it's going to cost a lot of money.
PATIENT: Money's no object. I've just won the Grand National!

29 PATIENT: I'm worried that I'm mad. I keep thinking I'm a packet of biscuits.
PSYCHIATRIST: A packet of biscuits? You mean those little square ones with lots of little holes in them?
PATIENT: That's right!
PSYCHIATRIST: You're not mad ...
PATIENT: Thank goodness!
PSYCHIATRIST: You're crackers!

30 PATIENT: I just don't seem to be able to get on with anyone.
PSYCHIATRIST: And why do you think that is?
PATIENT: How should I know, you moron!

31 PATIENT: My family thinks there's something wrong with me because I love pancakes.
PSYCHIATRIST: But there's nothing wrong with that. I myself love pancakes.
PATIENT: Really? Then you must come and see me! I've got trunks and trunks full of them!

32 PATIENT: My husband has developed this delusion that he is an aeroplane.
PSYCHIATRIST: Have him come in and see me tomorrow.
PATIENT: I'm afraid he can't come tomorrow. He's appearing in court for flying low over Haywards Heath.

33 PATIENT: The trouble is, my husband thinks he's a refrigerator.
PSYCHIATRIST: Well, that's not so bad. It's rather a harmless complex.
PATIENT: Well, maybe. But he sleeps with his mouth open and the light keeps me awake.

34 PSYCHIATRIST: Now tell me, do you normally stir your coffee with your right hand?
PATIENT: Oh, yes.
PSYCHIATRIST: Mmmm, that's odd. Most people use a spoon.

35 PSYCHIATRIST: So what's your job?
PATIENT: I'm a car mechanic.
PSYCHIATRIST: OK, get under the couch.

See Ethnic Jokes 3, Hollywood 6, Light-bulb Jokes 2, Suicide 2, Ugliness 3, Vanity 12, see also Hypochondria, Insanity, Psychology

Psychology

1 A psychologist is someone who goes to a strip-tease show and watches the audience.

2 While a conjuror gets rabbits out of hats, a psychologist gets habits out of rats.

3 PROFESSOR: Bagshawe, name the man who originated study into conditioned reflexes.
BAGSHAWE: Um ...
PROFESSOR: Does the name Pavlov ring a bell ...?

See also Fear, Insanity, Psychiatry

Public relations

1 Some are born great, some achieve greatness and some hire public relations officers.
Daniel J. Boorstin

See Hollywood 7; see also Advertising

R

Race

1 Is racial prejudice a pigment of the imagination?

2 What do you call a black hitch-hiker?
Stranded.

3 God is Black – and Boy is He Mad!
Bumper sticker

4 It is a great shock at the age of five or six to find that in a world of Gary Coopers, you are the Indian.
James Baldwin

See Fame 8, Heaven 1; *see also* Prejudice

Radio

1 A disc jockey is someone who talks until he gives you a headache and then tries to sell you something to cure it.

2 I started my career working on six different stations – four railway and two petrol.

3 I was a pioneer in radio. I was one of the first people to be switched off.

4 I'm not saying he's ugly but he's got a perfect face for radio.

5 I've got a two-way radio. It either works or it doesn't.

6 Radio is a device that allows people who have nothing to say to talk to people who aren't listening.

7 So tune in again next week: same time, same station, same jokes.

8 They say the longest word in the English language is the one that comes after, 'And now a word from our sponsors . . .'

9 How come you didn't get the job as a radio announcer?
They s-s-s-said I-I-I w-w-was t-t-too t-t-t-tall.

See also Advertising, Talkers, Television

Railways

1 Another thing commuters miss when they move away from the city is the train.

2 Don't race trains to level-crossings. If it's a tie, you lose.

3 My uncle used to be a train driver but he got the sack – for over-taking.

4 Does this train stop at Dover?
Well, if it doesn't, there's going to be one hell of a splash!

5 I want to catch the late train to Manchester.
Take the six thirty. That's usually as late as any.

6 Is this train on time?
We're just happy if it's on the track.

7 PASSENGER: Why did you build the station so far out of town?
STATIONMASTER: We wanted to have it near the track.

8 TRAIN PASSENGER: Return ticket, please!
BOOKING CLERK: Where to?
TRAIN PASSENGER: Back here, of course!

9 TRAIN PASSENGER: Single to Manchester, please!

BOOKING CLERK: That'll be nine pounds fifty. Change at Crewe.
TRAIN PASSENGER: I'll have my change here if you don't mind!

10 Which end of the train should I get off?
It doesn't matter. It stops at both ends!

11 PASSENGER: What time do we get to Birmingham?
GUARD: Ten fifteen.
PASSENGER: Is there any way I can get there sooner?
GUARD: Yes. Sit in the front carriage!

12 The train was making its usual slow progress through the West Country when it came to a juddering halt. After a few minutes, a passenger asked the guard what the problem was. The guard explained that there was a tortoise on the track.
'But we stopped because of a tortoise on the track five miles ago!'
'I know,' said the guard, 'but we've caught up with it again.'

13 Two drunks were staggering along the railroad tracks. One said, 'I've never seen so many steps in my whole life!'
And the other replied, 'I don't mind the steps, but this low railing is killing me.'

14 The most common of all antagonisms arises from a man's taking a seat beside you on the train, a seat to which he is completely entitled.
Robert Benchley

See The Army 2, Fish 3, Lateness 10, Manners 4, New York 3; see also Travel

Rain

1 Into each life some rain must fall – and usually on weekends.

2 It never stops raining in Rhyl. I tell you, it's a great place for anyone who ever wanted to live in a car-wash!

3 It was raining so hard, people were jumping into the river to save themselves from drowning.

4 It's raining cats and dogs!
I know. I just stepped in a poodle!

See Clothes 11, 12; see also Weather, Wind

Reagan, Ronald

1 For two weeks during his presidency, Ronnie and Nancy switched jobs – and he tried running the country for a while.

2 A triumph of the embalmer's art.
Gore Vidal

3 He has done for monetarism what the Boston Strangler did for door-to-door salesmen.
Denis Healey

4 I'm not worried about the deficit: it's big enough to take care of itself.
Ronald Reagan

5 Ronald Reagan is not a typical politician because he doesn't know how to lie, cheat and steal. He always had an agent for that.
Bob Hope

6 Ronald Reagan must love poor people, because he's creating so many more of them.
Edward Kennedy

7 They say hard work never hurt anyone, but I figure why take the chance?
Ronald Reagan

See also Congress, Conservatives, Politics and Politicians, The Presidency

Records

1 Dear Sir, I have a circular piece of

black plastic, about 12 inches across, with a hole in the middle.
Is this a record?

2 The only record I have ever wanted to break is the one my neighbour plays at two o'clock in the morning.

See Drink 58, Restaurants – Waiters 1; *see also* Success

Reincarnation

1 If reincarnation actually happens, I suspect I'm coming back as a sponge.

2 My uncle believed in reincarnation. In his will, he left everything to himself.

3 How long have you believed in reincarnation?
Ever since I was a young gerbil.

See also Death, Life

Rejection

1 I must decline your invitation owing to a subsequent engagement.
Oscar Wilde

Relaxation

1 I love lying back, relaxing in the bath. Sometimes I even put water in.

See also Games, Holidays, Sport, Work

Religion

1 Another 300 vicars were sacked last week, making a total of 2,000 holy unemployed.

2 I don't go to church much any more. I'm a Seventh Day Absentist.

3 I go to the bingo organized by my local church. The priest calls out the numbers in Latin so the atheists can't win.

4 I'm very religious – which means, of course, that I love my neighbour. Mind you, I really hate her husband!

5 I've joined a new church. It's very liberal. They've whittled it down to five commandments and five suggestions!

6 Our church welcomes all denominations – fives, tens, twenties . . .

7 She's so religious she wears stained-glass spectacles.

8 The meek will inherit the earth – as long as nobody minds.

9 We've got the most incredibly inspiring preacher. After every sermon, the congregation give him a kneeling ovation!

10 FATHER O'MALLEY: When are you going to give up and treat yourself to a taste of pork?
RABBI WEINSTEIN: On your wedding day!

11 FIRST PRIEST: Hello, I'm sure we've met before. My name's Brother Michael.
SECOND PRIEST: I don't remember the name but the faith is familiar.

12 FIRST RABBI: We've got to do something. Many of the young people in our synagogue are converting to the Quaker faith.
SECOND RABBI: I've noticed that too. In fact, some of my best Jews are Friends!

13 HOUSEHOLDER: Do you believe in the hereafter?
EVANGELIST: Yes, we do.
HOUSEHOLDER: Then, hereafter don't bother me again!

14 I'm just a poor preacher.
I know. I've heard your sermons.

15 Why do Baptists object to fornication?

They're afraid it might lead to dancing.

16 The bishop reprimanded a vicar for an indiscretion with his housekeeper. Apparently, they found his vest in her pantry and her pants in his vestry.

17 The plane had hit a patch of severe turbulence and the passengers were holding on tight as it rocked and reeled through the night. A little old lady turned to the minister who was sitting behind her and said, 'You're a man of God. Can't you do something about this?'

And he replied, 'Sorry, I can't. I'm in sales, not management.'

18 The wife of the churchwarden was taking her seat in the front row of the pews when she tripped and rolled over, revealing her underwear to the congregation.

Seeing her predicament, the priest stood in front of her and said, 'If any man should look at this poor, unfortunate woman, may the Lord strike him blind!'

And a man in the third row turned to his friend and said, 'I think I'll risk one eye.'

19 A Christian is a man who feels repentance on Sunday for what he did on Saturday and is going to do again on Monday.
Anon.

20 Every day, people are straying away from the church and going back to God.
Lenny Bruce

21 He charged nothing for his preaching, and it was worth it.
Mark Twain

22 If you want to see a man at his worst, see what he does to his fellow man in the name of God.
Anon.

23 In my opinion, parsons are very like other men, and neither the better nor the worse for wearing a black gown.
Earl of Chesterfield

24 Religion is man's search for reassurance that he won't be dead when he will be.
Anon.

See Cannibals 2, Food 27, Golf 13, 21, Graffiti 5, Laziness 16, 30, Marriage 38, 54, Morality 1, Names 4, School 17, Speakers and Speeches 15, Vanity 5, 16; see also Atheism, Catholics, Church, God, Heaven, Hell, Jews

Republicans

1 In this world of sin and sorrow there is always something to be thankful for; as for me, I rejoice that I am not a Republican.
H. L. Mencken

See also Congress, Conservatives, Politics and Politicians, Ronald Reagan

Restaurants

1 I went into this Chinese restaurant and asked for a karate chop and two veg.

2 I've just had a note from the canteen. They say that today they're using roast beef instead of chicken in the turkey sandwiches.

3 It was a really fancy restaurant. Before you could use the fingerbowl, you had to wash your hands.

4 It was the most authentic Mexican restaurant I've ever been to. When the waiter brought me a glass of water, he warned me not to drink it!

5 It's a terrific Chinese restaurant. They serve you all the food you can

eat for 50p. Trouble is, they only give you one chopstick.

6 On the menu at a vegetarian restaurant – veg and two veg.

7 The trouble with that restaurant is, it's so crowded nobody goes there any more.

8 There's a new Chinese restaurant opened in New York. It's got white chopsticks for blind people.

9 They'd run out of caviare. So they brought us a plate of tapioca and some dark glasses.

10 This place was incredibly expensive. An after-dinner mint was what you needed to pay the bill.

11 We were eating in this open-air café when it started raining. It took us an hour and a half to finish our soup.

12 Whenever I go to a restaurant, I always ask for a table near the waiter.

13 DINER: Have you got a buffet?
WAITER: It's 'boofay' – the 't' is silent.
DINER: Not when I drink it!

14 I know a place where we can eat dirt cheap.
I don't want to eat dirt at any price!

15 Will you join me in a bowl of soup?
Is it big enough for both of us?

16 A man goes into a café and says, 'I want a sausage burnt on one side to a crisp but uncooked in the middle, some .cold baked beans and a fried egg with a rock-hard yolk topped with some really greasy bacon.'
And the café owner says, 'But I can't cook a meal like that!'
And the man says, 'But you did yesterday!'

17 I went into this restaurant yesterday that advertises all you can eat for $1.99. So I filled my plate up at the counter, gobbled it down and went back for more.
But the manager stood in front of me, took my plate and said, 'That's all you can eat for $1.99!'

18 Courteous and efficient self-service.
Sign in restaurant window

19 Same-day Service!
Sign outside Ed Debevic's diner, Beverly Hills

See Crime 4, Doctors 53, Hard Times 2, Stinginess 1, 15; see also Drink, Food, Restaurants – Waiters

Restaurants – waiters

1 A man in Stoke-on-Trent recently went thirty-seven days without eating – then he finally gave his order to another waiter.

2 I asked for a bottle of the house red. He brought me the tomato ketchup.

3 Waiter, if this is coffee, bring me tea but if this is tea, bring me coffee.

4 CUSTOMER: There are fingerprints all over this glass!
WAITER: What other part of the body do you want it washed with?

5 DINER: Are you the same waiter who took my order?
WAITER: Yes, sir.
DINER: Well, you don't look a day older.

6 DINER: Do you serve crabs in this restaurant?
WAITER: We serve anyone, sir. Take a seat.

7 DINER: Excuse me, will my hamburger be long?
WAITER: No, sir, it'll be round.

8 DINER: Hamburger without onions, please.
WAITER: I'm sorry, we're right out

of onions. I'll have to make it without the tomatoes.

9 DINER: I'm sorry, waiter. I find I have just enough money to pay for my meal but I have nothing to tip you with.
WAITER: Let me add up that bill again, sir.

10 DINER: Is the fish fresh?
WAITER: I'll say. It's still chewing the bait.

11 DINER: Look out! You've got your thumb in my soup!
WAITER: Don't worry. It isn't very hot!

12 DINER: Waiter, call the manager. I can't eat this terrible food.
WAITER: There's no point, sir. He won't eat it either.

13 DINER: Waiter, my boiled egg is bad.
WAITER: Nothing I can do about it. I only laid the table.

14 DINER: Waiter, I don't like this cheese.
WAITER: But it's Gruyère, sir.
DINER: Well, bring me some that grew somewhere else!

15 DINER: Waiter, have you any wild duck?
WAITER: No, sir, but we have a tame one we could aggravate for you.

16 DINER: Waiter, do you have any stewed prunes?
WAITER: We do, sir.
DINER: Well, give them some black coffee and sober them up!

17 DINER: Waiter, do you have frog's legs?
WAITER: Yes, sir.
DINER: Good, hop over the counter and get me a cheese sandwich!

18 DINER: Waiter, I can't cut this steak!
WAITER: Hold on, I'll get a knife sharpener.

19 DINER: Waiter, this coffee tastes like mud!
WAITER: Well, it was ground only half an hour ago!

20 DINER: Waiter, I don't like all the flies in this dining room!
WAITER: Well, tell me which ones you don't like and I'll chase them out for you!

21 DINER: Wait a minute, what's your thumb doing on my steak?
WAITER: I don't want it to fall on the floor again, sir.

22 FIRST CUSTOMER: The service in this restaurant is terrible!
SECOND CUSTOMER: Yes, but the food is so bad I don't mind waiting!

23 I can't find any chicken in the chicken soup!
Well, you won't find any horse in the horseradish either!

24 These eggs just came up from the country.
Yes, but *which* country?

25 This is the best fish we've had for years.
Well, bring me some you haven't had for so long!

26 Waiter, what time is it?
Sorry, sir, this isn't my table.

27 Waiter, there's a fly in my soup.
They don't care what they eat, do they, sir.

28 Waiter, there's a dead fly in my soup.
Yes, sir, it's the heat that kills them!

29 Waiter, there's a fly in my soup!
Don't make a fuss, sir. They'll all want one.

30 Waiter, what's this fly doing in my soup?
Looks like the breaststroke to me, sir.

31 Waiter, this food isn't fit for a pig!
Hold on, I'll go and get some that is.

32 WAITER: Here is your wine, sir.
DINER: Thank you. What year is it?
WAITER: It's 1993, sir. It's on the top of all the newspapers.

33 WAITER: How do you like your coffee? It's Brazilian.
CUSTOMER: So that's where you've been!

34 WAITER: How did you find the steak, sir?
DINER: I just moved the potato and there it was.

35 We've got everything on the menu today, sir.
So I see. Bring me a clean one!

36 A waiter with a bad cut on his hand was lying on a bed in the casualty department of the local hospital. As a doctor passed him, he cried out, 'Doctor, please help me, I've been lying here for three hours!'
'I'm sorry,' said the doctor, 'this isn't my table!'

37 The customer had been waiting for ages for the soup to arrive. Finally, he caught the eye of the manager and asked, 'Excuse me, did the waiter who originally took my order leave any next of kin?'

See Britain and the British 4, Cannibals 5, Divorce 6, Supernatural 2; *see also* Coffee, Drink, Food, Restaurants

Retirement

1 At his retirement ceremony the boss told him, 'The way we see it, we're not so much losing a worker as gaining a parking space.'

2 At his retirement ceremony the boss told him, 'I know this is a day you've been looking forward to for some years now, but, believe me, not half as much as we have.'

3 At his retirement ceremony the boss told him, 'It's going to be very hard to replace you – mainly because the board doesn't think it's necessary.'

4 At his retirement ceremony the boss told him, 'We don't know how we'll ever replace you – mainly because we haven't quite worked out what it was you did.'

5 I get a regular monthly pension. The money may not be much, but the working conditions are terrific!

6 Look before you leap. Before you retire, stay home for a week and watch daytime television.

7 Retirement is that period in your life when you wake up in the morning with nothing to do and go to bed at night with it still not done.

8 Retirement means twice as much husband on half as much money.

9 Why is it that when you retire and time is no longer so important, they give you a watch?

10 You can always tell who's the guest of honour at a retirement lunch. He's the only one who yawns after the boss's favourite joke.

11 BOSS: I called you in because I want to discuss the question of retirement.
WORKER: But that's ridiculous. You're still a young man!

See Insurance 2, Poverty 9; *see also* Age, Birthdays, Middle Age, Old Age, Tributes, Unemployment, Work

Robbery

1 Excuse me, I'm doing a survey on self-defence. Would you know how to defend yourself against a karate attack?
No, I'm afraid I wouldn't.
Good! Give me your wallet!

2 JUDGE: Why is it that every time

you've been caught, you've been robbing a third-floor flat?

DEFENDANT: Well, that's my storey and I'm sticking to it.

3 Kleptomania. Is it catching?
No, it's taking.

4 Suddenly I looked out of the house and saw the police outside. So I jumped out of the back window and ran for my life.
But what about your loot?
I left it behind. I could never play the thing anyway.

5 One day I took my old aunt to one of the big department stores. She had a great time. I can still see her standing outside the main door with the silver glinting in her hair – and the store detective taking it out a fork at a time.

See Servants 7, Stinginess 28; *see also* Courtroom, Crime, The Law, Lawyers, Police, Prison

Romance

1 I know an awful lot about women – mostly from what I've been able to pick up.

2 I met her at a dance and she was the prettiest thing on the floor. I can see her now, lying there.

3 I met her in a revolving door and I've been going round with her ever since.

4 I met my wife at a dance. It was really embarrassing. I thought she was at home with the kids.

5 I told my secretary I wanted some old-fashioned loving – so she introduced me to her grandmother.

6 I've finally found the most wonderful woman. The trouble is, her husband wants her back.

7 I've got a new girlfriend. She reads modern novels, likes classical music and impressionist art and loves visiting museums. But then, nobody's perfect.

8 She's been mad about boys ever since she found out she wasn't one of them.

9 GIRL: If I come up to your room, do you promise to be good?
BOY: I promise to be fantastic!

10 I was at this party last night and there was this gorgeous young actress there and she kept annoying me all night.
I bet she didn't even look at you!
You're right. That's what kept annoying me!

See Post Office 5; *see also* Dating, Dating – Chat-up Lines, Kissing, Proposals, Sex, Sexual Attraction, The Single Life

S

Sailing

1 He not only lied about the size of his boat, he made me row it.

2 The day a man buys a boat is the second happiest day of his life. The happiest day, of course, is the day he sells it.

See Wealth 1; *see also* Boats and Ships, Holidays, The Navy, The Sea

Sales and selling

1 He calls himself an independent salesman. He takes orders from no one.

2 I tried selling doorbells door to door. But when I rang, the people who needed the product didn't know I was there!

3 If I were to paint you a picture of last year's sales, it would be a still life.

4 My motto is: a foot in the door is worth two on the desk.

5 The role of the receptionist is a very important one. She is the first person you see when you visit a company. And, if she's doing her job right, she's the *only* person you see when you visit a company.

6 What a salesman – he could sell underarm deodorant to the Venus de Milo!

7 FIRST SALESMAN: I only got three orders this week.
SECOND SALESMAN: What were they?
FIRST SALESMAN: Get out, stay out and don't come back!

8 FIRST SALESMAN: I made some very valuable contacts today.
SECOND SALESMAN: Yes, I didn't sell anything either.

9 A salesman called at the office of a very difficult potential buyer at the end of a hectic day.
As the prospect invited the salesman into his office, he said, 'You should count yourself lucky. Do you realize that already today I've refused to see fifteen salesmen?'
And the salesman said, 'I know. I'm them!'

10 The sales manager had run out of ways to motivate his men. Finally, he called them together and said, 'Today I'm launching a sales contest. And the man who wins gets to keep his job!'

11 The young woman selling cosmetics door to door in a posh district of town wasn't having much success when suddenly she had a bright idea. The next house she came to, when a woman opened the door, the young saleswoman said, 'I don't suppose you'd be interested in our new range of lipstick. The lady next door said it would be far too expensive for you.'

12 There were three stores next to each other on the high street all competing against each other for business. One day, the owner of the middle store walked out into the street and saw, hanging outside the store on one side, an enormous poster that read, 'Gigantic Sale Now On!' and outside the other an equally

large poster reading, 'Biggest Sale Ever!'

The shopkeeper thought for a moment, then dashed into his store, came out and put up a small sign that read, 'Entrance to Sale!'

13 Two hat manufacturers sent salesmen to Africa. Within a few days one of the salesmen cabled back to his company, 'Disaster – no one in Africa wears a hat! Am returning home immediately.'

At about the same time, the second salesman sent a cable to his company, 'Great news – no one in Africa is wearing a hat! Start production immediately.'

14 People will buy anything that's 'one to a customer'.
Sinclair Lewis

See The Army 11; *see also* Advertising, Bosses, Professions, Shopping, Unemployment, Work

Saving

1 I'm saving money because one day it might be worth something again.

2 Have you put anything away for a rainy day?
Yes, my wellingtons.

See also Banks and Banking, Money, Stinginess, Thrift

Scepticism

1 I respect faith, but doubt is what gets you an education.
Wilson Mizner

2 She believed in nothing; only her scepticism kept her from being an atheist.
Jean-Paul Sartre

See also Atheism

School

1 At the bottom of the student's report, the teacher wrote, 'If you won't believe half of what he says goes on in school, I won't believe half of what he says goes on at home.'

2 I hated my maths teacher. He did everything to embarrass me. One day he even asked me to count to ten – from memory!

3 I went to a tough school. I remember the teacher asking what comes at the end of a sentence and a kid says, 'An appeal.'

4 My brother went to a very exclusive school. You had to be sent there by a judge!

5 My school was so tough, the school magazine had an obituary column.

6 What I wanted to know when I was at school was why did the teachers get paid when it was the kids who did all the work?

7 When I was at school, my handwriting was so bad the teacher couldn't tell if I could spell or not!

8 When it came to education, my father wanted me to have all the advantages he never had. So he sent me to a girls' school.

9 Dad, can I have an encyclopedia?
Certainly not. You can walk to school like all the other kids.

10 FATHER: I'm ashamed of you. When I was your age, I could name all the presidents in order.
SON: Yes, but there were only two of them then!

11 I was very clever at school. Every time the teacher asked a question, I was the first to put up my hand.
You must have been clever.
I was. Because by the time I got

back, the question had been an-
swered.

12 I'm woried about you being at the
bottom of the class.
But, Mum, they teach the same
things at both ends.

13 If I cut two apples and four pears in
ten pieces what will I get?
Fruit salad.

14 So how were the exam questions?
They were easy. It was the answers
I had trouble with.

15 TEACHER: Alice, do you know how
to spell 'banana'?
ALICE: Yes, I do. I just don't know
when to stop.

16 TEACHER: Consider this sentence: 'I
don't have no fun at the weekend.'
How should I correct this?
PUPIL: Try and find a boyfriend.

17 TEACHER: Do you know what
Good Friday is?
STUDENT: No, what good is it?

18 TEACHER: I wish you'd pay a little
attention!
PUPIL: I'm paying as little as I can!

19 TEACHER: If you were to add 59,
725 and 27,640, then multiply by 7,
add and divide by 15 what would
you get?
PUPIL: The wrong answer.

20 TEACHER: If I had ten oranges in
one hand and seven oranges in the
other, what would I have?
PUPIL: Big hands.

21 TEACHER: Name five animals that
live in the jungle.
PUPIL: A lion . . . and four giraffes.

22 TEACHER: What comes after 'O'?
CLASS: Yeah!

23 TEACHER: What is the chief use of
cowhide?
PUPIL: To keep the cow in!

24 TEACHER: What is a 'fortification'?
PUPIL: Two twentifications?

25 TEACHER: You missed school yesterday, didn't you?
PUPIL: Not a bit!

26 TEACHER: You got almost 100 in
your exam.
PUPIL: You mean ninety-eight?
TEACHER: No, I mean two noughts.

27 TEACHER: You can't sleep in my
class!
STUDENT: If you didn't talk so much
I could!

28 What's your son going to be when
he leaves school?
At this rate, an octogenarian.

29 A seven-year-old was giving his
younger brother advice on starting
school. 'Whatever you do, don't
learn to spell "cat" – because if you
do, after that the words just get
harder and harder.'

30 I had a terrible time when I was
eleven years old.
First, I got tonsillitis, which was
followed by pneumonia. Then I got
appendicitis and that was followed
by poliomyelitis. After that I got
catarrh and finally ended up with
bronchitis. Then they gave me anal-
gesics and inoculations.
I honestly can't remember having
a worse spelling test.

31 On the first day of school the
teacher was getting to know her
new pupils. She pointed to a boy in
the front row. 'And what's your
name?'
'I'm Julie,' he replied.
'No,' said the teacher, 'I want
your proper name. You should say,
"I'm Julius."'
She then turned to the next little
boy. 'And what's *your* name?'
And the little boy said, 'I'm Bil-
ious.'

32 WOODWORK TEACHER: So, Eric,
what are you making?
ERIC: A portable.

WOODWORK TEACHER: A portable what?

ERIC: I don't know yet. I've only made the handle.

See Actors and Acting 21, Baldness 4, Beards and Moustaches 5, Catholics 2, Childhood 1, Farming 13, Middle Age 9, Parents 7, Unemployment 6; *see also* Education, The English Language, History, Languages, Maths, Teaching, University

Science

1 We need science to help us solve all the problems we wouldn't have if there were no science.

2 We owe a lot to Thomas Edison. If it wasn't for him, we'd be watching television by candlelight.

3 TEACHER: One of the first laws of physics is this: for every action there is an equal and opposite reaction. As an example, can anyone tell me what happens when you get into the bathtub?
STUDENT: Yes, the phone rings!

4 Science is always wrong. It never solves a problem without creating ten more.
George Bernard Shaw

See Lawyers 18, Medicine 2; *see also* Maths

Scotland and the Scots

1 A Scot is a man who keeps the Sabbath – and anything else he can lay his hands on.

2 I've just washed my kilt and I can't do a fling with it.

3 It was a Scottish wedding – the confetti was on elastic.

4 You know the difference between a Scottish wedding and a Scottish funeral?

At the funeral, there's one less drunk.

5 So you belong to a Scottish regiment. Do you have the right to bear arms? Of course, *and* we have the right to bare legs.

6 TOURIST: Is anything worn under that kilt?
SCOTSMAN: No, everything's in perfect working order.

7 What's the difference between the New York mafia and the Glasgow mafia?
One makes you an offer you can't refuse and the other makes you an offer you can't understand.

8 I deplore jokes which suggest that Scotsmen are miserly skinflints, such as the one about the Grand Canyon being started by a Scotsman who lost a penny in a ditch, or the one about the lad from Glasgow who killed his parents just so he could go on the orphan's picnic. Or even the one about the Scottish horserider who only bought one spur because he reckoned that wherever one side of the horse went, the other would go too.
I deplore them all. And why? Because some of my closest friends are Scottish . . .

9 You have to be very careful these days about stereotyping the Scots as mean.
There was a letter in *The Times* this week from an enraged Aberdonian. It said, 'If you print any more jokes about Scotsmen, I will have to stop borrowing your paper.'

See Sex 4; *see also* Britain and the British, England and the English, Stinginess, Thrift

Sea, The

1 I've developed my own cure for seasickness. It's called a tight collar.

2 We were shipwrecked. I would have sent an SOS if I could have spelt it.

See also Boats and Ships, The Navy, Sailing, Travel

Secrets

1 Don't worry, I can keep a secret. It's the people I tell it to who can't.

2 My wife thinks I'm too nosy – at least, that's what she keeps writing in her diary.

3 Secrets are things we give to others to keep for us.

4 Emily told me that you told her that secret I told you not to tell her.
Oh, no. I told her not to tell you that I told her!
Well, I told her I wouldn't tell you she told me what I told you not to tell her.

See Fishing 6; see also Gossip, Silence

Separation

1 My sister's broken up with her fiancé. She's sent back his letters, his Valentine's cards and his books of poetry, but she's keeping his jewellery for sentimental reasons.

2 What makes you think your husband is tired of you?
I haven't seen him for ten years!

See also Absence, Divorce, Marriage

Servants

1 Our maid has just started doing her spring clean. She's already picked up most of the tinsel.

2 People who keep servants would love to know how to keep servants.

3 She had to let the maid go because her husband wouldn't.

4 We've been terribly lucky. We've got a wonderful old family maid who's been with us for the last twenty meals.

5 FIRST MAID: I hate working at my new house. All day long it's, 'Yes, ma'am! Yes, ma'am! Yes, ma'am!'
SECOND MAID: It's worse at my new house. All night long it's, 'No, sir! No, sir! No, sir!'

6 That Mrs Mortimer is a fine lady to work for.
I like her. You can't do too much for her.
I don't intend to!

7 The butler was awakened by the sound of people moving around downstairs. Going to investigate, he discovered a pair of burglars making a swift exit through the window of a ransacked study.
He drew himself to his full height and intoned, 'And who shall I say called?'

See Families 8; see also Babysitters, Housework

Sex

1 A promiscuous person is someone who is getting more sex than you are.

2 Artificial insemination: copulation without representation.

3 As the male rabbit said to the female rabbit, 'This is fun . . . wasn't it?'

4 He'll chase anything in a skirt – which is why I'd never take him to see the caber-tossing at the Highland Games.

5 I really enjoyed reading The Joy of Sex. I couldn't put the wife down until I'd finished it.

6 I remember the days when 'safe sex' just meant that her parents were out for the evening.

7 I went to a conference yesterday on premature ejaculation. I got there five minutes early but it was already over.

8 I'm sorry, I don't sleep with strangers. What did you say your name was?

9 I've been experimenting with lots of new sexual positions. The next thing is to try them out on people.

10 My father told me all about the birds and the bees. Unfortunately, he didn't know anything about girls.

11 My father's stories about the birds and the bees were so fascinating, I was twenty-seven before I got interested in girls.

12 O, what a tangled web we weave, when first we practise to conceive!

13 Sex is hereditary. If your parents didn't have it, the chances are you won't either.

14 Sex is something that evolves over the years from triweekly to try weekly to try weakly.

15 That chorus girl? I never gave her a second thought – I was too busy with the first!

16 Two's company. Three's the result.

17 The three most popular things in life are a drink before and a cigarette afterwards.

18 They say that sex is bad for one – but it's fun for two.

19 You know what they say: to err is human, but it feels divine.

20 BOY: Do you smoke after sex?
GIRL: I don't know. I've never looked.

21 BOY: I dreamed about you last night.
GIRL: Did you?
BOY: No, you wouldn't let me.

22 BOY: I'll come straight to the point.

I'm only in town for a few hours so do you want to go to bed with me or not?
GIRL: Well, I wouldn't normally, but you've talked me into it.

23 FIRST WOMAN: I never made love to my husband before we got married. How about you?
SECOND WOMAN: I don't know. What's his name?

24 I took my girlfriend to the West Indies.
Jamaica?
It's none of your business!

25 MAN: Why don't you ever tell me when you have an orgasm?
WOMAN: Because you're never there!

26 PATIENT: Doctor, every time I sneeze, I feel terribly passionate. What should I take for it?
DOCTOR: Snuff.

27 PRIEST: Do you shrink from making love?
GIRL: If I did, I'd be a midget!

28 Q: What's the difference between frustration and panic?
A: Frustration is the first time you discover you can't do it the second time. And panic is the second time you discover you can't do it the first time.

29 What do you give the man who has everything?
Penicillin?

30 What's the difference between erotic and perverted?
Erotic is when you use a feather. Perverted is when you use the whole chicken.

31 A man sitting on a crowded bus was approached by a young woman who said, 'Would you mind giving me your seat. You see, I'm pregnant.'

And, getting up, the man replied,

'Certainly. But I must say, you don't *look* pregnant.'

And the young woman said, 'Well, it's only been about half an hour!'

32 My wife said to me in bed last night, 'Do you believe in free love?'

I said, 'Certainly not!'

She said, 'In that case, that'll be five pounds fifty.'

33 There was a young lady of Wheeling
Who professed to lack sexual feeling
Till a cynic named Boris
Just touched her clitoris
And she had to be scraped from the ceiling.

34 Two ducks booked into a hotel for a night of wanton passion but, as they started to get undressed, they realized that they had forgotten their condoms. So the man duck called room service and asked if they could send one up. Within a few minutes a waiter arrived bearing a condom on a silver tray.

The waiter said to the male duck, 'Shall I put it on your bill?'

And the male duck said angrily, 'What do you think I am – a pervert?'

35 A little coitus never hoitus.
Anon.

36 I'll come and make love to you at five o'clock. If I'm late, start without me.
Tallulah Bankhead

37 Nothing risqué, nothing gained.
Alexander Woollcott

38 Outside every thin girl there is a fat man trying to get in.
Katherine Whitehorn

39 Sex is only dirty when you do it right.
Bumper sticker

40 The pleasure is momentary, the position ridiculous and the expense damnable.
Earl of Chesterfield

41 When I'm good, I'm very good, but when I'm bad I'm better.
Mae West

42 I like two kinds of men: domestic and foreign.
Mae West

43 Fifty men outside? I'm tired – send ten of them home.
Mae West

44 Is that a pistol in your pocket or are you just glad to see me?
Mae West

See Actors and Acting 23, Advertising 4, Art and Artists 15, Babies 19, Catholics 4, Doctors 13, Law 13, Light-bulb Jokes 3, Limericks 4, 7, Marriage 53, Modern Times 6, Religion 15, 16, Shopping 12, Weddings 35; *see also* Beauty, Birth Control, Dating, Dating – Chat-up Lines, Honeymoons, Infidelity, Kissing, Romance, Sexual Attraction, The Single Life

Sexes, The

1 A woman without a man is like a fish without a bicycle.

2 A man without a woman is like a neck without a pain.

3 There'll never be an end to the war between the sexes. There's too much fraternizing with the enemy!

4 The only really happy people are married women and single men.
H. L. Mencken

See also Husbands and Wives, Men and Women

Sexual attraction

1 She's the sort of girl half the guys in

town want to marry – the other half already have!

2 To me a woman's body is a temple – and I try to attend services as often as possible.

3 She gave me a smile I could feel in my hip pocket.
Raymond Chandler

4 The trouble with life is that there are so many beautiful women and so little time.
John Barrymore

See Beards and Moustaches 2, Writers and Writing 12; *see also* Beauty, Dating, Dating – Chat-up Lines, Kissing, Romance, Sex, The Single Life

Shaving

1 Did you shave this morning?
Of course I did.
Well, next time stand a little closer to the razor.

2 GIRL: Hey, wait a minute. What's the idea of coming out tonight without shaving?
BOY: But I *have* shaved. You're looking at the back of my head!

See also Appearance, Barbers, Beards and Moustaches, Faces, Hair

Shopping

1 A bargain is something you cannot use at a price you cannot resist.

2 A supermarket is a place where you can find everything you want except the children when you're ready to leave.

3 An extravagance is anything you buy that is of no use to your spouse.

4 I found a real bargain in the supermarket. The normal 50p tin of baked beans was reduced from 75p to 65p!

5 I've just been out window-shopping. I had a great time. I bought four windows!

6 My wife buys everything that's marked down. Yesterday she came home with an escalator!

7 Now I know where all our money goes. My wife has just taken her supermarket trolley in for its 1,000-mile service.

8 Shopping is when a customer asks to see something more expensive; buying is when she asks to see something cheaper.

9 CUSTOMER: I want to buy a mousetrap and could you hurry please – I want to catch a bus.
SALESMAN: I'm sorry, sir, we don't stock them that big.

10 CUSTOMER: I'd like a bar of soap, please.
SALES ASSISTANT: Would you like it scented?
CUSTOMER: No thanks, I'll take it with me.

11 CUSTOMER: I want quite a few things, actually.
ASSISTANT: Have you got a list?
CUSTOMER: No, I always stand like this.

12 CUSTOMER: Do you keep stationery?
GIRL ASSISTANT: No, I wriggle about a bit.

13 CUSTOMER: Do you take anything off for cash?
SALES ASSISTANT: Sir, this is a shop, not a strip-tease joint!

14 SALES ASSISTANT: Madam, this cooker is very economical. It'll pay for itself in no time at all.
SHOPPER: Well, as soon as it does, send it over!

15 So why can't our Summer Special Sale continue to the end of August?

Because it would clash with the beginning of our Super Christmas Sale!

16 WOMAN: May I try on that dress in the window?
ASSISTANT: Well, we'd prefer it if you used the changing room.

17 A woman's place is in the mall.
Bumper sticker

See Credit 4; *see also* Advertising, Clothes, Credit, Credit Cards, Debt, Food, Money, Sales and Selling, Spending

Show business

1 Come and see the show!
Six gorgeous dancing girls!
Five gorgeous costumes!

2 PATIENT: I have no talent! I can't act, I can't dance, I can't sing! I want to get out of show business!
THERAPIST: Then why don't you?
PATIENT: I can't, I'm a star!

3 I've got this terrific new job in the circus – mucking out the elephants.
Mucking out the elephants! How many of them?
Twenty-five.
Twenty-five elephants! How much do they pay you?
Ten pounds a week.
Ten pounds a week for mucking out twenty-five elephants! If I were you I'd chuck it all in and get a decent office job.
What – and give up show business?

4 Oh, hello. I thought you'd retired.
But didn't you see me on television last week?
Yes – that's what made me think it.

See also Actors and Acting, Audiences, Circus, Comedians, Dancing, Films, Hollywood, Magic and Magicians, Music, Opera, Singing, Television, Theatre, Ventriloquists

Silence

1 Silence is having nothing to say and saying it.

2 Silence is the fool's greatest defence.

3 There's no one so wise as the man who says nothing at the right time.

4 If nobody ever said anything unless he knew what he was talking about, what a ghastly hush would descend upon the earth!
A. P. Herbert

See also Secrets, Talkers

Singing

1 He's a performer who was last heard at the Albert Hall – complaining about the price of his ticket.

2 I will now sing 'Somewhere My Love Lies Sleeping' with a male voice choir.

3 Last night I hit a high C – but how often am I going to back into a spear?

4 They say that once in every lifetime a really beautiful song comes along. Until it does, I'd like to do this one.

5 Tonight, for your delight, I'll be singing two of my favourite numbers: seven and forty-three.

See Childhood 4, Eskimos 1, 5, Introductions 18, 21, Mouths 1; *see also* Show Business, Singing – Insults, Song Titles

Singing – insults

1 He really has an unusual voice. It's like asthma set to music.

2 He's got a terrible voice. He couldn't be on key if he sat on a Yale lock!

3 He's got a singing voice that sounds like two chalk slates mating.

4 Him a singer? He couldn't carry a tune in an armoured car?

5 I once sang in front of the King of Sweden. At least I think I did. He said, 'If you're a singer, then I'm the King of Sweden.'

6 I'm sure he has a fine voice. It just seems such a pity for him to spoil it by singing.

7 OK, he's not much to look at. But he's even less to listen to.

8 She makes a noise like a cow that's just stood on its udder.

9 She's no singer. She couldn't carry a tune if it had a handle.

10 To be truthful, the way she carries a tune, she seems to be staggering under the load.

11 What he calls a voice, most people want to say excuse me after.

12 When he sings, you can't stop clapping – your hands over your ears.

13 How do you like my daughter's voice? They say she got it from me. You were very lucky to get rid of it!

14 My voice isn't big enough to fill an auditorium.
Well, it's certainly bad enough to empty one.

15 She's going off to London to have singing lessons.
Where did she get the money?
The neighbours all chipped in.

16 SINGER: Did you know I could sing like that?
CRITIC: I didn't know *anyone* could sing like that.

17 SINGER: Did you notice how my voice filled the hall?
CRITIC: Yes, and I also noticed that a lot of people left to make room for it.

18 With a voice like that, you ought to have your tonsils out.

But I've *had* my tonsils out.
In that case, you ought to have them put back in.

19 People who have heard me sing, say I don't.
Mark Twain

See also Hecklers, Insults, Singing

Single life, The

1 A bachelor is a man who is footloose and fiancée-free.

2 A bachelor is a man who learns to darn his own socks and sew on his own buttons – because he might get married some day.

3 A bachelor is a man who looks before he leaps – and then doesn't leap.

4 A bachelor is a man who profits by the mistake he doesn't make.

5 A bachelor is a man whose marriage vow is never to take one.

6 'What a simple life we bachelors lead,' I thought last night – as I stood in the kitchen washing my dish.

7 A bachelor is a man who's cheated some poor woman out of a divorce.

8 A bachelor is a man who believes in life, liberty and the happiness of pursuit.

9 A bachelor is a man who never chases a woman he can't outrun.

10 A wallflower is a woman who comes home from a dance wearing the same lipstick she went out with.

11 A wallflower is a man whose phone doesn't ring – even when he's in the bath.

12 Before she goes out on a date, her mother tells her to play easy to get.

13 He's a bachelor by choice. Sometimes his own, but mostly the choice of the women he's dated.

14 He's looking for a wife and he doesn't care whose.

15 I think – therefore I'm single.

16 She's waited so long for her boat to come in, her jetty's collapsed.

17 The only person who's asked her to get married is her mother.

18 Whenever I meet a man who would make a good husband, he already is.

19 I've proposed to four different men without avail.
Next time try wearing a veil.

20 MOTHER: When are you thinking of getting married?
DAUGHTER: All the time.

21 Why have you never married?
I don't want to make the same mistake once.

See The Office 4; see also Dating, Marriage, Men and Women, Romance, The Sexes

Skiing

1 I got a pair of water-skis for my birthday. All I need now is a lake with a slope.

2 Skiing is easy. I learned in just ten sittings.

See also Sport, Travel, Weather – Cold

Sleep

1 I drive my wife crazy. I don't talk in my sleep, I just grin.

2 I haven't slept for days. It's a good job I can sleep at night.

3 I used to snore so loudly I would wake myself up. But I'm cured now. I sleep in the next room.

4 Man is the only animal that goes to sleep when he's not sleepy and gets up when he is.

5 One night my uncle fell asleep in the bath with the taps running.

Didn't make a mess, though. He sleeps with his mouth open.

6 Sleep is such a wonderful thing, it's a shame you can't stay awake to enjoy it.

7 Sleep: that which, if you don't get enough of, you wake up half a.

8 Did you wake up grumpy this morning?
No, I let him sleep in.

9 Do you have any trouble falling asleep?
Certainly not. I can do it with my eyes closed!

10 Do you sleep soundly?
You ought to hear me!

11 I heard something this morning that really opened my eyes.
What was it?
An alarm clock.

12 PATIENT: Doctor, I don't seem to be able to sleep at night. What shall I do?
DOCTOR: Sleep nearer the edge of the bed. You'll soon drop off!

13 WIFE: I'm wide awake. I keep thinking there's a mouse under the bed.
HUSBAND: Well, start thinking there's a cat under the bed as well and let me get some sleep.

See Anxiety 3, Babies 11, Boxing 20, Coffee 3, Husbands and Wives 50, Laziness 11, Marriage 58, School 27, Speakers and Speeches 6, Taxes 14, Television 7; see also Insomnia

Small towns

1 I came from a town that was so small that the only thing that went out after ten o'clock was the lights.

2 I know that I'm back in my own home town if, when I use my electric razor, the street lights dim.

3 I spent a year in that town one night.

4 My home town was so small, the street map was actual size!

5 My home town was so small, the last one to bed had to turn out the light.

6 Nothing ever happens in our town. If we want excitement we go down to the department store and try on gloves.

7 Our town is so boring, the all-night diner closes at four in the afternoon.

8 Our town is so boring that the local paper prints the crossword puzzle on the front page.

9 Our town is so small that when they wanted to paint a white line down the middle, they had to widen the street.

10 Our town was so dull, they used to print the local paper three weeks in advance.

11 The place is so dull, a playboy is anyone who stays up to watch the eleven o'clock news.

12 We all look forward to Friday in our little town. That's the day we go down to the high street and watch the traffic lights change. It's at ten thirty if you're interested.

13 Anyone who's looking for excitement in our town just goes down to the supermarket to watch the bacon slicer. She's a smashing girl!

14 What a dump! I tell you, if God was going to give the world an enema, he'd start in Dimsby!

15 Do you have a village idiot?
No, we take it turns.

16 Where do you live?
Dimsby.
I'm sorry.
I said, 'Dimsby.'
I heard what you said, I'm just sorry.

See Lawyers 19; *see also* Bores, City Life, Poverty

Smells

1 Do you get fur from skunks?
I sure do. As fur as possible.

2 Your sister is spoiled, isn't she?
Not at all. That's just the perfume she's wearing.

See also Noses

Smoking

1 He likes to get good value from his cigars. In fact, he smokes them down so far, the ashes fall behind his teeth.

2 I kept reading in the papers that smoking was bad for you. So finally, I decided to give up reading the papers.

3 It has now been proved beyond reasonable doubt that smoking is one of the leading causes of statistics.

4 It's easy to stop smoking. All you need is an iron will, supportive friends – and a packet of wet matches.

5 She's the sort of girl who wears open-toed shoes – so she can pick up cigarette ends without bending down.

6 Smokers are people who puff on cigars, cigarettes and steps.

7 The problem is that trying to give up smoking makes me feel so angry. As soon as I stop smoking I start fuming.

8 Have you got a cigarette?
Lots of them, thanks.

9 This man took a kipper with him to the doctor's. And he said, 'Doctor, is it true smoking's bad for you?'
    The doctor replied, 'Of course it is!'
    And the man pointed at the kipper and he said, 'Well, it cured *him*.'

10 It has always been my rule never to smoke when asleep, and never to refrain when awake.
Mark Twain

11 Warning: when used as directed, cigarettes kill.
Anti-smoking advert

See Clothes 15, Funerals 3; *see also* Addiction, Drugs

Snobbery

1 He was so snobbish, he wouldn't even ride in the same car as his chauffeur.

2 To hear him talk, you'd think he begat his own ancestors.

3 One must not be a name-dropper, as Her Majesty remarked to me yesterday.
Norman St John Stevas

See Beach 3, Boats and Ships 1, Dogs 21; *see also* Ancestors, Aristocracy, Heredity, Wealth

Soccer

1 A friend of mine always books two seats when he goes to watch Chelsea. That's one to sit in and one to throw when the fighting starts.

2 As far as his team's concerned, he's the eternal optimist. He says they can still get promotion if they win eleven out of their last four games.

3 For a minute we were in with a great chance. Then the game started.

4 He's got one of the least demanding jobs in the country. He's the official scorer for Plymouth Argyle.

5 I used to be a half-back for Huddersfield Town. I tore the tickets in two and gave them half back.

6 I've started watching Luton Town. My doctor said I should avoid any excitement.

7 STRIKER: I had an open goal – but still I didn't score! I could kick myself!
MANAGER: I wouldn't bother. You'd probably miss!

8 Snow White arrived home one evening to find her house destroyed by fire. She was doubly worried because she'd left all seven dwarfs asleep inside. As she scrambled among the wreckage, frantically calling their names, suddenly she heard the cry: 'Chelsea for the Cup!'
   'Thanks goodness,' sobbed Snow White. 'At least Dopey's still alive.'

See also Sport

Sociology

1 How many sociologists does it take to change a light bulb? It isn't the light bulb that needs changing, it's the system.

2 What do you get when you cross a sociologist with a member of the mafia?
An offer you can't understand.

Song titles

1 'Come into the Pawn Shop, Myrtle, I Want to Get You Alone.'

2 'I Used to Kiss Her on the Lips, but It's All Over Now.'

3 'We Feed the Baby Garlic So We Can Find Him in the Dark.'

4 'She Forgot to Switch Off the Electric Blanket, So Now She's the Toast of the Town.'

5 'It's Better to Have Loved a Short Girl Than Never to Have Loved at All.'

6 'Don't Sit on the Gas Stove, Granny, You're Too Old to Ride the Range.'

7 'I Call My Husband Label Because He Sticks So Close to the Bottle.'

8 'They Call Me Luke Because I'm Not So Hot.'

9 'I'm So Miserable Without You It's Almost Like Having You Here.'

10 'She Was Only the Town Clerk's Daughter, but She Let the Borough Surveyor.'

11 'She Was Only a Red Indian's Daughter, but She Certainly Knew How.'

Space

1 The American space programme made medical history. It was the first time a capsule ever took a man.

2 If there are people on other planets, why don't they contact us?
Would you?

3 What was the *second* thing ever spoken on the moon?
'Hey, look at that. It's a full earth to-night!'

4 This morning I turned on the radio and got some amazing news. The newscaster said, 'We have some good news and some bad news for the people of the world. The bad news is that we have been invaded by thousands of Martians. The good news is that they eat politicians and pee petrol.'

See Knock-Knock Jokes 4; *see also* Modern Times, Travel

Speakers and speeches

1 I was just thinking, what an amazing coincidence – 600 of us having dinner together and we all ordered the same thing!

2 I'm speaking to you tonight under a considerable handicap. I'm sober!

3 It's certainly crowded in here to-night. Just be careful you don't put the spoons into somebody else's pocket!

4 My advice for speakers? If you don't know what to talk about, talk about three minutes.

5 My favourite advice to speakers: if you don't strike oil in the first two minutes, stop boring.

6 The best way to stay awake during an after-dinner speech is to give it.

7 You know what they say, all work and no plagiarism makes a dull speech.

8 Did I put enough fire into my speech?
I don't think you put enough of your speech into the fire.

9 Did the audience enjoy your speech?
I think so. When I sat down they said it was the best thing I'd ever done.

10 Did you make that speech up yourself?
Yes, right out of my head.
You must be.

11 FIRST POLITICIAN: Did you hear my last speech?
SECOND POLITICIAN: I certainly hope so!

12 So, I heard you went to a special school for help in curing your stutter. How did it go?
Peter Piper picked a peck of pickled peppers!
That's excellent!
S-s-s-sure. B-b-but it's r-r-really d-d-difficult t-to w-w-work it into a c-c-conversation.

13 A latecomer arriving fifteen minutes after the politician's speech had begun, asked a friend in the audience, 'What's the speech about?'
And the friend replied, 'He hasn't told us yet.'

14 The managing director, suddenly

remembering that he had to make an important speech that evening at a high-level conference, called in his assistant and asked him to write it for him.

'How long are you intending to speak for?' asked the assistant.

'About half an hour,' the MD replied.

The following morning, as the managing director arrived at his desk, the assistant brightly asked him how the speech had gone.

'It was an absolute disaster!' he replied. 'Half of the audience crept out and I could hardly hear myself speak because the other half were snoring! It would have been fine if it had lasted half an hour, as I told you, but you gave me a speech that lasted a whole hour!'

'No, I didn't,' said the assistant. 'I gave you a half-hour speech. But for safety reasons, I gave you two copies!'

15 The vicar was invited to speak at the monthly lunch of the Rotary Club. Also present at the meal was a reporter from the local newspaper, who enjoyed as much as anyone the vicar's light-hearted ecclesiastical anecdotes. At the end of his speech, the vicar approached the reporter and begged him not to print too many of his tales as he wished to use them at future local functions.

To the vicar's dismay, when he read the newspaper a few days later, the reporter had written, 'The vicar made an excellent speech but most of the stories he told cannot be repeated here.'

16 Way back in the days of ancient Rome, the emperor was enjoying one of his favourite spectacles – watching the Christians being thrown to the lions. But suddenly he realized that one Christian

seemed immune. As each of the lions approached him, he would whisper in its ear and it would slink away. The emperor had the Christian brought up to him and promised him that he could have his freedom if only he would reveal what he told the lions.

'There's no secret about it,' said the Christian. 'I simply tell them that if they eat me, they'll have to make an after-dinner speech.'

17 The American Democratic politician Adlai Stevenson found himself having to follow the comedian Fred Allen at a fund-raiser one evening. Fred Allen had been a smashing success with the audience and Adlai Stevenson was certain that his speech would suffer by comparison.

When he got up to speak, therefore, he said to his audience, 'Mr Allen and I were chatting before dinner and we decided it would be great fun to swap speeches – so I will now read his speech . . .'

18 The best audience is intelligent, well educated and a little drunk.
Alben W. Barkley

19 Winston [Churchill] has devoted the best years of his life to preparing his impromptu speeches.
F. E. Smith

20 The great orator always shows a dash of contempt for the opinions of his audience.
Elbert Hubbard

Openers

21 As I understand it, my job is to speak to you and your job is to listen. And I just hope we both finish at the same time.

22 But seriously, tonight is very special to me. It's not just the honour, it's not just the privilege of being invited to address you. It's the free meal. That – and the money.

23 Good ladies, evening and gentlemen ... I *knew* I should have practised this speech.

24 I imagine some of you have heard me speak before so you came early and grabbed a good seat – near the door.

25 I'm going to speak and hopefully you're going to listen, and if you should finish before I do, please raise your hand.

26 Ladies and gentlemen – I guess that takes care of most of you ...

27 Thank you. After such a flattering introduction, I can hardly wait to hear what I've got to say.

28 This is the second time I've given this speech. I delivered it last week at Pentonville Prison. So I apologize in advance to any of you who may have heard it before.

29 Tonight we all have something in common. None of us knows what I'm going to say next.

30 Well, I think we could all listen to our last speaker for ever. And I think we just have.

31 When I asked the chairman how long I should speak, he said, 'You can take as long as you like – but we're all off at nine o'clock.'

Closers

32 I'll close now because I see that there's only three minutes left before I'm supposed to finish – and I like to leave time for applause.

33 Since I've always believed that speeches should end on the same day they begin ... I'll close now.

34 And finally I'd like to thank you for your welcome, which was most cordial – and for your cordial, which was most welcome.

Savers

(for use when the expected laugh doesn't come)

35 Anyway, that's neither here nor funny.

36 Why don't I ever get English-speaking audiences?

37 Well, I'm glad I didn't give up my day job.

38 And so to continue on this serious note ...

39 I know you're out there – I can hear you breathing!

40 And here's another one you may not like ...

41 I'd love to see you all again – but not as a group!

42 OK, I'll just keep telling you these things and you just pick out the ones you like!

43 And that's just an example of the heady, carnival-like atmosphere I'm famous for generating.

See Inflation 4, Politics and Politicians 57, Religion 9, 14, 21; *see also* Awards, Bores, Conversation, Hecklers, Introductions, Talkers, Tributes

Spending

1 I've spent a fortune. Some of my money went on women, some on drink. The rest I spent foolishly.

2 OK, so I spend lots of money. But that's my only extravagance!

See also Banks and Banking, Credit, Credit Cards, Inflation, Money, Shopping, Wealth

Sport

1 Good sports are rarely good at sports.

2 He's decided to give up first-class cricket. But he'll still be playing for England.

3 I finally got a place in the Great Britain team for the Olympics – as a javelin catcher.

4 I went to a parachute-jumping class. The drop-out rate was incredible.

5 It's not whether you win or lose, but who gets the blame.

6 I come from a very athletic family. My brother once broke a leg throwing a ball. He forgot it was chained to his ankle.

7 I did the 100 metres in eight seconds.
But the world record holder can only do it in *ten* seconds.
Yes, but I know a short cut.

8 I wish I'd brought the piano to the stadium.
Brought the piano to the football game? Why?
Because I left the tickets on it.

9 I'm just off to see my brother. He's in the 6-mile bicycle race at Wembley Stadium.
The 6-mile bicycle race? But that finished three years ago.
I know, that's what I'm going to tell him.

10 Q: What do you find on a billiards table that you also find in men's trousers?
A: Pockets!

11 Our club manager won't stand for any nonsense. Last Saturday he caught a couple of fans climbing over the stadium wall. He was furious. He grabbed them by the collars and said, 'Now you just get back in there and watch the game till it finishes!'

12 Proficiency at billiards is proof of a misspent youth.
Herbert Spencer

See Advertising 9, Ethnic Jokes 1, Hospitals 21, Legs 1, The Office 6; *see also* American Football, Baseball, Boxing, Cricket, Exercise, Games, Golf, Horse-racing, Horses, Hunting, Ice Hockey, Sailing, Skiing, Soccer, Swimming, Tennis, Victory

Statistics

1 A statistician is someone who can put his head in the oven and his feet in the freezer and tell you, 'On average, I feel just fine.'

2 Statistics can, we know, be made to prove anything – even the truth.

See Smoking 3; *see also* Arguments, Maths

Stinginess

1 For a special birthday treat I took my girlfriend out to a really fancy restaurant. I made her laugh so hard, she dropped the tray.

2 He drinks only on special occasions – like when somebody else is buying.

3 He feels that two drinks are enough for anyone – especially if it's his turn to pay for the third.

4 He read in the paper that in India it costs just ten pounds to support a child for a year. So he sent his kids there.

5 He spent the first week of his holidays in Scarborough. And that's about all he did spend.

6 He's always the first person to put his hand in his pocket – and the last to bring it out again.

7 He's always got his nose in a book. He's too mean to use a handkerchief!

8 He's changed his name to Hilton so it'll be the same as the name on his towels.

9 He's so mean that when he sends his trousers to the laundry, he puts a sock in each pocket.

10 He's so mean, when he pays you a compliment he asks for a receipt.

11 He's so mean, the only fight he'd ever get into is a free-for-all.

12 He's the sort of person who likes to drink on an empty pocket.

13 I like to remain anonymous when donating money to charity, so I don't sign the cheque.

14 When he says it's not the money but the principle of the thing, you can bet it's the money.

15 He'll never pick up the bill. You've really got to hand it to him.

16 He's so mean, the things he does for people could be counted on his missing finger.

17 He's so stingy that one day, when he found a packet of corn plasters, he went out and borrowed a pair of tight shoes.

18 His heart is in the right place – in his chest.

19 I don't care how people treat me – just as long as they do.

20 I took my money out of the bank for a holiday. And after it had had one, I put it back in again.

21 I took this girl home in a taxi. She was so beautiful, I could hardly keep my eyes on the meter.

22 I'm afraid I can't contribute to your charity. My money is all tied up in cash.

23 I'm not saying my uncle is stingy, but last week he spilled some iodine so he cut his finger to use it up.

24 My uncle needed money so badly that he withdrew some from the bank!

25 My uncle suffers from a handicap. He's extremely hard of spending.

26 My uncle's found a new use for old razor blades. He shaves with them!

27 Stingy? He wouldn't even offer to buy a round of drinks at an AA meeting!

28 There was a smash and grab raid in Glasgow. The robbers would have got away with it but they went back for the brick.

29 What a party! The wine flowed like glue.

30 You're peeling off the wallpaper. I didn't know you were decorating. I'm not, I'm moving!

31 My uncle went into a store and bought a briefcase.
   The salesman said, 'Shall I wrap it for you, Sir?'
   And my uncle replied, 'No thanks, just put the wrapping paper and string inside.'

32 She asked her boss if she could have the day off to celebrate her silver-wedding anniversary.
   And the boss said, 'I suppose I have to put up with this every twenty-five years!'

33 The police arrested my uncle last week and charged him with breaking into a five-pound note. They let him go with a warning as it was his first offence.

34 He wouldn't give a duck a drink if he owned Lake Michigan.
   Anon.

See Bosses 7, Dancing 15, Gifts 4, 5; *see also* Borrowing and Lending, Debt, Flying – Economy, Hotels – Cheap, Money, Saving, Scotland and the Scots, Thrift

Stock market

1 He made a killing on the stock exchange. He shot his broker!

2 I used to think my broker was bearish. Then I thought he was bullish. Now I just think that he's rubbish.

3 My stockbrokers are a legend in the City for accurately predicting the 1929 crash – sixty years too late.

4 The stock market was in a terrible state. One day the Dow Jones was unchanged and they called it a rally.

5 Can we trust the City any more? The way things are going, the future of 'invest' seems to be 'investigation'.

6 There was a tremendous turnaround in the market today. A stockbroker who jumped out of a window on the twelfth floor, saw a computer screen on the seventh floor and did a U-turn.

7 They call him a broker because, after you see him, you are.

8 Wall Street had just voted him Man of the Year. Unfortunately the year is 1929.

9 When I saw how badly my shares were doing, I tried to call my broker – but his ledge was busy.

10 You know you've gone to the wrong stockbroker when you ask him to buy you 1,000 shares in IBM and he asks you how to spell it.

11 I'd have to be an idiot to buy shares in your company!
Fine. How many do you want?

See also Bankruptcy, Banks and Banking, Borrowing and Lending, Business, Credit, Hard Times, Inflation, Money, Wealth

Strength

1 He had a terrible accident in the army and lost a vital organ. But he's so tough, he grew another one.

2 I'm so strong I can tear a phone book in half the hard way – one page at a time.

3 Some people are so strong they can tear a telephone book in half. He has trouble with a wet Kleenex.

See also Exercise

Stupidity

1 I'm worried about the guy who's just joined our club. At the bottom of the application form, where it says 'Sign here', he wrote 'Pisces'.

2 Brains aren't everything. In his case, they're nothing.

3 When he graduated from nursery school, he was so excited he could hardly shave!

4 Don't call me stupid! I've got more brains in my little finger than I've got in my whole head.

5 He came home soaking wet from a drive-in car wash. He forgot to take the car.

6 He couldn't tell you which way the lift was going if you gave him two guesses.

7 He doesn't understand the concept of Roman numerals. He thinks we just fought World War Eleven.

8 He heard the country was at war – so he moved to the city.

9 He is a bit slow. It takes him an hour and a half to watch *Sixty Minutes*.

10 He was born on 2 April – a day too late.

11 He's almost got it right. He changes his oil every day and his shirt every 10,000 miles.

12 I caught him standing in front of the mirror with his eyes closed. He said he was trying to see what he looked like when he was asleep.

13 I was a little confused this morning.

I held the egg in my hand and boiled my watch.

14 I was so confused this morning that I stood in front of the bathroom mirror, trying to remember where I'd seen myself before.

15 I'm afraid he's at home, suffering from a freak accident. He was struck by a thought.

16 I'm not saying he's stupid, but if he had a pet zebra he'd call him Spot.

17 Is he intelligent? I don't know. He says he knows a lot – but he just can't think of it.

18 Is he stupid? If you gave him a penny for his thoughts, he'd have to give you change!

19 Is she stupid? She wanted to tighten the clothes-line, so she moved the house.

20 It took him five hours to look up 'vegetarian' in the dictionary. He didn't realize it was in alphabetical order.

21 My brother is so stupid, when he gets amnesia he actually gets smarter.

22 My uncle invented a new type of parachute. It opens on impact.

23 Our Catholic priest is not too bright. He thinks Vat 69 is the Pope's telephone number.

24 She's so stupid, she thinks Taco Bell is the Mexican phone company.

25 Stupid? He can't count to twenty without taking his shoes off.

26 The mind is like a TV set. When it goes blank, it's a good idea to turn the sound off.

27 What he lacks in intelligence, he makes up for in stupidity.

28 You bet he's stupid. He had to take his IQ test twice to get it up to double figures.

29 What makes you so stupid?

I don't know. But whatever it is, it works.

30 You've got your shoes on the wrong feet.
I know. I must have had my legs crossed when I put them on.

31 I drove into a garage in a little country town and I asked the man there if he could tell me if my rear indicator lights were working. So he stood at the back and I flicked the switch and he said, 'Yes, they are. No, they're not. Yes, they are. No, they're not . . .'

32 Stupidity often saves a man from going mad.
Oliver Wendell Holmes Jr

See Children 26, Success 5; *see also* Bores, Ethnic Jokes, Failure, Hecklers, Insults, Losers

Success

1 A friend is always delighted at your success, provided it doesn't exceed his own.

2 Behind every successful man, there stands an amazed woman.

3 He owed his success to his first wife and his second wife to success.

4 If at first you don't succeed, try reading the instructions.

5 Most of the world's greatest successes are achieved by someone either being clever enough to know it can be done – or too stupid to know it can't.

6 Success is simply a matter of luck. Ask any failure.

7 Success is trying to make enough money to pay the taxes you wouldn't be paying if you hadn't made so much money in the first place.

8 Success is relative – the more success, the more relatives.

9 The recipe for success combines two ingredients, luck and pluck – the luck in finding someone to pluck.

10 The secret of my success? I started at the bottom – and kissed it.

11 You're looking at a success story. I started off with nothing and look at me now. I'm 100,000 pounds in debt!

12 I'm a self-made man!
I accept your apology.

13 All you need in life is ignorance and confidence, and then success is sure.
Mark Twain

14 Nothing recedes like success.
Walter Winchell

See also Failure, Jealousy, Losers, Luck, Victory, Wealth

Suicide

1 Suicide is the sincerest form of self-criticism.

2 I told my psychiatrist I had suicidal tendencies.
He said, 'From now on you pay in advance.'

See Men and Women 12, Mothers-in-law 9; *see also* Death

Summer

1 These summer nights are getting hotter than ever. I woke up this morning with a sort of tingling sensation, and then I realized my water bed was perking!

2 You know it's summer when the chair you're sitting on gets up when you do.

3 Summer is the time when it's too hot to do the job it was too cold to do in the winter.

4 Do you summer in the country?
No, I simmer in the city.

See also Beach, Drought, Holidays, Swimming, The Sun, Weather – Hot

Sun, The

1 Mum, can I go out and watch the eclipse?
Of course you can – but don't stand too close.

2 I got up at dawn this morning to see the sunrise.
Well, you couldn't have picked a better time.

See The Environment 5, Holidays 20; *see also* Summer, Weather – Hot

Supernatural, The

1 A seance is simply sitting down with a few choice spirits.

2 A woman went to a seance to get in touch with her late husband, who'd been a waiter. As soon as the lights dimmed, the medium went into a trance and the table began to move.
    The woman cried, 'George! George! Is that you? Speak to me!'
    And a ghostly voice said, 'I can't. It's not my table.'

See also Fortune-telling

Superstition

1 My brother's very superstitious. Yesterday morning, he got up at seven, found that he had seven pounds in his pocket, caught the number seven bus into town and then found that in the seventh race that day there were seven horses. So he put seventy-seven pounds on horse number seven and sure enough – it came in seventh.

See Weddings 6

Swearing

1 I'm sorry, there's no room for vulgarity on this programme. It's already far too full of filth and obscenity.

2 Swearing is a bad habit that should not be indulged in by other people.

3 Swearing is what is said when you don't know what to say.

4 In certain trying circumstances, urgent circumstances, desperate circumstances, profanity furnishes a relief denied even to prayer.
Mark Twain

See Theatre 1; see also Arguments, The English Language, Manners

Swimming

1 Where did you learn to swim?
In the water.

2 I thought I could trust the people who use my pool, but all I know is that when I filled it last year, I put in 10,000 gallons and when I emptied it last week, I took out *11,000* gallons.

See Holidays 11; see also Beach, Pollution – Water, Sport, Summer

Sympathy

1 Sympathy is what one person offers another in return for the details.

2 Sympathy: what you give to someone when you don't want to lend him money.

3 I can sympathize with everything, except suffering.
Oscar Wilde

4 To be sympathetic without discrimination is so very debilitating.
Ronald Firbank

See also Accidents, Death

T

Talkers

1 A woman's word is never done.
2 He just can't stop talking. He'd make a great neighbour for anyone with a windmill.
3 He talks 100 words a minute, with gusts up to 120.
4 When all is said and done, he never is.
5 He's a man who regards free speech not so much as a right but more as a continuous obligation.
6 He's a man who can talk for hours without a note – or, for that matter, without a point.
7 I don't always know what she says. She can talk 50 per cent faster than I can listen.
8 I once went out with a girl with a terrible stutter. By the time she said she wouldn't, she had.
9 I used to think that there was no such thing as a perpetual-motion machine until I saw her mouth in action.
10 I've never really been on speaking terms with her. Listening terms, yes, but speaking terms, no!
11 When things go wrong at home, I always give my wife a good listening-to.

See Drink 29, Limericks 2, Radio 9, Theatre 5; see also Bores, Conversation, Speakers and Speeches

Taxes

1 If you ask the Inland Revenue, this country is a land of untold wealth.

2 It's getting harder and harder to support the government in the style to which it has become accustomed.
3 It's ridiculous! The average citizen works six months a year for the government. Government *employees* don't work six months a year for the government!
4 People who complain about paying their income tax can be divided into two types: men and women.
5 Taxation: the process by which money is collected from the people in order to pay the salaries of the people who do the collecting.
6 The Eiffel Tower is the Empire State Building after taxes.
7 The Lord giveth and the Inland Revenue taketh away.
8 The reason the government is worried about lowering taxes is that it might establish a dangerous precedent: the right of people to keep their own money.
9 When your ship comes in, it's always docked by the government.
10 You've got to hand it to the tax collector. If you don't, he'll come and get it.
11 They say a fool and his money are soon parted – and the rest of us just wait to be taxed.
12 Taxation without representation may have been tyranny – but it was definitely a lot cheaper.
13 A Communist government won't let you make much money. A capitalist government lets you make as

much money as you like – they just won't let you keep it.

14 The taxman was surprised to receive a letter which read, 'Dear Sir, Last year I cheated on my tax and I can't sleep for thinking about it. I am therefore enclosing a cheque for 2,000 pounds. If I find that I still can't sleep, I'll send you the balance.'

15 A taxpayer is someone who works for the federal government but who doesn't have to take a civil service examination.
Ronald Reagan

16 I'm proud to be paying taxes in the United States. The only thing is, I could be just as proud for half the money.
Arthur Godfrey

See Business 1, Prison 3, Success 7; *see also* Accountants, Debt, Economics, Government, Money, Politics and Politicians, Wealth

Taxis

1 Did you know that taxis are soluble? They dissolve in the rain.

2 The great thing about being a cab driver is that you get to go to work every day in a taxi.

3 Why do cabbies drive like they own the road when they don't even own the cab?

4 Call me a taxi, my good man!
Certainly, sir. You are a taxi!

5 PASSENGER: Take me anywhere!
TAXI DRIVER: Sorry. I'm not going in that direction.

6 PASSENGER: Ten pounds? You can't fool me. I haven't ridden in taxis for years for nothing!
TAXI DRIVER: But I bet you've tried!

See Drink 38, Stinginess 21, Wealth

7; *see also* Cars, City Life, Driving, Travel

Teaching

1 Good teachers cost a lot but bad teachers cost a lot more.

2 Teaching is the fine art of imparting knowledge without possessing it.

3 The student teacher was asked to fill in a form when she arrived at college. At the top was the question: Give two reasons for becoming a teacher. She wrote, 'July and August.'

4 A schoolmaster should have an atmosphere of awe, and walk wonderingly, as if he was amazed at being himself.
Walter Bagehot

5 A teacher who is not dogmatic is simply a teacher who is not teaching.
G. K. Chesterton

6 I am inclined to think that one's education has been in vain if one fails to learn that most schoolmasters are idiots.
Hesketh Pearson

7 The members of the most responsible, the least advertised, the worst paid, and the most richly rewarded profession in the world.
Ian Hay

8 When a teacher calls a boy by his entire name, it means trouble.
Mark Twain

See Bores 2; *see also* Children, Education, School

Teenagers

1 Adolescence is a period of rapid and remarkable change. Between the ages of twelve and seventeen, for

instance, a parent can age as much as twenty years.

2 Adolescence is the time when your daughter starts to put on lipstick and your son starts to wipe it off.

3 It's not easy arguing with my kids. My trouble is, I'm not young enough to know everything.

4 My son is always ready to give me the benefit of his inexperience.

5 My teenage son said to me last night, 'Dad, how do you expect me to be independent, self-reliant and stand on my own two feet on the tiny allowance you give me?'

6 She's at that awkward age when she's stopped asking us where she comes from and started refusing to tell us where she's going.

7 Teenage is the period between hop-scotch and real Scotch.

8 Teenagers today know everything – except how to make a living.

9 Today the accent is on the young. But the stress is on the parents.

10 Today's teenagers are alike in many disrespects.

11 We've given my son a hint. On his bedroom door we've pinned a sign: Check-out time is eighteen.

12 Like its politicians and its war, society has the teenagers it deserves.
J. B. Priestley

13 Never lend your car to anyone to whom you have given birth.
Erma Bombeck

See Cars 29, Home 3, Problems 2, Telephones 6; *see also* Adolescence, Children, Families, Fathers, Mothers, Parents, Telephones

Teeth

1 His teeth have so many cavities, he talks with an echo.

2 I know she's got all her own teeth. I was with her when she bought them.

3 I wouldn't say her teeth protrude that much, but the other day *I did* catch her eating an apple through a tennis racket.

4 If you want to keep your teeth in good condition, brush them after every meal – and mind your own business.

5 My dentist advised me to use striped toothpaste – to make my teeth look longer.

6 My dentist said, 'Frankly, I've seen better teeth on a comb.'

7 She's got so much bridgework that every time I kiss her I have to pay a toll.

8 She's only got one tooth – but it certainly comes in handy for opening beer bottles!

9 She's the only girl I know who wears her teeth parted in the middle.

10 The bad news is that my new girl-friend has terrible buck teeth. But the good news is that every time we kiss, she combs my moustache.

11 Can you recommend anything for yellow teeth?
How about a brown tie?

See Lies 8, Poverty 16, Weather – Cold 4; *see also* Dentists, Mouths

Telephones

1 I don't know what to do. My boss won't let me make personal calls at the office and my wife and daughter won't let me make them at home.

2 It used to be something that strong men did, tearing the phone book in half. Nowadays they do it with a phone bill.

3 My daughter is a very popular young woman. The only time the phone doesn't ring is when it's for me.

4 Why is it that wrong numbers are never out when you call?

5 Why is it that wrong numbers are never engaged?

6 Did you read about that woman who hadn't used a telephone in more than thirty years?
That's what happens when you have teenagers in the house!

7 Answer the phone! Answer the phone!
But it's not ringing.
Why leave everything till the last minute?

8 Do you believe in free speech?
Of course I do.
Good. Can I use your phone?

9 HUSBAND: I can't believe it, I've never seen you put the phone down after only ten minutes! How come?
WIFE: It was a wrong number.

10 I'm sorry to call you in the middle of the night.
That's all right I had to get up anyway to answer the phone.

11 No, this is not the Jones's house. You must have a wrong number.
Are you sure?
Have I ever lied to you before?

12 The young businessman was just setting up on his own and, sitting in his brand-new office on the first morning, he heard someone coming up the stairs. Determined to give the impression of a go-ahead company, he picked up the phone as the visitor entered the office and pretended to be discussing a multi-million-pound deal.
Finally, after five minutes of high-powered negotiation on contracts and down-payments and bank guarantees, he put the phone down and faced the visitor.
'Sorry about that. Can I help you?'
And the visitor said, 'Sure, I've come to install the phones.'

13 Well, if I called the wrong number, why did you answer the phone?
James Thurber

Television

1 A television audience is lots of people with nothing to do watching lots of other people doing it.

2 He's got a perfect face for television – it's already blurred.

3 I did my first television show a year ago and the very next day one million television sets were sold. And the people who couldn't sell theirs threw them away.

4 I heard of one programme that was so dreadful, the studio monitors were switched to another channel.

5 I watched a very thought-provoking programme on television last night. The thought it provoked was, 'Why am I watching this programme?'

6 I've been watching so much television in the last year, I've had to have my eyeballs retuned.

7 Some television is most refreshing. You feel really good when you wake up.

8 Television is just radio with eyestrain.

9 Television is the device which has

changed a generation of children from an irresistible force into immovable objects.

10 Television is called a medium because so little of it is rare or well done.

11 There's a new television quiz show coming up with a first prize of one million pounds. A presenter I know already has his agent negotiating to get him the job – as a contestant.

12 There's no question that television has a beneficial educational effect. It's driving people to read books.

13 We never turn our television off. In fact, the only way we can change the channel now is with the fire tongs.

14 When he first appeared on television, the critics coined a new slogan: The show must go off.

15 When I really want to be entertained, I've got this massive 6-foot screen. It's made of bamboo and paper and I stick it right in front of the television and open a good book!

16 Years ago most people thought televison was impossible – and many of them still do

17 When I was a kid we didn't have a television, so my dad bored a hole through the wall into the house next door and we used to watch the wrestling every night – till we discovered that the neighbours didn't have a television either.

18 Dealing with network executives is like being nibbled to death by ducks.
Eric Sevaraid

19 Imitation is the sincerest form of television.
Fred Allen

20 Television is just chewing gum for the eyes.
Fred Allen

21 Television is a device which permits people who haven't anything to do, to watch people who can't do anything.
Fred Allen

22 Television has raised writing to a new low.
Sam Goldwyn

23 Television criticism is like describing an accident to an eyewitness.
Jackie Gleason

24 The viewer who skips the advertising is the moral equivalent of a shoplifter.
Nicholas Jackson

See Marriage 13, Retirement 6; see also Actors and Acting, Advertising, Children, News, Show Business

Tennis

1 He plays tennis so badly that his opening serve is match point!

See also Sport

Texas and Texans

1 A Texan friend of mine gave his son a cowboy outfit for Christmas – a 20,000-acre cattle ranch!

2 I knew this short guy from Dallas who was so rich, he didn't wear elevator heels – he just had Texas lowered.

3 A Texan died and went to heaven and St Peter greeted him at the gate.
'Welcome,' he said. 'Where do you come from?'
And the man said, 'Texas.'
St Peter replied, 'Well, come on in – but you're not going to be satisfied.'

4 If I owned Hell and Texas, I'd rent out Texas and live in Hell.
General Philip H. Sheridan

See also America and the Americans, Beverly Hills, Wealth

Thanksgiving

1 Thanksgiving is a day when the turkey gets stuffed in the morning and the family in the afternoon.

2 The Puritans celebrated Thanksgiving Day to commemorate being saved from the Indians. We continue to celebrate it to commemorate being saved from the Puritans.

3 So what size turkey did you have?
It was so big we had to call in an upholsterer to stuff it!

See also Christmas, New Year, Parties

Thatcher, Margaret

1 Attila the Hen.
Clement Freud

2 She cannot see an institution without hitting it with her handbag.
Julian Critchley

3 She's very democratic. She'll talk down to anyone.
Austin Mitchell

4 The parrot on Ronald Reagan's shoulder.
Denis Healey

5 The Prime Minister tells us she has given the French President a piece of her mind – not a gift I would receive with alacrity.
Denis Healey

See also Conservatives, Government, Houses of Parliament, Politics and Politicians

Theatre

1 The play closed because of too many four-letter words – from the critics!

2 So how are the acoustics in the new theatre?
Perfect. The actors can hear every cough!

3 What was the play about?
About thirty minutes too long.

4 Why are you leaving? It's only the interval.
But look, it says on the programme, 'Act Two – one month later'.

5 The theatregoer was getting increasingly annoyed at the two women in the row in front who were talking to each other throughout the play. Finally, he leaned forward and said to one of the women, 'Excuse me, but I can't hear a word.'
'I should hope not,' said the woman. 'This is a private conversation.'

6 Opening night: the night before the play is ready to open.
George Jean Nathan

See Crime 24, Dating 40, Films 1, Literature 3; see also Actors and Acting, Audiences, Dancing, Films, Opera, Show Business, Singing, Theatre – The Critics

Theatre – the critics

1 A theatre critic is someone who stones the first cast.

2 My seat, unfortunately, was facing the stage.

3 The play was so terrible I asked the woman in front of me to put her hat on.

4 A critic is a person who surprises the playwright by informing him what he meant.
Wilson Mizner

5 If you will only take the precaution to go in long enough after it commences and to come out long

enough before it is over, you will not find it wearisome.
George Bernard Shaw

6 No worse than a bad cold.
Harpo Marx

7 People laugh at this every night, which explains why democracy can never be a success.
Robert Benchley

8 Some laughter was heard in the back rows. Someone must have been telling jokes back there.
Robert Benchley

9 There is less in this than meets the eye.
Tallulah Bankhead

See also Actors and Acting, Theatre

Thrift

1 I've just given my wife a lecture on extravagance and, believe me, there's going to be some changes made. For a start, I'm giving up smoking.

2 Thrift is a terrific virtue – especially in your ancestors!

3 My problem lies in reconciling my gross habits with my net income.
Errol Flynn

See also Banks and Banking, Flying – Economy, Hotels – Cheap, Money, Saving, Spending, Stinginess

Tidiness

1 I'm fanatically tidy. I may only have one book in my library but at least it's in alphabetical order!

2 I've decided it's time to tidy up my room. Last night the phone rang and I couldn't find it.

3 My aunt is so obsessively tidy that when you ring her doorbell it sprays you with room-freshener.

4 My wife has an obsession with tidiness. If I get up in the middle of the night to go to the bathroom, by the time I get back the bed's made.

5 My wife is obsessively tidy. I just bought her a cuckoo clock and she's started putting paper under it.

See Psychiatry 16; see also Appearance, Cleanliness, Homes – Squalid, Housework

Timidity

1 He refuses to sleep with his wife on the grounds that she's a married woman.

2 He's so cautious, he looks both ways before crossing his legs.

3 He's so polite, he won't open an oyster without knocking on the shell first.

4 I'm not a yes-man. When my boss says, 'No,' I say, 'No.'

See also Anxiety, Failure, Fear, Indecision, Losers

Tom swifties

1 'I've lost my crutches,' said Tom lamely.

2 'I'm looking for a gift for my wife,' said Tom presently.

3 'I'm glad I remembered my umbrella,' said Tom drily.

4 'I can't feel a thing,' said Tom insensitively.

5 'They've run out of Angostura,' said Tom bitterly.

6 'I think I've got the measles,' said Tom infectiously.

7 'I'm dead,' said Tom breathlessly.

See also Cross Jokes, Light-bulb Jokes

Trades unions

1 Both management and unions agree that time is money. They just can't agree on how much!

2 I'd support any strike for shorter hours. I think sixty minutes is far too long.

3 My dad was a trades unionist. He used to begin our bedtime stories with, 'Once upon a time and a half . . .'

4 The management were going to cut wages by fifty pounds a week, but don't worry, I've got it backdated to 1 January.

5 BOSS: Why are you people always at my throat?
SHOP STEWARD: Because it keeps us away from the area you expect us to kiss!

6 FIRST TRADES UNIONIST: I see the daffodils are out.
SECOND TRADES UNIONIST: How does that affect us?

7 A shop steward was telling a meeting of his members that the management had agreed to all their demands.
'From now on, all wages are doubled, holidays are increased to ten weeks per annum and we only have to work on Fridays.'
And a man from the back shouted, 'Not every bloody Friday?'

8 Dear Sir,
If we are to stop the militant minorities from taking over our trades unions, we ordinary members have got to be prepared to stand up and be counted.
Yours faithfully, A. N. Other.

9 The worker went to his shop steward and complained that he'd been underpaid by five pounds this week.

'What about last week?' asked the shop steward.
'Last week they overpaid me by five pounds.'
'I'll have to do something about this,' said the steward.
'We can overlook the occasional mistake, but two weeks in a row . . .'

See Marriage 33; *see also* Bosses, Politics and Politicians, Unemployment, Work

Travel

1 A commuter is someone who goes up to the city every day in order to make enough money to sleep in the country.

2 A tourist is someone who travels to find things that are different and then complains when they are.

3 Hawaii, where all the girls wear grass skirts and where, when all the men go courting, they take a lawnmower.

4 I just got back from my holidays and I'm still suffering from bus lag.

5 It was a nightmare journey. The bus was so crowded even the driver was standing.

6 It's a nightmare travelling in London these days. The other day I had to stand all the way from Marble Arch to Hammersmith – and I was in a taxi.

7 Last year I took my wife on a trip around the world. This year she wants to go somewhere else!

8 On the buses now, they demand exact change.
Can you believe that?
Let me tell you, they can have their exact change just as soon as they take me to my exact destination!

9 Rome wasn't built in a day. It just looks like it!

10 There are plenty of places to stay in the desert. We stayed in a bedouin breakfast.

11 These days tourists are travelling further and further afield in the hope of avoiding the tourists.

12 Yes, I do a lot of travelling. I've been to nearly as many places as my luggage.

13 I travelled from London to Brighton seventeen times without a ticket.
How did you manage that?
I walked.

14 I waited ages for a number 36 bus.
But it never came.
So what did you do?
Well, eventually two number 18s came along so I got on them.

15 PASSENGER: I say, driver, do you stop at the Ritz?
DRIVER: What, on my wages!

16 PASSENGER: Inspector, where do I catch the number 47 bus?
INSPECTOR: In the small of the back if you don't get on the pavement.

17 Q: Where are the Seychelles?
A: On the Sey shore!

18 TOURIST: Me come in great silver bird.
NATIVE: Oh, really? Well, I always go by plane.

19 Travelling across the desert we met some traders with camels.
Bedouins?
Bedouins, goodouins, all sorts, really.

20 The missionaries were hacking their way through the jungle when they came upon a native village in a clearing. As the natives rushed towards them, one of the missionaries held up his hand to stop them and began to address them.

'I come from a peaceful land,' said the missionary.
And the natives cried out as one, 'Wongabonga!'
'A land where we love our fellow men,' he continued.
'Wongabonga!' the natives cried again.
'A land where every man is equal.'
'Wongabonga!'
'And we have travelled many days through the jungle to show you how you can change your lives to be as happy and contented as we are back in our own land.'
'Wongabonga!'
Just then the missionary noticed a small herd of cattle at the side of the clearing.
'That's an interesting breed,' he said. 'Do you mind if I go over and have a closer look at them?'
And one of the natives said, 'Of course not, but be careful you don't step in the wongabonga!'

21 It was a very windy day in the Himalayas and a sherpa spotted a young mountaineer floating down under a parachute.
'That's very dangerous,' he told the mountaineer. 'Coming down here in a parachute.'
'But I didn't come down in a parachute,' protested the mountaineer, 'I went up in a tent!'

22 When you're safe at home you wish you were having an adventure; when you're having an adventure you wish you were safe at home.
Thornton Wilder

See Drink 52, Husbands and Wives 26; *see also* Boats and Ships, Cars, Driving, Flying, Holidays, Hotels, Languages, Modern Times, Railways, Taxis

Tributes

1 After just two years working here, he was given the key to the executive washroom. Then, after he'd scrubbed the place clean, he had to give the key back.

2 Every once in a while we honour a man of high achievement, transparent integrity and penetrating intellect. Not today, though!

3 He started at the top and steadily worked his way down.

4 He's a humble and modest man – and with good reason.

5 He's a man who's been admired for years – and none of them recently.

6 He's been called a rotten, low-down stinker. But that's just his family's opinion!

7 I have to say to you that, in all the years I have known him, no one has ever questioned his intelligence. In fact, I've never heard anyone mention it.

8 I've been delving into his past and I've discovered that there's a Henry Harris that nobody knows – until tonight!

9 In many ways he's been like a son to me – insolent, ungrateful, disrespectful . . .

10 Of course, there's a lot to be said in his favour. But it's not nearly so interesting.

11 She's so effervescent. In fact, I can't remember a time when she effervascent.

12 Since I met him nearly ten years ago, there hasn't been a day when I haven't thought about him. And I haven't thought about him today either!

13 Success hasn't changed him. He's still the same lousy skunk he always was!

14 They say at the office that he does the work of two men: Laurel and Hardy.

15 This is a man who started at the bottom – and sank.

16 This is a man who has no equals – only superiors.

17 This is the man who, when it started to rain, said to Noah, 'It's only a light shower.'

18 This man is an inspiration to us all. Let's face it, if *he* can make it, then anyone can.

19 What can I say about our guest of honour? Well, there are some things that go without saying. Unfortunately, he isn't one of them.

20 What can I say about our guest of honour that hasn't already been said about toxic waste?

21 Women should like him. They shrink from his touch!

22 What can I tell you about him? He's just a terrific guy. I couldn't tell you all the things he's done for me over the years – but he's asked me to try.

23 He said that tonight I should simply tell the truth – no matter how flattering.

24 Meeting Franklin Roosevelt was like opening your first bottle of champagne; knowing him was like drinking it.
Winston Churchill

See also Awards, Failure, Farewells, Insults, Introductions, Retirement, Speakers and Speeches, Tributes – Responses, Unemployment

Tributes – responses

1 And now, the case for the defence . . .

2 I won't take long. This suit is due back in twenty minutes!

3 I'm sure I don't deserve an honour like this, but then, what's my opinion against thousands?

4 What an amazing coincidence! While you were saying all those wonderful things about me, I was thinking exactly the same thing!

See also Awards, Speakers and Speeches, Tributes

Truth

1 Truth may be stranger than fiction, but fiction is truer.

2 As scarce as truth is, the supply has always been in excess of the demand.
Josh Billings

3 Men occasionally stumble over the truth, but most of them pick themselves up and hurry off as if nothing had happened.
Winston Churchill

See also Lies

U

Ugliness

1 He was so ugly, he used to model for death threats!

2 He's so ugly, Frankenstein's Monster went to a Halloween Party as *him*!

3 He's so ugly that when he goes to therapy, the psychiatrist makes him lie face down!

4 I wouldn't say he's ugly, but on Halloween his parents send him out as he is.

5 I'm not saying he's ugly, but he looks good in anything but the mirror.

6 I'm not saying she's ugly, but at her wedding everybody kissed the groom.

7 I'm not saying he's ugly, just that he looks as if his hobby is stepping on rakes!

8 She looks like a million dollars – all green and crumpled!

9 She was in the beauty salon for three hours. And that was just for the estimate.

10 She's turned many a head in her day – and a few stomachs.

11 There's still one man who thinks she's a ten – her shoe salesman!

12 BOY: At least you're beautiful on the inside.

GIRL: Trust me to be born inside out!

13 A woman is walking down the street with a duck under her arm when she is accosted by a drunk.

The drunk says, 'Yecchh. Where'd you get that repulsive thing?'

And the woman replies, 'Sir, it happens to be my duck!'

And the drunk says, 'I know, I was talking to the duck!'

See Art and Artists 12, Birth 5, Photography 5, Radio 4; *see also* Appearance, Faces, Figures – Fat, Figures – Thin, Hecklers, Insults, Plastic Surgery

Unemployment

1 THE SACK AND HOW TO GIVE IT

I just don't know what we'd do without you. But we're going to try.

Tell me, how long have you been with us – not counting tomorrow.

You'll find a little extra in your pay packet this week – your cards.

Look, you made a mistake and I'd like to help you out. Which way did you come in?

The official reason you're leaving is because of illness and fatigue. I'm sick and tired of you.

Look, I'll put my cards on the table. They're just there beside yours.

Look, you made a mistake but it's not a resigning matter. Not at all. You're fired!

I'm putting you in charge of our Building and Loan Department. I want you to leave the *building* and leave us *alone*.

We're extending our flexi-time experiment. From today you can go home any time you like – and stay there.

Despite all the suggestions I've made over the years, I've been unable to fire you with enthusiasm. Until now.

It's not that you aren't a responsible worker. In fact, you've been responsible for more screw-ups than any worker we've ever had.

You've always been shy. Now what we'd like you to be is retiring.

You've got that resigned look about you again. This time, why don't you put it in writing?

2 My boss said to me this morning, 'I'm going to mix business with pleasure. You're fired!'

3 He's got a BA, an MA and a PhD. They only thing he doesn't have is a JOB.

4 Looking on the bright side of unemployment – when you get up in the morning, you're already at work!

5 On the plus side, the good thing about unemployment is that it certainly takes the worry out of being late for work.

6 The government has discovered a great new way of cutting down on unemployment. They're going to raise the school-leaving age to forty-seven.

7 The government has announced radical new plans to cut the length of the dole queues. They're going to get people to stand closer together.

8 Things are so shaky at work, they hand out your calendar one day at a time.

9 We've got a fantastic fire-alarm system in our office. The moment somebody gets fired, the whole office knows about it.

10 After what he said today, I'm never going to work for that man again!
What did he say?
He said, 'You're fired!'

11 Do you have anything to say before I fire you?
Yes. How about a raise?

12 One employee complained to the boss when she was sacked, 'How can you fire me. I do the work of three people!'
And the boss replied, 'Tell me who the other two are and I'll fire them too.'

See Actors and Acting 4, 7, Hard Times 21, Religion 1, Sales and Selling 10; see also Bosses, Business, Retirement, Work

University

1 The problem with a liberal arts education is that it leaves you well rounded but not pointed in any particular direction.

2 Can you tell me what happened in 1066?
I can't even remember what happened last night!

See American Football 1, Banks and Banking 16, Jews 3, The Law 20; see also Education, School, Teaching

V

Vanity

1 He had a dreadful accident while out walking. He was hit by a passing motorboat!

2 He's a self-made man who insists on giving everyone the recipe.

3 He's a terrible egotist. He's more interested in himself than me.

4 He's always believed in love at first sight – ever since he first looked in a mirror.

5 He's going through a religious conversion. He no longer believes he's God!

6 He's so vain, he's got a mirror on his bathroom ceiling just so he can watch himself gargle.

7 He's so vain, he's planning to take his own hand in marriage.

8 He's vain all right. He joined the navy so the world could see him.

9 I am not conceited – although I have very right to be.

10 I am writing a book. It's called *Famous People Who Have Met Me*.

11 I don't think I'm particularly good-looking. But what's my opinion against that of thousands of others?

12 I used to be so conceited that I had to see a psychiatrist. But now, after only three months' treatment, I'm one of the nicest people you could hope to meet.

13 I wouldn't say he was conceited, but half an hour after he's left the bathroom the mirror is still warm.

14 I've never heard him say an unkind word about anyone – mainly because he only talks about himself.

15 Is he vain? The last time I saw him, he was strolling down Lovers' Lane holding his own hand.

16 My uncle is deeply religious. He worships himself.

17 Sometimes he gets carried away with his own importance – but not far enough.

18 Vain? The only time you'll find him *not* looking in the mirror is when he's backing into a parking space.

19 Do you think I'm vain?
No. Why do you ask?
Well, people as good-looking as me usually are.

20 A writer was called as an expert witness in a libel case. When he was asked to identify himself, he said, 'I'm Harold Hotchkiss, England's greatest living novelist.'
At the end of the day, his wife came over to him and said, 'Darling, your evidence was wonderful. But couldn't you have been a little more modest when giving your name?'
And the writer said, 'But I had no choice. I was under oath!'

21 As the new patient made himself comfortable on the couch, the psychiatrist picked up his pad and said, 'Good morning, as this is the first time we've met, perhaps you'd like to tell me something about yourself.'
'Where would you like me to start?' said the patient.
'Why not start with the first thing you can remember.'

'OK, in the beginning I created heaven and earth . . .'

22 When you're as great as I am, it's hard to be humble.
Muhammad Ali

See also Actors and Acting, Egotists

Ventriloquists

1 DUMMY: I know he's still alive, I can hear myself breathing!

2 He was a terrible ventriloquist. His lips moved even when he wasn't saying anything.

See also Show Business

Victory

1 As always, victory finds 100 fathers, but defeat is an orphan.
Count Galeazzo Ciano

2 To the victor belong the toils.
Adlai Stevenson

See also Defeat, Records, Sport, Success, War

W

War

1 The real war hero is the man who prevents it.

2 A nuclear war wiped out the whole planet. The only living things left alive were two monkeys in the middle of the African jungle.

One turned to the other and said, 'Ok, let's start again!'

3 All wars are popular for the first thirty days.
Arthur Schlesinger Jnr

4 Old soldiers never die – just young ones.
Graffito

5 Retreat, hell! We're just advancing in another direction.
Marine General P. O. Smith

6 War is the continuation of politics by other means.
Karl von Clausewitz

See Ireland and the Irish 3, Parents 2, Stupidity 7, 8; see also The Army, The Navy, Victory

Water

1 I never drink water. I'm afraid it could become habit-forming!

2 If the formula for water is H_2O, is the formula for an ice cube H_2O squared?

3 There's a lake in Norway so clear that if you look into it you can see people drinking tea in China.

See Restaurants 4, Wealth 18; see also Drought, The Environment, Pollution – Water, Swimming

Wealth

1 A millionaire friend of mine has just bought himself a new yacht. The first one got wet.

2 Abroad on holiday, the billionaire came across a wishing well. Not having a coin handy, he threw in a cheque!

3 Better to have been nouveau than never to have been rich at all.

4 He must be rich. He's got a walk-in wallet.

5 He spends the summer in a little place he's just bought up north. It's called Canada.

6 He was so rich, he even got a boy for his dog.

7 He was so rich he used to go to drive-in movies in a taxi.

8 He was so rich, whenever he cashed a cheque, the bank bounced.

9 He was so rich, the NatWest opened a branch in his living room.

10 He was so rich, even his chauffeur had a chauffeur.

11 He was so rich, he used to give away his new Mercedes when the ashtrays got full.

12 This guy's so rich he has two swimming pools – one for rinsing.

13 He's so rich he has four cars – one for each direction.

14 I came into money through a lucky stroke. My uncle had one and left me everything!

15 I don't knock the rich. I've never got a job yet from a poor person!

16 I made my money the old-fashioned way. I inherited it!

17 It's nothing but the best for him. He even has two nose specialists – one for each nostril.

18 My uncle is so rich he has Perrier on the knee!

19 The billionaire built himself a house so large, it was in four area codes.

20 There was this Texan who was so rich, he had an unlisted telephone company.

21 Wealth can certainly be a curse – especially if your neighbours have it!

22 What motivated you to become a millionaire?
I was trying to reach an income my wife and kids couldn't live beyond!

23 It is the wretchedness of being rich that you have to live with rich people.
Logan Pearsall Smith

24 The greatest luxury of riches is that they allow you to escape so much good advice.
Arthur Helps

See Aristocracy 6, Homes 8, Hospitals 12, Poverty 28, Wills 2; see also Banks and Banking, Beverly Hills, Borrowing and Lending, Golddiggers, Inflation, Money, Texas and the Texans

Weather

1 And now the weather: tomorrow will be muggy, followed by Toogy, Weggy, Thurgy . . .

2 Hello, is that the weather forecaster? I just wanted to let you know that this morning I shovelled 3 feet of 'partly cloudy' off my drive.

3 I don't think the sun is coming out today.
Well, would *you* come out on a day like this?

4 We went away on holiday for a week and it only rained twice: once for three days and once for four.

5 Did you have any trouble in the floods?
I'll say. I had to float out of the bedroom on my double bass.
And what about your wife?
She accompanied me on the piano.

6 How did you find the weather in Spain?
I just went outside and there it was!

7 The sky was dark with clouds.
There was a storm brewing?
No, they were just the empties coming back from Manchester.

8 After a week of the worst storms anyone could remember, most of the town was under water and the emergency services were stretched to the limit. At the rescue headquarters they took a call from a panic-stricken local man.
'You've got to help me. I'm standing in 2 feet of water!' he cried.
'You're standing in 2 feet of water?' replied the operator. 'I'm afraid we've got to help people who're far worse off than you.'
'But you don't understand. I'm up here on the fourth floor!'

9 Driving home after work, the man was caught in a terrible blizzard. When the car got stuck in a snowdrift, he climbed into the back seat and spent the night shivering and trying to sleep. The next morning, staggering to a nearby telephone box, he called his boss and said, 'I won't be in today. I haven't got home yesterday yet.'

See Tributes 17; *see also* Rain, The

Sun, Weather – Cold, Weather –
Hot, Wind

Weather – cold

1 It was so cold, the hens were laying
eggs from a standing position.

2 It was so cold, I had to put my food
in the refrigerator to warm it up.

3 It was so cold last night that I fell
out of bed and cracked my pyjamas.

4 It was so cold that my teeth were
chattering all night – and they
were in a glass on my bedside
table.

5 My room is so cold that in the
winter it steams up on the *outside* of
the windows.

6 My room's so cold that every time I
open the door the light goes on.

7 You know it's below freezing when
you comb your hair outside and it
breaks!

8 You know what they say: 'Many
are cold but few are frozen.'

See Ethnic Jokes 8; *see also* Eskimos,
Weather

Weather – hot

1 It was so hot in town today that I
saw a dog chasing a cat and they
were both walking.

2 It was so hot in town yesterday,
women weren't wearing their
minks, just carrying the appraisals.

3 The heat was terrible – 106 in the
shade. But it didn't worry me. I
stayed in the sun.

See also Drought, Holidays,
Summer, The Sun, Weather

Weddings

1 We had a very quiet wedding. The
vicar had laryngitis!

2 A morning wedding is a good idea.
Then, if the marriage doesn't work
out, at least you haven't wasted the
whole day.

3 A wedding ring is like a tourniquet.
It stops your circulation!

4 Being a romantic sort of girl, she
insisted on getting married in her
grandmother's dress. She looked
absolutely gorgeous – but her poor
grannie nearly froze to death.

5 Brides today are wearing their wedding dresses shorter – and more
often.

6 Call me superstitious, but I believe
that it's unlucky to see the bride
before the wedding – and sometimes
for thirty years after.

7 I had so much fun at my stag night,
I postponed the wedding.

8 I say this to the bride's father: you're
not so much losing a daughter as
gaining a bathroom.

9 I'll never forget my wedding day.
You never saw two happier people
than her mother and father.

10 I'll never forget my wedding. I've
tried, but the wife won't let me.

11 It was one of those quiet weddings.
I didn't turn up!

12 NERVOUS GROOM: Is it kisstomary
to cuss the bride?

13 Ours was a small wedding. Just my
parents, her parents and the obstetri-
cian.

14 People said their marriage wouldn't
last. They left the church together,
didn't they?

15 She wanted a formal wedding – so
her father painted the gun white.

16 The best man is the one chosen to
keep the bridegroom from escaping
before the ceremony.

17 The time had come to take a wife.
The question was, whose wife to
take?

18 The trouble was, I went into marriage with both eyes closed. Her brother closed one and her father closed the other.

19 The trouble with being best man at a wedding is that you never get the chance to prove it.

20 Watching her walk up the aisle, her friends knew she would make him happy. After all, she'd made five men happy the week before.

21 We had a nice wedding – just a quiet family affair. Just me, the wife and the kids.

22 We had a very quiet wedding. Her father put a silencer on his shotgun!

23 They had a shotgun wedding – the bride's father said, 'He does.'

24 What a wedding it was! All our friends were there, throwing old shoes. And her father was there, trying them on!

25 What a wonderful wedding. The bride looked stunning and the groom looked stunned!

26 When the vicar said, 'For better or for worse,' he meant that the groom couldn't do better and the bride couldn't do worse.

27 GIRLFRIEND: Is it going to be a white wedding?
BRIDE: Only if it snows!

28 GUEST: How soon do you expect the nuptials?
GROOM: Right after the wedding!

29 They say it's unlucky to postpone a wedding.
Not if you keep postponing it!

30 Have you kissed the bride?
Not recently.

31 USHER: Are you a friend of the groom?
GUEST: Certainly not, I'm the bride's mother!

32 We planned a runaway wedding.
How do you mean?
Every time we planned it, I ran away.

33 An old man approached a smartly dressed young man at the wedding reception and asked, 'Excuse me, are you the bridegroom?'
And the young man shook his head sadly and replied, 'I'm afraid not. I was eliminated in the semifinals.'

34 BRIDE: My perfect plum!
GROOM: My pretty peach!
MINISTER: I now pronounce you fruit salad!

35 MOTHER: Did you enjoy the wedding, dear?
LITTLE GIRL: It was lovely, Mummy – but what does 'fornication' mean?
MOTHER: What was the bride wearing?
LITTLE GIRL: She was really beautiful! She had a long white dress and a veil and she was carrying a lovely bouquet of flowers. But, Mummy, what does 'fornication' mean?
MOTHER: How lovely! And did you have lots of nice things to eat?
LITTLE GIRL: Yes, I had prawns and chicken and two helpings of ice-cream. But, Mummy, what does 'fornication' mean?
MOTHER: Well dear, it's a *very* naughty word. Where did you hear it?
LITTLE GIRL: At the wedding, Mummy. I heard the bride say to the groom, 'Fornication such as this, we really should have had champagne.'

36 Every bride has to learn it's not her wedding but her mother's.
Luci Nugent Johnson

See Arguments 13, Cricket 5, Figures – Fat 20, 25, Films 1, Golf 26, Hollywood 9, Husbands and Wives

Wills

1 My uncle had the shortest will ever. It read, 'Being of sound mind, I spent all my money.'

2 One of the richest men in Beverly Hills wrote in his will, 'To my son, Robert, I leave twenty million dollars – and he should be glad I didn't cut him out of my will completely.'

3 She left him because he had a will of his own – and it wasn't made out to her.

4 Where there's a will, there's a lawsuit.

5 You know what they say: where there's a will, there's relatives.

See Dating – Chat-up Lines 5, Reincarnation 2; *see also* Death, Families, Funerals, The Law, Lawyers

Wind

1 It was so windy on the motorway today, I was doing sixty-five in neutral!

2 It was so windy the other day, one of our hens laid the same egg six times.

3 It was so windy yesterday, I saw Siamese twins looking for each other.

See also Weather

Wives

1 A wife is a woman who stands by her husband through all the trouble he wouldn't have had if he'd stayed single.

2 Every man should have a wife – preferably his own.

3 If your wife does not cause all your troubles, she at least conveniently symbolizes them at times.
Don Herold

See also Husbands and Wives, Marriage, Women

Women

1 A woman is like a tea-bag; you never know how strong she is until she gets in hot water.
Nancy Reagan

2 Life's a bitch and so am I.
Bumper sticker

See also Feminism, Husbands and Wives, Men and Women, Women – The Male View

Women – the male view

1 If you want to know why they're called the opposite sex, just express an opinion.

2 There's only one way to handle a woman – but no one knows what it is.

3 The way to fight a woman is with your hat – grab it and run.
John Barrymore

4 Women would rather be right than reasonable.
Ogden Nash

See also Husbands and Wives, Men – The Female View, Men and Women, Women

Work

1 Don't get me wrong. I love the job. It's the *work* I hate!

2 Hard work never hurt anyone who hired somebody else to do it.

Work

3 He's a distinguished man of letters. He works for the Post Office.

4 He's got a very important job. He goes to work in a taxi every day. You would too if you were a taxi driver!

5 I don't like drinking too much coffee at work. It makes me toss and turn at my desk all day.

6 I have a perfect attendance record. I haven't missed a tea-break in three years!

7 I took one of those job-assessment tests at work the other day. The report said my aptitudes and abilities were best suited to some form of early retirement.

8 I used to have a job testing mattresses in a bed factory but I had to leave. I hated the way they kept waking me up for my tea-break.

9 I'm a key man at the Foreign Office. I lock up at night!

10 I've got a new job. I'm a lifeguard at a water-bed factory!

11 It takes him an hour to get to work – after he's got there.

12 My brother is working as a dustman. He gets fifty pounds a week and as much as he can eat.

13 My brother's just started as a police reporter. Every day he has to report to the police.

14 My brother just got a job replacing a machine that found the work too boring.

15 My first job was as a doorman – but I kept getting arrested for loitering.

16 My husband's a plant manager. And all he does all day is water them.

17 There's nothing wrong with work as long as it doesn't take up too much of your spare time.

18 My sister's a stripper. She's up on the roof now, getting the lead off!

19 My uncle has a very important job, working for the Yum Yum Soup company. He's a proofreader for their alphabet soup.

20 My uncle was a road-sweeper but he was fired because he couldn't keep his mind in the gutter.

21 They sacked him because he'd only been there three weeks but he was already two months behind in his work.

22 Where my uncle works, he has 500 people under him. He's a security guard at the cemetery!

23 Why did I become a baker? Because I kneaded the dough!

24 Work? I love it! I could stand around and watch it all day.

25 BOSS: You should have been back from lunch at two o'clock. It's now three. Where have you been?
JUNIOR: I've been having my hair cut.
BOSS: In the firm's time?
JUNIOR: Well, it grows in the firm's time, doesn't it?
BOSS: Yes, but it doesn't *all* grow in the firm's time!
JUNIOR: Well, I didn't have *all* of it cut off!

26 EMPLOYEE: When will my raise become effective?
BOSS: As soon as you are.

27 How many people work in this office?
About half of them.

28 I used to be a dresser in a strip-tease club for ten pounds a week.
Ten pounds a week? That's not very much.
It was all I could afford.

29 I used to be a tree-feller in the Sahara. But there aren't any trees in the Sahara.
Not now there aren't.

30 My wife knitted this sweater in less than a week and thought nothing of it.
Well, I don't think much of it either.

31 What time does your secretary start work?
About two hours after she gets here!

32 Why did you go into the cement business?
Because I've always been a good mixer.

33 Why do you want a raise?
Well, sir, somehow my family found out that other people eat three meals a day.

34 Two business partners were discussing the new receptionist, who was starting work that morning. 'I suppose we'd better start by teaching her what's right and what's wrong.'
'OK, *you* teach her what's right . . .'

35 By working faithfully eight hours a day, you may eventually get to be a boss and work twelve hours a day.
Robert Frost

36 I owe, I owe, so off to work I go!
Bumper sticker

37 The longer the title, the less important the job.
George McGovern

38 Work is the greatest thing in the world, so we should always save some of it for tomorrow.
Don Herold

39 Work is the refuge of people who have nothing better to do.
Oscar Wilde

See America and the Americans 4, Banks and Banking 8, Circus 3, 4, Holidays 22, Honeymoons 5, Las Vegas 3, Luck 8, Weather 9; *see also* Bosses, Business, Laziness, The Office, Professions, Retirement, Unemployment

Worry

1 He's such a worrier, he's beginning to wonder what wine goes with fingernails.

2 If only I knew what I was so worried about, I wouldn't be so worried.

3 When I look back on all these worries, I remember the story of the old man who said on his deathbed that he had had a lot of trouble in his life, most of which had never happened.
Sir Winston Churchill

See also Anxiety, Fear, Timidity

Writers and writing

1 He's a writer whose books will be read long after Shakespeare, Dickens and Henry James are forgotten. But not until then.

2 He's been a writer ever since he was a teenager. In fact, as soon as he left school he began to write for money – in every letter his parents got from him.

3 I began as a writer as soon as I left university and within six months I'd sold several articles – my watch, my overcoat, my typewriter . . .

4 It took me more than a year to finish my first book. I'm a very slow reader.

5 My brother's a failed author. He writes books nobody wants to read and cheques nobody wants to cash.

6 AGENT: So how are you getting on with that mystery drama you're writing?
WRITER: Well, I've been working on it for twelve months solid and it's still not right.

AGENT: A case of all work and no play!

7 FIRST WRITER: I once got ten pounds a word.
SECOND WRITER: How was that?
FIRST WRITER: I talked back to the judge!

8 I finally had a story accepted!
Fantastic! How?
I got home at three in the morning and my wife believed every word of my explanation.

9 I once wrote for *The New Yorker*.
What happened?
What do you think? They sent me one.

10 I'm a writer.
Well, what a coincidence. I'm a reader!

11 A writer is somebody for whom writing is more difficult than it is for other people.
Thomas Mann

12 All a writer has to do to get a woman is to say he's a writer. It's an aphrodisiac.
Saul Bellow

13 Almost anyone can be an author; the business is to collect money and fame from this state of being.
A. A. Milne

14 I have made this letter longer than usual, only because I have not had the time to make it shorter.
Blaise Pascal

15 I never think at all when I write. Nobody can do two things at the same time and do them both well.
Don Marquis

16 I write for *Reader's Digest*. It's not hard. All you do is copy out an article and mail it in again.
Milt Kamen

17 If you want to get rich from writing, write the sort of thing that's read by persons who move their lips when they're reading to themselves.
Don Marquis

18 In composing, as a general rule, run your pen through every other word you have written; you have no idea what vigour it will give to your style.
Sydney Smith

19 No man but a blockhead ever wrote, except for money.
Samuel Johnson

20 There is an impression abroad that everyone has it in him to write one book; but if by this is implied a good book the impression is false.
W. Somerset Maugham

21 What is written without effort is in general read without pleasure.
Samuel Johnson

22 Writers seldom write the things they think. They simply write the things they think other folks think they think.
Elbert Hubbard

23 Writing is the only profession where no one considers you ridiculous if you earn no money.
Jules Renard

See Films 3; *see also* Books, Books – The Critics, Critics, Journalism, Libraries, Literature, Literature – The Critics, Newspapers

READ MORE IN PENGUIN

BY THE SAME AUTHOR

The Penguin Dictionary of Modern Humorous Quotations

From Anon and Woody Allen ('Not only is there no God, but try getting a plumber on weekends'), Miss Piggy and Dorothy Parker, to Mae West ('To err is human, but it feels divine'), Morecambe and Wise and P. G. Wodehouse, the last hundred years offer a rich banquet of humour. Even Belgium, golf and inflation have inspired witty remarks, while sections on Eating and Drink, Politicians and Poets, Animals and Americans, Sex, Drugs and Rock 'n' Roll all include countless gems. Fred Metcalf's clearly cross-referenced anthology, the first of its kind since 1949, provides a superb selection – ideal for after-dinner speakers, would-be wags ('Next to being witty yourself, the best thing is to quote another's wit') and anyone in search of hours of amusement.